T0319892

Job Creation

Job Creation

The Role of Labor Market Institutions

Edited by

Jordi Gual

Professor of Economic Analysis for Management, IESE, International Graduated School of Management, University of Navarra, Barcelona, Spain and Research Fellow, Centre for Economic Policy Research, London, UK

Edward Elgar
Cheltenham, UK • Northampton, MA, USA

Published by
Edward Elgar Publishing Limited
8 Lansdown Place
Cheltenham
Glos GL50 2HU
UK

Edward Elgar Publishing, Inc.
6 Market Street
Northampton
Massachusetts 01060
USA

A catalogue record for this book
is available from the British Library

Library of Congress Cataloguing in Publication Data
Job creation: the role of labor market institutions / edited by Jordi
  Gual.
        1. Job creation—Congresses. 2. Full employment policies–
  –Congresses. 3. Unemployment—Congresses. 4. Job creation—Europe–
  –Congresses. 5. Job creation—United States—Congresses. I. Gual
  1 Sole, Jordi.
  HD5713.J6 1998
  331.12'042—dc21   98–12820
                                                                        CIP

ISBN 1 85898 789 X

Printed and bound in Great Britain by
Biddles Ltd, Guildford and King's Lynn

Contents

Contributors

Professor **Carlos Cavallé**
Dean of IESE, Universidad de Navarra, Spain.

Professor **Colin Crouch**
Professor of Sociology, European University Institute, Florence, Italy
and University of Oxford, Oxford, UK.

Dr **Anthony Ferner**
Principal Research Fellow, Industrial Relations Research Unit, Centre for
International Employment Relations, Warwick Business School,
University of Warwick, Coventry, UK.

Professor **Jordi Gual**
IESE, Universidad de Navarra, Spain and CEPR, London, UK.

Professor **Stephen Nickell**
Institute of Economics and Statistics, Oxford University, Oxford, UK.

Professor **Paul Osterman**
Sloan School of Management, Massachusetts Institute of Technology, US.

Professor **Vicente Salas**
Universidad Autónoma de Barcelona and Universidad de Zaragoza, Spain.

Professor **Dennis J. Snower**
Department of Economics, Birkbeck College, University of London and
CEPR, London, UK.

Preface

European labor markets continue to be in a state of bewilderment. A sign of this is the controversial French proposal to adopt a 35-hour working week and the Aubry Plan which envisages the creation of 350,000 low-skill jobs. The Italian and Spanish labor markets have jumped on the bandwagon. Meanwhile, economists continue to argue that the solution to Europe's employment problem is unlikely to lie in reducing the working week, particularly if this is done by law. European labor markets need more flexibility and deregulation, not new, rigid structures. Economists argue that the French plan is more an attempt by the French Socialist Party to make good its electoral promise to create 700,000 jobs than a practical solution that would benefit both workers and employers.

Europe continues to display an inability to generate enough better-paid jobs. With the exception of the UK, the EC countries' job creation figures are not satisfactory, and no clear paths have been forged towards the resolution of this dilemma. The problem persists both in terms of its conceptual definition and in the steps to be taken. And it probably persists because Europe has yet to bring the job problem to the fore; not because it does not consider the problem to be important, but because it has a higher priority – the single currency. Until Europe clarifies the present and future of monetary union and sets in motion the policies, programmes and mechanisms required to ensure the euro's success, it will not have enough time on its hands to focus on the problem of creating jobs.

Jacques Delors' White Book was a promising first step, and for many it was well conceived. It had created concern and offered solutions. However, I would claim that the euro project caused a hiatus following the White Book that has not yet come to an end. If politicians were truly interested in tackling the problem head-on, they would find more than enough arguments to do so. Unemployment among the young, which affects 40 per cent of those under 25 in Spain and 25 per cent in France and Belgium, is consequential enough to require the adoption of practical measures.

We all know, in addition, that Europe's low demographic growth is reducing the young population at a time when life expectancy overall is growing. This means that there will be fewer and fewer young people who will have to work to support an ever-growing and ageing population.

This poses a serious problem for the welfare state, which has been discussed on repeated occasions from a speculative and perhaps theoretical perspective. But it is obvious that here, too, no practical solutions in line with the dimensions of the problem have been found.

We must also face the problem of the long-term unemployed, which constitutes another important concern for every European nation. We know that half of the unemployed over the age of 45 in Europe fall into the long-term category, and therefore the chances are that they will remain out of the job market. We need to think about what it means for a country when human resources at the peak of their skills and abilities remain unproductive. And when, instead of contributing through their work to the well-being of society, they are asking society to subsidize their unemployed status.

Unemployment is not only an economic problem, but also a human problem, as it represents an assault on the dignity of a person – a dignity that entails the right of each person to a job according to his or her skills and ability, and sufficiently well compensated. Europe has not taken this grave problem seriously because it cannot, due to a lack of political will and because there are other priorities.

In the debate on job creation, frequent reference is made to the situation in the United States. Those in favour of flexibility of job markets underscore the advantages of the American model and offer it as an example that should be followed. Fortunately, there are others who remind us that the American model has achieved success in one of the aspects demanded by an individual's dignity, namely job creation, at the cost of inadequate pay at the lower echelons of the skills ladder. However, the American system also provides the low paid with greater opportunities to improve their position in the more or less near future, compared with their European counterparts, who start from a position of unemployment. Therefore, we should ask ourselves whether the principles of flexibility that characterize the American model have certain features that could usefully be applied to the European model. An example can be found in the case of the Netherlands, a country which, as we know, had an unemployment rate of nearly 14 per cent some 10–12 years ago, one of Europe's highest at the time. The Dutch, with their pragmatic style, and without giving up their welfare state, adopted a series of institutional measures that have borne fruit, halving unemployment without substantially cutting social benefits.

The Dutch adopted three measures to increase flexibility in employment. The first altered the work contract, enabling part-time hiring with the proviso that these contracts can gradually acquire the same social benefits as full-time contracts. The second affected the contributions made by companies to social security, which have been cut in order to lower production costs. The third measure lowered the personal income tax rate for the lowest-paid workers, which translates in the long term into a rise in average wages without increasing labor costs.

The Dutch have realized that lowering labor costs is an important factor in job creation, when coupled with adapting to the diverse needs of job-seekers, many of whom are satisfied with shorter working hours.

What has been said thus far reaffirms the idea that although politicians are not in the best position to deal with the entire, overall problem, there is still quite a bit of room for action in the field of job creation, by fine-tuning legislation to improve the efficiency of markets and the institutions involved.

Another important issue for job creation is trends. The question is, can monetary union facilitate growth by itself and can growth, in turn, create jobs? If both answers are yes, then we can breathe more easily and the unemployed can wait it out. However, in my opinion, neither of the two questions has a clear-cut, positive answer. With regard to the first question, the situation is so perplexing that few dare to claim that monetary union in itself will bring growth. But this should not come as a surprise, since the goals of monetary union are essentially political, not economic.

With regard to the second question, it is clear that sustained economic growth like that experienced in recent years has led to job creation in the United States – but not in Europe, simply because we follow two different economic models. The European model is of growth by increased productivity, whereas the American model is growth by job creation.

Alongside these two models, there are two other factors which can also affect job markets and job creation. These are, of course, globalization and the spread of technology. Globalization is clearly a growing phenomenon whose consequences have not yet been sufficiently analysed. What we do know is that the market deregulation that is central to globalization is at present allowing capital and production to flow away from the EU, with obvious consequences for employment.

As for the spread of new technologies, these accentuate the globalization process and therefore produce similar effects. However, in the more developed countries, new information technologies, when applied in deregulated markets like the US, are net job creators. It is to be hoped that this will also be the case in Europe in the coming years, when these technologies are applied to similar levels as in the US.

The Third International Conference on Job Creation ("What Kind of Labor Market Do We Want?"), held in Barcelona on 19–20 June 1997, explored these themes in depth, as the papers published in this book will clearly demonstrate.

The conference was the latest in a series organized by IESE, reflecting our deep concern with the problems of job creation and unemployment in Europe. For several years now IESE and its staff have been working on these issues, which are so important for all our futures.

We have, I believe, succeeded in developing a vision that combines academic rigour with a practical appreciation of the realities of business and commerce.

I am confident that *Job Creation: the Role of Labor Market Institutions* will help the academic and business worlds – not to mention the world of politics – to reach a better understanding of the many complex issues surrounding job creation and unemployment. My thanks go to all those who took part in the 1997 conference for their excellent contributions; and I wish to thank Jordi Gual in particular for editing this important new book.

Carlos Cavallé
Dean of IESE, University of Navarra
Anselmo Rubiralta, Professor in Business Administration

1. The employment debate: employment performance and institutional change

Jordi Gual[*]

1.1. INTRODUCTION

Industrialized economies have faced growing labor market problems over the last two decades. In continental Europe, insufficient job creation has led to sustained high rates of unemployment, particularly among the young and the long-term unemployed. In the US, the economy has created many jobs over the last twenty years but real wages have stagnated and there is growing inequality in labor markets.

Job creation and the quality of jobs are thus fundamental social problems all over the industrialized world. They are also becoming increasingly important in developing countries as they progress in their development strategy (witness, for example, the problems experienced by South Korea in its attempt to liberalize the labor market).

This book brings together a distinguished group of academics from various fields with the goal of providing a broad assessment of how changes in labor market institutions can improve employment performance.

It is well known that job creation does not constitute, on its own, a legitimate maximand in standard economic analysis. Economists like to discuss social welfare optimization, the maximization of some function of profits and consumer welfare. Nevertheless, how increased social welfare translates into variables such as participation rates and youth unemployment rates constitutes a key public policy concern.

Moreover, from the perspective of the role of firms in society, it is also important to analyse how firms can simultaneously maximize the returns to shareholders and provide rewarding jobs and professional careers to their employees while operating in increasingly complex markets, where technological change and globalization are drastically changing the very nature of work.

The objective of this introductory chapter is to provide a framework which places the contributions in this book within a broad perspective of

1

the international debate on employment performance. To do so, I shall survey a range of academic research that tackles the issue of how institutional change can improve job creation.

The survey is not comprehensive for at least two reasons. First, the vast amount of research and analysis that has been devoted to the subject by scholars in the fields of humanities and social sciences makes it virtually impossible to provide a summary in a single, short and manageable chapter. I shall be selective and focus on a few chosen research topics which are of interest, both in terms of the relevance of the questions being asked and with regard to the issues addressed by the chapters in this book. The second reason why this survey is incomplete has to do with the background of its author. Being trained as an economist, I have an obvious tendency to present a skewed view of labor market problems, emphasizing the contributions of research in economics. The Third International Conference on Job Creation,[1] at which the chapters in this book were initially presented, brought together specialists from economics, industrial relations and sociology, but I am afraid that this introductory chapter does not do full justice to the contributions from disciplines other than my own.

I shall approach the debate on employment and the role of labor market institutions by placing firms at the very centre of the analysis. It is enterprises and entrepreneurs, with their initiative and commitment, that create new jobs. It is also the firm that determines the nature of jobs, their quality and other important characteristics such as their location. Thus, it is firms – through their strategies and their decisions on internal organization – that drive the job creation process.

Of course, firms do not operate in a vacuum. They are subject to a wide set of restrictions imposed by existing institutions and to external influences arising from the evolution of technology and other forces (that is, political changes) which are enlarging the markets in which they operate.

I take both technological change and globalization as two exogenous[2] trends that are influencing firms' behaviour in many dimensions and, in particular, in the way firms grow, employ people and organize themselves internally.

Technological progress and globalization affect jobs and their nature within a given economic area. The way these trends alter the job creation processes is crucially determined by a large set of social institutions of which the most important is, of course, the labor market itself. But the nature of the business system, the structure of education and training systems, and the organization of other product and service markets also matter. Figure 1.1 summarizes the relationships between trends, institutions and the job creation process. The framework depicted by this chart:

1) stresses the role of the exogenous factors of change in labor relations (technology and globalization);

2) highlights the key role of institutions in shaping the reaction of the economy to those changes; and

3)   focuses on how firms adapt to the global trends and to their specific institutional environment and how that process of adaptation changes the nature (and number) of jobs.

The key role of institutions is fairly intuitive. How firms adapt to external forces and how that impacts on their employment and training policies is crucially dependent on the institutions of labor markets, among others. For example, it has been widely argued that changes in technology and more open international markets are hurting the low skilled in industrialized countries. The nature of the impact is, however, very different depending on the institutional context. In Europe those trends have resulted in an increase in unemployment among the low skilled. In the US, the result has been a declining relative wage.

Figure 1.1 highlights the fact that the job creation process takes place at the firm level but under the influence of trends which impact firms through social institutions. It will provide us with a road map into the employment debate, and should help us focus on the key determinants of the job creation process (labor market institutions and the strategies of firms) so that we place the role of trends and other institutional features in perspective. Before turning to a detailed analysis of labor institutions we shall review next the main results from the extensive research conducted on technology and globalization. We shall look as well at some of the more important non-labor market institutions that are likely to influence employment performance.

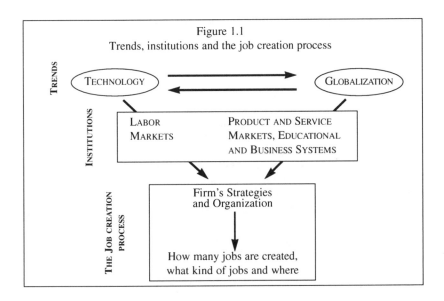

Figure 1.1
Trends, institutions and the job creation process

1.2.   THE FACTORS OF CHANGE

1.2.1. Technology

Technological change is commonly perceived as a major factor behind the observed trends in world labor markets. It is important to clarify, however, that the effect of technology on jobs can be traced to three conceptually distinctive phenomena. First, technological change might have been accelerating over the last twenty years, displacing workers who have not yet been absorbed by a lagging rate of job creation. Second, technological change may be biased, with increased use of labor-saving technologies. And third, the nature of technological progress may have changed so that, even without acceleration or bias, new technology is characterized by features that provoke rapid changes in the qualifications demanded from the workforce.

1.   Accelerated technological change

Casual evidence on the speed of technological progress points to very remarkable changes. For example,[3] in recent years computing power has been doubling every 18 months and the price per unit of computing power is falling at cumulative rates of 35 per cent. Similarly, transmission capacity in telecommunications has soared and today transatlantic fibre-optic cables can carry 1.5 million simultaneous conversations, whereas the figure was a bare 138 in 1960.

This informal evidence, however, is in conflict with the ongoing debate on the productivity slowdown in OECD countries. Total factor productivity increases (that is, productivity increases excluding those which are associated purely with the increased use of labor and capital) have been low over the last twenty years and this has prompted substantial amounts of research and policy analysis aimed at reversing that trend.[4]

Nevertheless, the reasons behind the productivity slowdown remain unclear, especially since the slowdown is at odds with casual evidence and observed (massive) investment in new technologies, particulary computing. One possible explanation would point to a misguided (or inefficient) use of the new technologies. Recent research by Hitt and Brynjolfsson (1996) has explored this possibility systematically. These authors find that investment in information technologies does in fact increase productivity. However, they also find that most of the benefits of new technologies are passed on to consumers in the form of lower prices, so that investment in new technologies does not necessarily increase business profitability.

This brings us to an alternative explanation of the productivity slowdown which has been the subject of a large research effort in recent years. If the benefits of new technologies are enjoyed by consumers in the form of lower prices, maybe what is happening is that the conventional measures of productivity are not taking these price declines into account appropriately.[5] This type of consideration underlies the US Consumer Price Index (CPI) Commission Report[6] which argues that inflation has been overestimated in the US over the last decades, thus leading to an underestimation of productivity growth. The measurement problems are particularly acute in service industries.[7] These industries represent an increasing share of industrialized economies and this would reinforce the idea that we might actually have experienced a period of unprecedentedly strong productivity growth and not a slowdown. Accelerated technical change may lead to higher unemployment if growth is uneven across sectors and requires employment reallocation.[8] Then, faster growth reduces the duration of job matches, which directly increases the job separation rate and reduces the rate of creation of new vacancies. Both effects raise the equilibrium rate of unemployment. These negative effects, however, are counterbalanced by the fact that faster productivity growth will also raise the returns to vacancies and thus increase the exit rate from unemployment.

In the end, it is difficult to conclude on the basis of both theory and evidence that accelerating technical change is a fundamental factor behind changes in the labor market. Even if technology has moved forward at a rapid pace recently, periods of accelerated technological change have also been observed in the past and have not led to changes in employment as drastic as those that we observe today.[9]

2.   *Biased technical change*
Recent trends in technology could have a significant impact on employment if they were characterized by a bias against the use of labor relative to other productive factors, such as capital or energy. Similarly, biased technical change could favour skilled versus unskilled labor, lowering the relative wage of unskilled workers (in a non-intervened market such as that of the US) or increasing unemployment among the less skilled (in the presence of downward rigidities in the wage formation process, as in Europe). Evidence on the importance of this demand shift towards less labor, and in particular less-skilled labor, has indeed been assembled in several studies.[10] The data show that the observed pattern of unemployment and wages by skill levels can only be explained by very strong demand shifts, given that from the supply side we have witnessed a relative increase in the supply of educated workers.

It is clear, however, that this negative effect of technical change on jobs is not always the result of exogenous changes in technology. In fact, in Europe strong rates of unit labor cost increases, particularly at the time of the oil shocks in the 1970s, and the excessive cost of labor promoted by labor regulations (see below) may in some countries have promoted technical change that aims at reducing the use of labor. The bias is, thus, the result of firms' choices when facing relative costs of inputs which penalize labor artificially through high taxes and social security contributions.

Biased technical change promoted by excessive wage and non-wage increases (particularly for low-skilled workers) must certainly play a role as a factor explaining the surge of unemployment in recent years. However, one can legitimately wonder whether that is all. Many people have argued that the current changes in technology are simply different from any progress the world might have experienced in the past. For some of them for example (The Luddites of the twenty-first century, and Jeremy Rifkin in his 1996 best-seller *The End of Work*) it is all too easy to jump to conclusions: the new kind of technological change will truly destroy jobs and, this time, we are told, they will be gone for ever.

3.   *The nature of technological progress*
Is the current technological revolution different from previous ones? And what do we mean by different?

In the past there have been huge technical advances such as the introduction of electricity and railways. Those changes have already revolutionized the economy and the world of business. Is the current revolution, based on computing and telecommunication technologies, any different?

At least two strands of literature have pointed out and explored features of the current technological change which make it unique and which may have far-reaching implications for the nature of jobs.

The first line of work has emphasized the idea that new technologies are leading to a knowledge-based economy, and that such an economy will be characterized by increasing returns, with increased abilities, wealth and productivity concentrating in a small number of firms (and individuals) (Romer 1986; Arthur 1996). Reich (1991) has explored these issues informally, in particular linking them to globalization and the implications for the nature of jobs and worker compensation. According to Reich, only what he calls "symbolic analysts" (people working in the identification and resolution of problems through the development and manipulation of symbols such as data, words and images) will be able to command ever-higher compensations. These people will enjoy access to a world market and exploit the increasing returns of their activities (the same idea can be deployed in many markets), while individuals undertaking routine production (or service) work will be facing competition from workers in many other countries and, thus, confronting lower wages and/or fewer work opportunities.

The second strand of papers has explored the implications of the information revolution for production processes and the internal organization and skills of the labor force. In this literature the introduction of flexible machine tools, programmable multi-task production equipment and computerized data systems has resulted in wide-ranging changes within firms, altering traditional Tayloristic organizational forms, and inducing new and different demands on employees (see Milgrom and Roberts 1990; Lindbeck and Snower 1996; and the contribution by Dennis Snower in this volume).

Overall, existing research on technological progress as a factor of change in employment and labor relations seems to indicate that both the bias of technical change and its changing nature have had a profound impact on the job creation process. In particular, the analysis of how the nature of technological progress affects jobs is a promising research programme to which we will come back in the analysis of changes in the strategies and internal organization of firms (section 1.5 below).

1.2.2. Globalization

Globalization trends are also highlighted as key contributing factors to the turmoil experienced in the labor markets of industrialized nations. As with technology, casual observation leads many commentators to conclude that low-cost labor-intensive producers from around the globe are displacing increasingly larger shares of economic activity, and thus jobs, in the industrialized nations.

It is true that there has been a change in the political climate which has fostered the globalization trend, with many countries adopting free trade and foreign direct investment (FDI) regimes, and with the promotion of trade and investment liberalization through the World Trade Organization.

Nevertheless, despite the rhetoric, globalization is not anything new in the trade domain. The data show that world trade has been increasing fast over the last ten years, but not faster than a few years ago. World exports grew at an anual rate of 4 per cent between 1990 and 1995, but the rate was 6 per cent between 1970 and 1980, and even higher in the 1960s.

The debate on the employment effects of trade has been surveyed in detail in Gual (1996b).[11] The main result of this controversy is that the impact of trade is predominantly of an inter-industry nature. That is, trade alters the specialization of countries and leads to industrial restructuring, with declining employment and wages in some sectors, and increasing ones in others.[12] Aggregate employment is thus unaffected. Nevertheless, difficulties in sectoral reallocation could – as in the case of technological change – lead to temporary drops in employment. As we shall explore in detail below, institutions play a fundamental role in this sectoral reallocation process. In fact, institutions can convert a temporary drop into a permanent one in a phenomenon which is known as hysteresis.[13]

What has been remarkable over the last ten years has been the worldwide increase of cross-border direct investment flows. Between 1983 and 1987 the average worldwide FDI flows were US$75 billion. The figure for the period 1988–95 is almost 200 billion. The chapter by Anthony Ferner in this book (Chapter 7) provides an interesting perspective on a debate which has up to now been much less explored, even if it is potentially much more important.

As argued by Ferner, the impact of FDI trends on employment is an issue which has led to a strong debate in some European countries (notably France[14]). As with trade, the overall beneficial nature of cross-border direct investment justifies a detailed analysis of its implications for labor markets. Fear of job losses, or the introduction of pure assembly plants, has been prominent in social debates on this issue and the employment risks may prevent advances in the liberalization of investment flows. However, no conclusive evidence has been produced on the subject, particulary if we look not only at jobs but also at their nature.

On the one hand, inward FDI may lead to job creation, when new investments add capacity to the economy. It may lead, however, to short-term job destruction if the foreign investors displace more labor-intensive local producers. In the long-term, though, increased productivity should lead to improved living standards, with beneficial effects on output and jobs.

Similarly, outward FDI may deflect investment funds abroad and could reduce the capital available to domestic workers. It has been argued, thus, that this type of FDI can delocalize jobs. The analysis here is, however, difficult since it must be based on comparisons with counterfactuals, that is, with a potential situation where outward FDI does not take place. In many industries, domestic investment is not the alternative to investing abroad. Indeed, not investing abroad may lead to a permanent loss of competitive advantage and, possibly, the ultimate erosion of the remaining domestic activities. The economics literature has developed consistent and comprehensive models of FDI (Markusen 1995) but the implications for jobs have been addressed only recently and results on this issue are still preliminary.[15] Chapter 7 in this book looks at data on the scale of employment in multinational companies, analyses the developments in the world economy which explain this process of relocation and shows that the relocation danger has been grossly exaggerated. Nevertheless, Ferner contends that there are some reasons for concern in relation to potential social dumping, as well as with regard to competition in high-skill sectors coming from low-wage economies.

1.3. JOB CREATION AND NON-LABOR MARKET INSTITUTIONS

Now, I shall briefly review research on the institutions, other than those of the labor market, which affect employment performance most directly. I shall focus on the functioning of product and service markets, and on the role of the educational system. It is clear, though, that the nature of work and the relations between firms and their employees are going to be affected by a broader set of determinants. Workers' attitudes to work, the incentives to take up new job opportunities, the attitude of management towards employee participation and many other relevant dimensions of the employment relationship will be influenced very much by the business system.[16] This system comprises a wide array of institutions: the cultural system, which covers the norms and rules that govern the exchange relationships between economic actors; the political system, which includes the roles of the state in society; the financial system, which determines the distribution and pricing of capital; and the labor system, which in this broad sense refers to the regulations which delineate how skills are developed, certified and exchanged between individuals and organizations (subjects which are addressed later). We shall not pursue these topics here but it is worth stressing that from the point of view of research on job creation in industrialized western economies, the main merit of this sociological approach is to draw our attention to the role that culture and values play in determining the attitude of firms and employees towards the changing nature of the employment relationship. For example, the nature of hierarchical relations within the firm is strongly affected by the predominant values in society. The development of flat organizations which emphasize team work and strong interactive relations betwen teams and the central coordination body might be less appropriate in cultural systems where "remote paternalism" predominates (see Whitley 1996). In general, the analysis of cultural aspects is important when we analyse how firms adapt their strategy and organization to the changing competitive environment. The changing nature of human resource management policies at the firm level is going to be directly affected by the cultural context.

1.3.1. Product and Service Markets

The role of efficient product and service markets as factors contributing to job creation has been the subject of substantial debate in policy circles. The beneficial employment effects of deregulating and increasing competition in product and service markets has been voiced by influential business reports (McKinsey Global Institute 1994) and has drawn the attention of policy makers (see OECD 1994). Nevertheless, academic research on the subject is scarce.[17]

At the conceptual level, the standard macroeconomic analysis of the inflation and unemployment trade-off provides the appropriate framework.[18] Rigidities and non-competitive behaviour in product markets play a dual role, similar to that played by labor market imperfections. First, they tend to increase the lowest possible rate of unemployment. Such a rate (known as the non-accelerating inflation rate of unemployment or NAIRU), is determined by the appearance of inflationary pressures and those are facilitated when firms face no competition or operate in highly regulated markets. In these markets cost increases are passed on to the consumers even if the economy is in a slump. Second, product market imperfections make it more costly (in terms of lost output and jobs) to reduce the inflation level. That is, the short-run inflation unemployment trade-off is worsened. If firms can sustain mark-ups in recessions, it becomes harder to slow down price increases, and stronger policy-induced economic contractions are needed.

The empirical and policy relevance of these arguments remains, however, unclear. There is no doubt that fostering more competition in markets, where either collusion is pervasive or firms abuse a dominant position, has beneficial effects through lower prices, increased output and more employment. However, within a liberalized open economy, there are not many markets where such non-competitive behaviour prevails. In modern industrial markets a large part of observed mark-ups reflect superior product positioning by firms that have invested heavily in R&D or brand development. The anti-trust case in those situations is far less clearcut.

As for deregulation, its practical employment impact is subject to similar caveats. Although some macroeconomic benefits may be obtained in terms of more flexible price formation, the overall employment impact of lifting regulations will to a large extent be contingent on the nature of the regulatory framework before and after the changes. Although the effect of deregulation in the general economy is bound to be positive – in terms of welfare, output and jobs – as efficiency is increased in many markets,[19] in some sectors regulatory conditions may have led to an excessive use of labor, so that employment declines after liberalization. This has been confirmed in *ex-post* assessments of deregulation such as the comprehensive one produced by Winston (1993) with respect to the US.

The fact that deregulation leads to increased jobs only indirectly, and may be detrimental to employment in easily identifiable sectors, is a major obstacle to regulatory reforms.

Beyond this comparative statics perspective, deregulation and increased competition are perceived by many as key components of a dynamic business environment which facilitates firm growth and job creation.[20] The link between a more competitive environment and higher innovation is confirmed by the empirical industrial organization literature,[21] but how this translates into jobs is a more open issue. Higher innovation creates jobs but also destroys them, increasing turnover in the labor market.[22]

This underlines the need for coordinated deregulation of product and labor markets. It also highlights the fact that high turnover with the entry of new firms in new activities will only be possible if there is a parallel change in the supply of skilled labor. This is, in fact, the subject to which I turn next.

1.3.2. Educational Systems and the Skills Mismatch

One of the main explanations of the employment problems confronted by developed countries over the last years relies on what is known as the skills mismatch; that is, the idea that trends in technology and the globalization of markets have created a gap between the skills demanded by firms and those possessed by the labor force.

It is important to recognize that if the mismatch story is to be relevant, it cannot be simply a temporary phenomenon. It has to be grounded on some basic failure in the process of skills acquisition by the workforce, otherwise a change in the demand for skills would be matched gradually by a change in the qualifications of the labor force, and the mismatch would not be a permanent phenomenon.[23]

Views on skills acquisition have been very much influenced by Gary Becker's theory of human capital (Becker 1962, 1975).

The main argument of Becker can be summarized in a simple fashion. He divided training into two categories: general training, which was useful to all firms in the economy, and specific training, or training which was useful only at the level of one specific firm. In the first case, the benefits of training accrue fully to employees, since there is competition in the market for labor services and the acquired training translates into a higher wage rate. In such a situation, employees would be willing to invest in training since they would expect to enjoy all the returns to their investment. In the case of firm-specific training the returns to investments in training accrue to the specific firm and would be shared between employees and employers who would thus also be willing to split the costs.

The analysis of Becker has been very influential and underlies the view that the market for skills is a market that should not be subject to government intervention because the incentives of employers and employees will on their own provide the appropriate levels of training in the economy. Such a vision is no doubt behind the free market approach to training predominant in the economies of the UK and the US.

Nevertheless, the existence of potential market failures in the education market has long been recognized. It is widely accepted that the productivity of workers depends not only on their own level of training but also on the training of fellow workers with whom they work. Thus, from a social point of view, the investment in education and training by a single individual provides benefits beyond those that are reaped by him or her through the increase in the productivity of other workers. Such an externality is not taken into account by private individuals when deciding how much to invest in education. This is the kind of market failure which has been at the root of the policy of general education subsidies commonly observed in many industrialized economies. Such a policy, by the way, is more common for general and university education than for professional training, although it is not clear why that is the case.

The Becker paradigm has been criticized on several grounds. First, in the case of firm-specific training, the idea that the returns to training investment will be appropriated by both the employer and the employee is unclear. This is a typical situation of what is known as the hold-up problem, which we have already reviewed when discussing job security provisions. If the investment is firm specific, the negotiation power of workers *ex post* is low, and foreseeing this, they may decide not to invest in training to begin with.

More fundamentally, the sharp distinction between general and firm-specific training is probably inaccurate (see Booth and Snower 1996). Training is usually useful to a limited number of firms in a given industry or set of industries. Thus, in general, firms will enjoy some market power in the labor market and will be able to extract some rents from workers (see also the discussion on minimum wages, above). As a consequence, they will be paying a wage below the marginal productivity of labor and, therefore, appropriating some of the returns to training. This will negatively affect the incentives of individuals to acquire training.

Similarly, if training is useful not only to a single firm but to a group of firms, although this might lessen the hold-up problem, it will clearly affect the incentives of firms to provide more skills to their workers, since labor mobility could mean that firms are in fact subsidizing their competitors (what is known as the "poaching externality").

The recent book edited by Booth and Snower (1996) surveys other potential externalities. Among these, probably the most important refers to the existence of failures in the credit market. As already mentioned, human capital cannot be used as collateral and that might lead to underinvestment in education by talented individuals who face liquidity constraints. In his contribution to this book, Snower argues that some of the market failures in the training domain may actually be exacerbated by the organizational revolution and the move from Tayloristic organizations to new organizational forms.

Research on the impact of skill acquisition systems on the employment prospects of individuals and on the performance of firms and industries has followed several routes. Much of the work has dealt with the comparative institutional analysis of alternative training systems. This research typically compares market-based approaches, such as those of the US and the UK, with more institutionalized systems like those of Germany and Japan, and systems based more on taxation incentives such as that of France (examples of this type of institutional research are the contributions of Shackleton 1995 and Hyman 1992).

This kind of research offers a rich detail of evidence and appraises the effectiveness of systems by looking at a broad number of issues and a variety of programmes, including an analysis of their effectiveness. This is in fact very important because government intervention in training is also subject to substantial government failures, even when the government is not the direct provider of training (see Booth and Snower 1996).

Alternatively, some recent work (Mason et al. 1996) has examined the relationship between workforce skills, product quality and industry performance by comparing companies located in different countries and competing in the same industry using distinct quality-skills strategies. These authors argue that the choice of strategy by firms conditions their demand for skills, affects performance and also sends important signals to the workforce in terms of the potential returns to investment in the acquisition of additional skills. This kind of work is extremely interesting as it points out effective ways in which training systems can be coupled with the competitive position of firms so that the training-enterprise system avoids the low-skill-bad-job trap.

1.4. THE ROLE OF LABOR MARKET INSTITUTIONS

The key role played by labor market institutions in determining how firms and workers react to a changing economic environment was recognized long ago. Traditionally, institutions have been the focus of research within the "industrial relations" and sociology literatures.

Economists have only more recently focused on the role of institutions and, wherever useful, they have deployed modern economic analysis techniques to study issues such as collective bargaining, or the incentives that specific institutions – such as unemployment insurance – have on employee behaviour. Recent work has even tried to analyse the extent to which labor market institutions fit together and in relation to other societal institutions (Freeman 1996).

Apart from the attempts by Freeman to provide a more comprehensive approach, the economics literature has advanced in the analysis of labor market institutions in a very systematic but compartmentalized way.[24] Using economic analysis and the traditional methodology of economics, the functioning of specific institutions has been modelled and the theoretical implications have often been tested with different data sets. This line of research has produced interesting insights, evidence and some controversies. Its reliability depends very much on the extent to which one can handle each institution in isolation.[25]

From a very different perspective sociologists have also provided interesting views on the employment debate (that is the contribution of Colin Crouch in this book, Chapter 6, developing the perspective of the neo-institutional school). Arguably, some of the criticisms of the deregulation case defended by many economists and international organizations such as the International Monetary Fund (IMF) and the Organization for Economic Cooperation and Development (OECD) rely on a caricature of the "mainstream economics" framework which stresses the virtues of full labor market liberalization. As argued below, however, mainstream economic analysis recognizes many labor market imperfections that may justify regulation.

Some of the most interesting contributions of the institutional school are its focus on employment rather than unemployment, the detailed study of the role of female employment, and the thorough analysis of the employment patterns of the young and the elderly.

By focusing on these perspectives, Crouch's contribution in this book provides an explanation of the impact of institutions on employment performance which complements the standard economics-based approach that I shall review later. For example, Crouch points out that the analysis of the labor market should not focus on unemployment data, since – among other problems – these data are often biased by the fact that qualification as unemployed entitles individuals to unemployment benefits (and increases government spending).[26] Because of these effects, both individuals and the government are likely to adopt behaviours which may distort the interpretation of the data.

Similarly, Crouch analyses employment rates (computed taking into account all the population between the ages of 15 and 80) by focusing on female employment. His analysis shows that this type of employment accounts for the greatest absolute differences among countries as well as the most recent rates of growth. Southern European countries show the lowest female employment rates, with the exception of Portugal, which scrapped the relevant legislation after the 1974 change of political regime.

Overall, the approach of the neo-institutional school highlights the importance of appraising labor market problems within a broad perspective that takes into account the role of ideology and political and social groups (see also Whitley 1996).

The importance of the political economy of institutional reform is clear. Leaving aside the United Kingdom, labor market reform in European Union (EU) countries has been very slow and patchy, despite high and rising unemployment figures. As we have seen above, the key role played by society's institutions and social actors in the workings of the labor market has long been recognized. However, only recently have researchers explored in a systematic way the broader political implications of labor market reform. Gilles Saint-Paul (1996) has shown in detail the potential distributional consequences of altering key labor market institutions and how the distribution of the gains and losses from reform affects the different political constituencies and the viability of change.[27] Turning back to the more narrow economic analysis point of view, I review next some of the most interesting results and relevant issues reported in the literature.

1.4.1. The Economic Analysis of Institutions

As usual in economics, the analysis of labor market regulations starts from the benchmark case of a perfectly competitive market. In such a market, firms are willing to pay to workers the value of their marginal productivity and workers supply their work effort, taking into account their opportunity cost in terms of forgone leisure.

Economic analysis is prompt to recognize that the market for labor is not akin to the market for many products and services and, as a consequence, several potential market failures have been examined closely. Labor market institutions are thus appraised as policy tools which may be used to guarantee a proper functioning of the market.

What are the fundamental market failures identified in the economic literature? First, the existence of imperfect competition in the market, either due to union activity (a monopoly on the seller's side) or to the existence of a single buyer of labor services (a monopsony). Second, the asymmetric nature of the information available in the market regarding the characteristics of jobs (for example, in terms of health and safety). Third, the existence of uncertainty about the future behaviour of both labor demand and supply, together with the impossibility of creating a market for contingent labor contracts due to informational deficiencies. A couple of examples illustrate the nature of this market failure.

First, workers may not be able to obtain insurance that covers temporary future drops in income. They may lack the required collateral (human capital cannot be used), or simply the market for that kind of insurance may collapse because of adverse selection (only workers who are more likely to experience falls in income want to obtain insurance, and this raises the premium too much).

Similarly, it might be difficult for firms and workers to commit freely to a long-term relationship: once a worker has acquired firm-specific knowledge, he or she is locked in. The firm need not fully compensate the worker for all the investment in order to retain him or her and this may discourage the investment (which could otherwise be socially productive) to begin with. Writing a complete contingent contract for this problem may be extremely difficult, and it is even more difficult to verify it or enforce its compliance (informational problems are particularly acute with regard to both worker's effort and firm's productivity).

Economic analysis provides, thus, efficiency benchmarks which may be used in the analysis of labor market institutions. It cannot be used to advocate a total deregulation of labor markets. Rather, it is useful because it points out which regulatory features are justified from the perspective of overall economic efficiency and which have to be justified on some other ground.

I shall review next some of the most important institutions prevalent in today's western labor markets: minimum wages, unemployment insurance, collective bargaining regulations and job security provisions.[28]

Minimum wages

According to the conventional view, minimum wage policies pursue equity objectives – guaranteeing an adequate level of wages to the less skilled – but should be assessed negatively from the efficiency point of view. From this perspective, minimum wages would be set typically above the market-clearing level, thus leading to a lower employment level than the one which would be observed in a free market. Following this conventional approach, the minimum wage would be an inefficient way to attain redistribution objectives. The alternative optimal policy is based on a negative income tax, which preserves the wage advantage of the low skilled and restores the living standard through direct subsidies.

Recent research conducted by some American economists has sparked a controversy over this conventional analysis. Researchers such as Card and Krueger (1995)[29] have pointed out that many firms do not in fact face a flat supply of labor at the ongoing wage rate, but rather an upward-sloping schedule so that an increase in the wage rate elicits a slight increase in labor supply and, similarly, a decline in wages does not imply that all workers are ready to be employed somewhere else. Firms are, to a certain extent, monopsonists.

In these circumstances, firms tend to employ too few workers (hiring the marginal worker raises the cost of all infra-marginal ones) and a minimum wage could in fact lead to an increase in jobs as opposed to a decline, while improving overall efficiency.

The extent to which this argument has empirical validity has been investigated by several authors in recent work within the standard economics literature (see, for example, Dolado et al. 1996). This evidence seems to indicate that minimum wages are unlikely to constitute a serious factor preventing job creation in Europe at the aggregate level,[30] although they appear to be a more relevant issue for young workers.[31] The results do not point, therefore, to a major overhaul of the minimum wage system but they do support the need to change the current arrangements and allow the minimum wage to vary according to age.

Unemployment insurance

Unemployment insurance is a labor market institution which also basically pursues equity objectives. Nevertheless, a plausible efficiency case for state intervention[32] has been made, arguing that a private market where workers would insure against the possibility of becoming unemployed would not exist because of the presence of an adverse selection problem. Only workers with large probabilities of being fired and losing their jobs would be willing to pay for an insurance which, as a consequence, would become too expensive.

Even if state-provided unemployment insurance must exist, research on its impact on unemployment has shown that the design of the institution is very important. The key results show that both higher benefit levels and longer benefit duration worsen the unemployment rate. Benefit duration is found to be particularly important (Katz and Meyer 1990).

Recent research by Bover et al. (1996) has also shown that these effects are quantitatively important. For example, when workers have been on the dole for three months it is found that the probability that a worker without benefits will leave unemployment is double that of a worker who is enjoying benefits.

Empirical econometric research has thus confirmed the basic intuition that unemployment benefits will make the unemployed more selective in their search for jobs and, sometimes, will actually discourage job search. This will prolong unemployment spells and decrease the employability of the labor force in the face of rapidly changing technological and demand conditions.

In his chapter in this book (Chapter 2), Stephen Nickell argues that unemployment benefits, by encouraging the growth of long-term unemployment (LTU) versus short-term unemployment, are contributing not only to higher unemployment levels, but also to higher degrees of unemployment persistence.

Nickell's empirical results confirm that higher levels of benefits contribute to higher levels of LTU, that real wages are negatively correlated with changes in unemployment and that this correlation is higher when LTU levels are high. Indeed, higher LTU levels arise when overall unemployment declines and the proportion of LTU in the pool of unemployed increases. Nickell's results show that as unemployment declines (raising the proportion of LTU) the downward sensitivity of wages to unemployment declines, thus fostering unemployment persistence.

Collective bargaining

The debate about the labor market institutions which might be more appropriate for collective bargaining has been heavily influenced by the work of Calmfors and Drifill (1988). The conventional approach from the point of view of economic analysis had been that the existence of unions would be detrimental to employment. The argument was straightforward: unions concentrate the bargaining power of workers and this leads to a monopoly situation where the only seller of labor services is the union. This bids wages up, but always at the expense of employment.

Researchers in political science and industrial relations had always emphasized the alternative view, whereby the existence of unions coupled with strong employers' organizations (in a regime that became known as corporatism) was to be preferred, as negotiators would set their wage agreements taking into account the effects for the whole country: the potential impact on inflation and macroeconomic stability. The work of Calmfors and Drifill provided a systematic empirical and theoretical analysis of both hypotheses. The authors found that the relationship between the degree of bargaining centralization and macroeconomic performance (as measured by the rate of real wage increases) was not monotonic. In fact, real wage increases were in general higher for intermediate bargaining systems, in which negotiations where undertaken at the industry and/or regional level. The best results were obtained either in fully decentralized systems (such as those of the US) or in very centralized ones (such as Sweden or Austria).[33]

The discussion on the nature of the bargaining system should, however, take into account considerations other than the macroeconomic impact on wages and inflation. Since macroeconomic policies have tended to be more stable in recent years, a centralized reaction to a shock that reduces the competitiveness of a country is becoming less valuable. At the same time, the centralized determination of wages might hurt many firms in an economy which is increasingly working under a large variety of market conditions. Similarly, it is not clear how exactly the choices of the unions' and employers' leaders will take into account the interest of the economy as a whole. As the Spanish experience shows, the negotiation interests of the unions might concentrate on employed workers with fixed contracts, the insiders, thus disregarding other constituencies.[34]

Chapter 2 in this book, by Stephen Nickell, looks at the impact of collective bargaining on unemployment persistence rather than on employment levels. Nickell argues that coordinated bargaining by unions – counteracted by coordination on the part of employers – improves the power of insiders and thus strengthens a negative job security effect which creates persistence. This works as follows: low unemployment in this period, relative to the previous period, increases job security and thus diminishes wage moderation, dampening the positive evolution of unemployment levels. Insider power, according to Nickell's results, strengthens this perverse mechanism.

Job security provisions

Employment protection legislation includes provisions on redundancy payments and advance notice requirements, as well as on the conditions accepted by courts to justify a dismissal as based on a valid cause. This legislation is usually justified on equity grounds. However, in an uncertain world access to information will be asymmetric: working conditions or pay may be subject to external factors (technology or product demand) about which the employer may have better information than the employees.[35] In such a world, complete contingent labor contracts cannot be written and specifying restrictions on contracts may serve efficiency purposes. Nevertheless, even if job security provisions may be justified on an efficiency basis, this does not imply that it is easy to determine the most appropriate form of correcting the market failure (what kind and what level of employment protection should be offered).

Apart from their welfare and distributional impact, job security provisions have an effect on employment and wages. This has been investigated by economists and the prevailing evidence shows that employment protection regulations have a very minor direct effect. Employment is unaffected since firms engage in less firing in economic downturns, but foreseeing that, they also engage in less hiring to begin with;[36] wages, however, tend to be lowered by employment protection regulation (Bertola 1990), thus reflecting the fact that the rent captured by workers with this regulation is, at least partially, lost in terms of wages.

The predominant view is, therefore, that these regulations shift rents from firms to workers without necessarily leading to lower employment creation (Layard et al. 1994, p. 108). The most significant impact on jobs arises when the legislation discriminates between different groups of workers. Then, the regulation favours insiders who resist the acceptance of lower nominal wage increases despite the existence of high unemployment (Lindbeck and Snower 1989; and Bentolila and Dolado 1994).

Nickell emphasizes in this book the negative effect of these regulations on the persistence of unemployment. Job protection schemes may not affect the level of unemployment (if we consider a long enough time span), but they do seem to augment the degree of persistence. Nickell points out that persistence does not in itself reduce social welfare. In fact, slow adjustments to negative shocks could be defended on equity grounds. Nevertheless, it should be pointed out that job protection schemes could diminish efficiency by limiting the adjustment possibilities of small firms to negative shocks (large firms can usually adjust employment because they experience a large enough regular flow of employees who leave the company).

1.5.   FIRMS' STRATEGIES AND THE CHANGING NATURE OF JOBS

I started this introductory chapter by emphasizing that the conceptual framework would place enterprises at the centre of the analysis. Indeed, jobs are created as new firms appear in the market or old firms expand their activities successfully. This process of firm creation and expansion is based on the effective adaptation of existing firms and potential entrepreneurs to the changing demands of the market and the potentialities of new technologies. So far we have focused on how institutions influence the demand for labor by firms, the supply behaviour of individuals and the whole employment relationship. It is worth stressing, though, that new skilled jobs appear if firms are able to react to the challenges of technologies and new markets, and can adapt internally to the new scenario. Jobs are preserved if firms and employees can also adapt. It is therefore important to explore how firms can adapt their strategy and their internal organization and employment practices to confront these challenges, and how this adaptation changes the nature of work.

1.5.1. Organizational Changes

One of the distinctive features of the current technological revolution is its extremely important impact on two types of costs which affect crucially the internal organization of firms.[37]

The first cost that has declined dramatically is the cost of communications. Thanks to revolutionary progress in telecommunications, it is today cost-effective to disseminate huge amounts of information within the firm. Similarly, information collected in market transactions can be channelled at low cost and used for decision-making.

The effective use of information within the firm relies, of course, on the sharp reduction of computing costs. Technological progress in this domain has allowed the development of computerized systems that handle vast amounts of information about the market and internal production flows. More generally, it has permitted the appearance of programmable, multi-task flexible equipment.

The increased availability of information, the ease with which it can be processed and the increased flexibility of production and service-provision systems have a profound impact on the way firms may organize themselves internally.

The immediate implication of this kind of technical change is to alter the way production processes are organized and even how products are designed. For example, they may facilitate broader product lines, reduce batch sizes, shorten product cycles, facilitate made-to-order production and reduce work in process.

In fact, some of the broad trends that we observe in modern industrialized economies may be seen as parts of the same phenomenon. In many companies we have seen dramatic *organizational changes*, with significant reductions in the labor force (downsizing), the elimination of middle managers and, sometimes, a complete redesign of the company processes (reengineering).

The investigation on the shift towards a new production paradigm has been motivated by well-known management accounts of the process.[38]

In a series of papers, Paul Milgrom and John Roberts have focused on manufacturing and have emphasized the systemic nature of this process by stressing how the effective introduction of the new technologies requires changes in several organizational aspects of the firm due to the complementarities between different aspects of production strategies and organization.

The impact goes, indeed, beyond the pure production process. Changes in information flows, new flexible multi-task equipment, and the general reorganization of activities within firms lead to a reorganization of work and the way tasks are carried out. This imposes new requirements on the labor force and may call for a new system of human resource management (HRM) practices.[39]

Altogether the nature of work is changing in many organizations and, concomitantly, there is a new approach to employee–employer relations.

As far as job definitions are concerned, the tendency is to move away from repetitive, mechanical activities towards a new concept of multi-task flexible jobs, with substantial work rotation and team work.

Simultaneously, there has been a marked increase in the introduction of innovative supportive HRM policies. The general spirit of these innovations has been to increase the participation of employees, to foster new relationships with management, to facilitate team activities and to increase profit sharing and other forms of innovative financial compensation schemes.

1.5.2.   New Organizational Forms and Firm Strategy

In fact, reengineering processes, the introduction of innovative work practices and other organizational changes should be understood as reflecting the competitive reaction of enterprises in an environment which is rapidly changing under the influence of new technologies, increased competition through globalization and deregulation, and changing consumer preferences as income per capita rises.

To the extent that organizational changes are the result of competitive moves in the marketplace, they will be contingent on the strategies followed by companies and the market environment they experience. Indeed, the work by Paul Osterman in this book (Chapter 4) and elsewhere shows that such a link does exist for the case of innovative human resource management practices.

Osterman distinguishes between innovative work arrangements (such as self-directed work teams; job rotation; use of employee problem-solving groups; and total quality management) and HRM policies (fundamentally rules on hiring, compensation and training) and argues that firms focusing on a quality-based competitive strategy will be more likely to use innovative HRM policies, as opposed to firms operating on the basis of low-cost strategies.

In fact, the effects of new work practices on firms and the determinants of their rate of adoption have been explored in detail in several papers.[40]

This type of work points to four main conclusions. First, HRM practices do not have an impact as independent measures but rather when they form part of packages or bundles of policies undertaken by firms in this area. Second, when that is the case, HRM bundles may be very important in quantitative terms in the sense of significantly affecting performance. Third, despite this fact, few firms adopt sets of consistent[41] HRM practices. And fourth, this insufficient adoption may be explained by a large variety of causes.

One of the possible causes is that the adoption of a bundle of HRM policies has to fit with the overall business strategy of the firm and with the nature of technology in the industry. This is consistent with the work of Osterman and has been explored in a few empirical industry-specific papers. For example, McDuffie (1995)[42] explores empirically the relation between bundles of HRM practices and firm performance. He argues that the introduction of flexible production systems – with the reduction of buffers in the production process – makes the introduction of innovative HRM practices a key component for success. His empirical results confirm this thesis in the automobile industry. It remains to be seen how the fit process between strategy and HRM policies works in other manufacturing or service industries.

Indeed, results in this area are not yet conclusive and other researchers find that the adoption of high-performance work practices invariably improves performance and seems to be unrelated to business strategy (Huselid 1995). As reviewed elsewhere,[43] the ambiguity of these results may be linked to the specification and empirical problems inherent in this type of studies thus far.

A second potential explanation for the insufficient adoption of consistent HRM policies could be that labor market institutions and other societal restrictions prevent firms from undertaking change. This has not been explored in detail, but in a context of rapidly changing technologies, the ability of (labor market) institutions to adapt to the changing requirements of firms can be a key determinant of the success of a country in the creation of rewarding jobs. As argued above, the job creation process can be in jeopardy if social inertia and legal restrictions prevent change. From the public policy point of view, it is important to assess what design of labor markets and business and educational systems facilitates the adaptation process. Before tackling this point, I turn next to the issue of the extent to which the changes triggered by the organizational revolution play any role in the trends observed in modern labor markets.

1.5.3. The Impact on Labor Markets

Whatever the exact nature of the relationship between firm strategy and the organizational revolution, it is clear that changes within firms could play a significant role in actual labor market outcomes. Indeed, from a theoretical perspective Lindbeck and Snower (1995, 1996) have explored the implications of some of the observed trends in production systems (and to a lesser extent of the sometimes coincidental innovative work practices) for the labor market. Their argument is based on the increased importance of the returns from (informational and technological) task complementarities relative to the returns from specialization. They show that advances in information and production technologies, together with increases in the supply of employees with general human capital, can explain the changing fortunes of workers in labor markets, with increased jobs and employment opportunities for what they call versatile workers, relative to non-versatile workers. Lindbeck and Snower conclude that the organizational revolution could be an additional factor (together with skill-biased technological change, international trade and insufficient training) explaining the increase of labor market inequalities.

The chapter by Osterman in this book also considers the possible implications of the organizational revolution for the quality of work. It does so by looking at the main features of contingent employment. In fact, the chapters in this book by both Osterman and Vicente Salas (Chapter 5) argue also, without a formal model in this case, that the move towards new organizational forms may induce the segmentation of the labor market between core and periphery employees. These authors do not focus on the internal reorganization of the firm (the redesigning of how tasks are bundled into jobs) but rather emphasize the redefinition of the boundaries of the firm brought about by new technologies and increased competitive pressures. Firms may decide to focus on "core" competences and, as a consequence, provide job security and other benefits to "core" employees.

The data presented by Osterman show two remarkable aspects of contingent employment. First its dual nature. Even though most contingent employment is associated with low-quality jobs (with low wages, low social benefits and low training), there is also a non-negligible segment of qualified contingent jobs.[44] Second, that most contingent employment seems to be driven by conventional motivations related to the increased importance of peak demand, rather than by the organizational revolution.

Altogether, this type of evidence may lead the analyst to conclude that the increasing weight of contingent employment in modern economies is a result of the well-known trends in labor markets (that is biased technological change, third world competition) and has little to do with organizational changes within firms. This conclusion is, however, unwarranted. As pointed out by Salas in his chapter, the evidence collected thus far is very tentative since we know very little about internal labor markets. Indeed, one of the key points made by this author is that the organizational revolution could, in itself, facilitate job preservation and the increased availability of high-quality jobs. That is why public policy, through the choice of institutions which may facilitate organizational change, is important.

1.5.4. The Policy Implications

From the perspective of public policy, the organizational revolution questions the adequacy of the traditional policy instruments used in most western economies and may call for an active intervention whereby institutional change is promoted with the objective of facilitating the adoption of new organizational forms at the firm level.

Snower discusses how institutions such as centralized bargaining, unemployment security benefits and job security legislation, as commonly implemented, become counterproductive in the context of the organizational revolution.

New organizational forms are characterized by the increasing importance of multi-tasks, which makes it difficult to apply the traditional principle of centralized bargaining –"equal pay for equal work"– in wage negotiations.

Similarly, the unemployment benefit system tends to discriminate against workers who might be willing to supply their services on a temporary or part-time basis. As discussed above, the demand for this type of workers (with low or high levels of training) will increase as firms adopt new organizational forms and keep only core employees within the boundaries of the company. According to Snower, the trend towards increased temporary work will make job security legislation largely irrelevant, and in fact quite counterproductive, to the extent that acquired rights extend to occupational mobility.

Public policy, however, should not only adapt to the organizational revolution. It can actually play a role in its promotion. In fact, Salas argues that public policy, through the design of key labor market institutions, can be a crucial determinant of the nature of employment relations and thus facilitate organizational change at the enterprise level.

According to Salas, who focuses on the Spanish situation, institutional changes may promote a reorientation of the strategy of Spanish firms, from the current focus on low-cost competition towards a higher value-added approach. Such a goal can be achieved by moving away from what the author qualifies as traditional explicit labor contracts towards a new relational contract. This type of contract is more open-ended, leaving more room for adjustment to new circumstances. It is based on the commitment of both employers and employees to a long-run relationship, with implicit job security in exchange for increased worker participation and internal occupational mobility.

In principle, this type of (incomplete) contractual relationship is more appropriate in a turbulent business environment, but decision rights under unforeseen circumstances (residual decision rights) are ascribed to the firm and this change in the balance of power within companies is likely to prevent the change in the contractual regime. Salas suggests that employers' investments in general multi-task training and government regulations promoting information exchanges (worker representation on corporate boards) could be institutional changes which would give credibility to the new contractual relationship and facilitate change.

1.6. FINAL REMARKS

Institutions play a key role in the determination of the employment performance of a country. Key indicators, such as the rate of job creation, the unemployment rate or the participation rate, are to a large extent established by the complex interaction of several social, economic and political institutions.

This book focuses on the role of labor market institutions although, as this introductory chapter has made clear, a much broader range of economic and social institutions is likely to influence employment performance.

I believe that emphasizing the role of institutions is the appropriate analytical approach. Today it is widely recognized that insufficient job creation, low participation rates and high unemployment rates are structural problems. These are difficulties that will not go away with cyclical growth, or – as some analysts have appallingly argued – with a (distant) decline in the rate at which new and reduced cohorts of youngsters enter the labor force. Only structural – that is, institutional – change can improve employment performance.

Institutional change is, however, very difficult. Institutions, whether they are legal constructs or social norms, are prone to substantial inertia, often embodying a complex network of conflicting interests and opposing social groups. Under many circumstances, the beneficiaries of inherited institutions block potential changes which could be highly beneficial from a global point of view.

Institutional rigidities are particularly unfortunate in the world economy at the turn of the twentieth century. The rapid pace of technological change, the very nature of new technologies and the globalization process impose new and changing demands on firms, individuals and society at large.

Spurred by increasingly competitive markets, firms are quickly reacting to this challenge and undergoing a profound organizational revolution. Social institutions must be adapted to the new circumstances. They should ease the adjustment of firms but at the same time cushion the social impact, ensuring social cohesion and facilitating the adaptation of individuals.

Furthermore, as argued by Salas in this book, public policy should not only accommodate institutional change, but rather it should lead the way towards increased institutional flexibility and adaptability.

Institutional reforms may comprise a wide range of structural changes.

At the company level, reengineering and firm reorganization are strong institutional changes which may adversely affect individuals. At the country level, equally strong social shocks may be produced by the reduction of unemployment benefits, the introduction of firm-level bargaining, the reduction of job security provisions and other reforms in employment relationships.

These and other institutional reforms imply profound changes in the distribution of rents and economic power in the economy. In some cases, institutional restructuring increases the uncertainty about the future distribution of rents and job opportunities. Indeed, these foreseen or suspected income redistribution changes lie behind the slow pace of structural labor market reform which has been observed thus far, particularly in most of continental Europe.

The recognition of the strong impact of institutional reform on employment performance and income distribution across the whole economy makes it clear that institutional change must be systemic, encompassing a wide range of institutions with the objective of ensuring enough political support for change, spreading as much as possible across the population the gains and losses from reform.

NOTES

* I wish to thank professors Carlos Cavallé and Jordi Canals for their continuous encouragement in the preparation of this volume.

  My thanks also to Edurne Pérez-Yarza and Teresa Sanjaume. They provided excellent support in the organization of the conference and the edition of this volume.

1 IESE, Barcelona, 19–20 June 1997.

2 Of course, complete exogeneity is too extreme. There is a feedback mechanism and technology and globalization are also the result of firms' strategies. Indeed, the literature on endogenous growth in economics makes it clear that innovations take place as a result of the pursuit of profit motives by individual firms (Romer 1986). Foreign direct investment is also endogenous in the recent economics literature on the subject (Markusen 1995). As usual, the establishment of a conceptual framework requires that we abstract from some of the features of the real world, so that we can centre the analysis on the issues of direct interest. It is therefore reasonable to assume when examining the job creation process that technological change and globalization are exogenous.

3 See *The Economist* (1996) and Butler et al. (1997).

4 For example, influential reports such as the Made in America project led by Dertouzos et al. (1989).

5 See Baily and Gordon (1988).

6 For a succinct account of the report, see Boskin et al. (1997).

7 See Gordon (1996).

8 This intuitive idea has been formalized by Aghion and Howitt (1994). In general, however, very little research supports a positive relationship between technological change and unemployment. As Layard et al. (1994) point out, unemployment is untrended over the very long term and this suggests that there is no long-term relationship between productivity changes and unemployment.

9 Indeed, the period with the stronger rate of growth of output (not total factor productivity) for the currently developed countries corresponds to the golden years after the Second World War (a rate of 3.7 per cent on average for 16 countries between 1950 and 1970) and the last two decades do not show a slow growth (2.2) if one compares it with the rates observed between 1870 and 1950 – with averages ranging from 1.2 to 1.5 per cent (see Barro and Sala-i-Martin 1995, p. 6).

10 See Juhn et al. (1991), Berman et al. (1994) and Machin (1996). See also note 23.

11 Some recent (opposing) contributions to the debate include Lawrence (1996) and Rodrik (1997).

12 See Revenga (1992), Sachs and Shatz (1994), Lawrence and Slaughter (1993) and Freeman (1995).

13 See Gual (1996a).

14 See Arthuis (1993).

15 See Feenstra and Hanson (1995); Lawrence (1994, 1995); Messerlin (1995) and Slaughter (1995).

16 Whitley (1996).

17 For a detailed survey, see Gual (1997).

18 Beyond the standard macroeconomic model, which is based on the idea that there is only a short-term trade-off between inflation and employment, some authors have introduced new arguments in favour of a more active demand management policy. For example, Drèze (1996) argues that even purely temporary drops in demand can have permanent negative effects on employment, and Akerloff et al. (1996) have shown that when stable inflation is set too low there might be negative permanent effects for employment.

19 Note that in some markets where market failures are pervasive, full deregulation may decrease efficiency.

20 The empirical literature on growth has also used a liberalization variable as a factor contributing significantly to the growth of GDP per capita.

21 See, for example, Geroski et al. (1995) and Nickell (1995).

22 This is, of course, the point made by Aghion and Howitt (1994).

23 Work by Machin (1996) and Haskel and Martin (1996) suggests that indeed economies such as those of the UK and the US have suffered major changes in the nature of labor demand, with a significant shift towards skilled employment, without the supply of skilled labor being able to keep pace. Moreover, Machin also shows that most of the observed demand changes do not take place across establishments or industries but rather within specific work sites, often in relation to R&D workplaces. This would point to biased technological change as the major factor inducing labor demand changes.

24 Bertola and Rogerson (1997) provide an example of a joint analytical treatment of

two institutions. These authors argue that the remarkable similarity in job turnover rates between the US and Europe despite the difference in job security institutions may be explained by the joint impact of job security provisions and other institutions (such as collective bargaining) that compress wages and prevent the adjustment of the market through wages in the presence of demand shocks.

25 As pointed out by Alogoskoufis et al. (1995), it is difficult to assess empirically the impact of each of these institutions in isolation because their presence is highly correlated in cross-country analysis.

26 The need to focus on employment rates rather than unemployment rates has also been emphasized by Murphy and Topel (1997).

27 Mancur Olson's theory of collective action provides a related approach. This author argues that the increase in European unemployment is secular and due to the formation of special interest groups which shape policy and maintain the status quo (see Olson 1995).

28 This review is not comprehensive since I do not consider other relevant labor market institutions such as the impact of taxes on labor, restrictions on non-standard labor contracts, and regulations on working time and on the structure of compensation and wage differences across workers.

29 See also Neumark and Wascher (1995) and Deere et al. (1995).

30 Machin and Manning (1997) do not find any evidence for a group of countries including France, the United Kingdom, the Netherlands and Spain.

31 This effect is captured by Bazen and Skourias (1997) for the case of France.

32 The case for insurance, private or public, is also based on the ideas of labor income volatility and job search. Unemployment insurance could be an appropriate instrument to guarantee a smooth income stream to workers over their lifetime since human capital cannot be used as a collateral for borrowing. Unemployment payments may also facilitate the process of looking for an appropriate job and, thus, contribute to overall economic efficiency.

33 The complexity of the relationship between the structure of collective bargaining and employment outcomes makes it difficult to provide a clearcut empirical assessment. The OECD has recently obtained inconclusive results (see OECD 1997) despite the fact that a related result (the negative impact of collective bargaining on wage dispersion) appears to be confirmed by the data.

34 See Bentolila and Dolado (1994).

35 Alogoskoufis et al. (1995).

36 Nevertheless, employment protection regulations reduce turnover and this may be detrimental to sectoral reallocation in periods of fast technological change (Alogoskoufis et al. 1995, p. 114). Moreover, as argued by Bertola and Rogerson (1997), advance notification requirements may play a significant role. The advance notice would allow workers with a higher chance of finding a job to avoid entering the unemployment stock and, as a consequence, those who do enter unemployment will be less likely to find a job within a short time span.

37 Butler et al. (1997) argue that technological changes, by drastically reducing the cost of economic interactions, are going to alter fundamentally the boundaries of the firm, diminishing integration and fostering horizontal cooperation.

38 Womack et al. (1990) and Hammer and Champy (1993).
39 Indeed, Milgrom and Roberts do refer to the implications for jobs and HRM policies (for example, employment guarantees are explored in Milgrom and Roberts 1995) but centre their attention on the consequences for the internal organization of the firm (that is, the structure of production and vertical integration; see Milgrom and Roberts 1990).
40 See Osterman (1995), Ichniowski and Shaw (1995), Ichniowski et al. (1996 and 1997).
41 This type of research deals jointly with new work arrangements and new policies. Consistency – as required for example by Ichniowski et al. (1996), p. 312 –means, therefore, fit between the new ways of organizing work (for example, teams) and HRM policies (such as compensation).
42 See also Arthur (1992).
43 See Portales and Gual (1997).
44 In a recent paper Segal and Sullivan (1997) argue that part of the growth of the temporary jobs industry is associated with the supply side of the market (people willing to offer their services on this basis). Similarly, they argue that the rapid growth of this industry is having beneficial effects in the labor market and the macroeconomy. Many firms use temporary workers as a way of recruiting new employees, and the increased match between supply and demand in the labor market may explain (in the US) the extraordinarily low (non-inflationary) unemployment rate achieved in recent years.

REFERENCES

Aghion, P. and P. Howitt (1994), "Growth and unemployment", *Review of Economic Studies*, **61**, 474–494.
Akerlof, George et al. (1996), "The macroeconomics of low inflation", *Brookings Papers on Economic Activity*, **1**, 1–76.
Alogoskoufis, G. et al. (1995), *Unemployment: Choices for Europe*, Centre for Economic Policy Research, Fifth Report on Monitoring European Integration, London: CERP.
Arthuis, Jean (1993), "Les délocalizations contre l'emploi." A report to the French Senate.
Arthur, Jeffrey B. (1992), "The link between business strategy and industrial relations systems in American steel minimills", *Industrial and Labor Relations Review*, **45** (3), April, 488–506.
Arthur, W. Brian (1996), "Increasing returns and the new world of business", *Harvard Business Review*, July–August, 100–109.
Baily, M.N. and R. Gordon (1988), "The productivity slowdown, measurement issues and the explosion of computer power", *Brookings Papers on Economic Activity*, **2**, 347–431.
Barro, Robert J. and Xavier Sala-i-Martin (1995), *Economic Growth*, Advanced Series in Economics, New York: McGraw-Hill.

Bazen, S. and N. Skourias (1997), "Is there a negative effect of minimum wages on youth employment in France?" *European Economic Review*, **41** (3–5), 723–732.

Becker, G.S. (1962), "Investment in human capital: a theoretical analysis", *Journal of Political Economy*, Supplement, **70**, 9–49.

Becker, G.S. (1975), *Human Capital*, New York: Columbia University Press.

Bentolila, S. and J. Dolado (1994), "Labor flexibility and wages: lessons from Spain", *Economic Policy*, **18**, April, 53–99.

Berman, Eli, John Bound and Zvi Griliches (1994), "Changes in the demand for skilled labor within U.S. manufacturing industries", *Quarterly Journal of Economics,* **109** (2), 367–397.

Bertola, Giuseppe (1990), "Job Security, Employment, and Wages", *European Economic Review*, **34** (4), 851–886.

Bertola, G. and R. Rogerson (1997), "Institutions and labor reallocation", *European Economic Review*, **41** (6), 1147–1172.

Booth, Alison L. and Dennis J. Snower (eds) (1996), *Acquiring Skills*, Centre for Economic Policy Research, Cambridge: Cambridge University Press.

Boskin, M.J. et al. (1997), "The CPI Commission: findings and recommendations", *American Economic Review Papers and Proceedings*, **87** (2), 78–83.

Bover, Olympia, Manuel Arellano and Samuel Bentolila (1996), "Unemployment duration, benefit duration, and the business cycle", Mimeo, Economic Service, Bank of Spain, April.

Butler, P. and J. Driffill (1997), "A revolution in interaction", *McKinsey Quarterly*, **1**, 4–23.

Calmfors, Lars and J. Driffill (1988), "Centralization of wage bargaining. Bargaining structure, corporativism, and macroeconomic performance", *Economic Policy*, **6**, April, 14–61.

Card, David and Alan B. Krueger (1995), "Time series minimum-wage studies: A meta-analyis", *American Economic Review*, **85** (2), May, 238–243.

Deere, Donald, Kevin M. Murphy and Finis Welch (1995), "Employment and the 1990–1991 Minimum-Wage Hike", *American Economic Review*, **85** (2), May, 232–237.

Dertouzos, M.L., Richard K. Lester and Robert M. Solow (1989), *Made in America. Regaining the Productive Edge*, The MIT Commission on Industrial Productivity. Cambridge, MA: MIT Press.

Dolado, Juan, Francis Kramarz, Stephen Machin, Alan Manning, David Margolis and Coen Teulings (1996), "The economic impact of minimum wages in Europe", *Economic Policy*, **23**, October, 317–372.

Drèze, Jacques H. (1996),"Employment in Europe" in Jordi Gual (ed.), *The Social Challenge of Job Creation*, Cheltenham, UK: Edward Elgar, 29–54.

The Economist (1996), "The Hitchhiker's Guide to Cybernomics", 28 September, 3–50.

Feenstra, R.C. and G.H. Hanson (1995), "Foreign investment, outsourcing and relative wages", National Bureau of Economic Research,Working Paper, No. 5121, May.

Freeman, R.B. (1995), "Are your wages set in Beijing?", *Journal of Economic Perspectives*, **9** (3), Summer, 15–32.

Freeman, R.B. (1996), "Does it Fit? Drawing lessons from differing labor practices" in

Jordi Gual (ed.), *The Social Challenge of Job Creation*, Cheltenham, UK: Edward Elgar, 70–88.

Geroski, P., P. Gregg and J.V. Reenen (1995), "Market imperfections and employment", *OECD Jobs Study Working Papers,* 5, Paris: OECD.

Gordon, Robert J. (1996), "Problems in the measurement and performance of service-sector productivity in the United States", National Bureau of Economic Research Working Paper, No. 5519, March.

Gual, Jordi (1996a) "Four myths on employment" in Jordi Gual (ed.), *The Social Challenge of Job Creation*, Cheltenham, UK: Edward Elgar.

Gual, Jordi (ed.) (1996b), *The Social Challenge of Job Creation*, Cheltenham, UK: Edward Elgar, 3–25.

Gual, Jordi (1997), "El empleo y la desregulación de los mercados de bienes y servicios", *Papeles de Economía Española*, 72, 326–341.

Hammer, Michael and James Champy (1993), *Reengineering the corporations*, New York: Harper.

Haskel, Jonathan and Christopher Martin (1996), "Skill shortages, productivity growth and wage inflation" in Alison Booth and Dennis J. Snower (eds), *Acquiring Skills*, Centre for Economic Policy Research, Cambridge: University Press, 147–174.

Hitt, Lorin M. and Eric Brynjolfsson (1996), "Productivity, business profitability, and consumer surplus: three different measures of information technology value", *MIS Quarterly*, June, 121–142.

Huselid, Mark A. (1995), "The impact for human resource management practices on turnover, productivity and corporate financial performance", *Academy of Management Journal,* 38 (3), 635–672.

Hyman, J. (1992), *Training at Work. A Critical Analysis of Policy and Practice*, London: Routledge.

Ichniowski, Casey and Kathryn Shaw (1995), "Old dogs and new tricks: determinants of the adoption of productivity-enhancing work practices", *Brookings Papers in Economic Activity Microeconomics*, 1, 65.

Ichniowski, Casey, Kathryn Shaw and Giovanna Prennushi (1997), "The effects of human resource management practices on productivity: a study of steel finishing line", *American Economic Review*, 87 (3), June, 291–313.

Ichniowski, Casey, Thomas Kochan, David Levine, Craig Olson and George Strauss (1996), "What works at work: overview and assessment", *Industrial Relations*, 35 (3), July, 299–333.

Juhn, C., Murphy, K.M. and R.H.Topel (1991), "Why has the natural rate of unemployment increased over time?" *Brookings Papers on Economic Activity,* 2, 75–142.

Katz, L. and B. Meyer (1990), "The Impact of potential duration of unemployment benefits on the duration of unemployment", *Journal of Public Economics*, 41, 45–72.

Lawrence, Robert Z. (1994), "Trade, multinationals and labor", National Bureau of Economic Research Working Paper No. 4836, August.

Lawrence, Robert Z. (1995), "U.S. wage trends in the 1980s: the role of international factors", *Federal Reserve Bank of New York Economic Policy Review*, 1 (1), January, 18–25.

Lawrence, Robert Z. (1996), *Single World Divided Nations? International trade and*

OECD labor markets. Washington, DC: Brookings Institution Press/OECD Development Center.

Lawrence Robert Z. and Matthew Slaughter (1993), "Trade and U.S. wages: giant sucking sound or small hiccup?" *Brookings Papers on Economic Activity Microeconomics* **2**, 161–226.

Layard, R.G., Nickell, S.J. and R.A. Jackman (1994), *The Unemployment Crisis*, Oxford: Oxford University Press.

Lindbeck, Assar and Dennis J. Snower (1989), *The Insider–outsider Theory of Employment and Unemployment*, Cambridge MA: MIT Press.

Lindbeck, Assar and Dennis J. Snower (1995), "Restructuring production and work Centre for Economic Policy Research Working Paper, No. 1323, December.

Lindbeck, Assar and Dennis J. Snower (1996), "Reorganization of firms and labor market inequality", *American Economic Asssociation Papers and Proceedings*, **86** (2), May, 315–321.

Machin, Stephen (1996), "Changes in the relative demand for skills" in Alison Booth and Dennis J. Snower (eds), *Acquiring Skills*, Centre for Economic Policy Research, Cambridge: Cambridge University Press, 127–146.

Machin, Stephen and Alan Manning (1997), "Minimum wages and economic outcomes in Europe", *European Economic Review*, **41** (3–5), 733–742.

Markusen, J. (1995), "The boundaries of multinational enterprises and the theory of international trade", *Journal of Economic Perspectives*, **9** (2), Spring, 169–189.

Mason, Geoff, Bart Van Ark and Karin Wagner (1996), "Workforce skills, product quality and economic performance" in Alison Booth and Dennis J. Snower (eds), *Acquiring Skills*, Centre for Economic Policy Research, Cambridge: Cambridge University Press, 175–197.

McDuffie, John Paul (1995), "Human resource bundles and manufacturing performance: organizational logic and flexible production systems in the world auto industry", *Industrial and Labor Relations Review*, **48** (2), January, 197–221.

McKinsey Global Institute (1994), *Employment Performance*, Washington, DC: November.

Messerlin, P.A. (1995), "The impact of trade and foreign direct investment on labor markets: the French case", OECD Jobs Study, Working Paper No. 9.

Milgrom, Paul and J. Roberts (1990), "The economics of modern manufacturing: technology, strategy, and the organization", *American Economic Review*, **80** (3), June, 511–528.

Milgrom, Paul and J. Roberts (1995), "Complementarities and fit. Strategy, structure, and organizational change in manufacturing", *Journal of Accounting and Economics*, **19**, 179–208.

Murphy, K.M. and R. Topel (1997), "Unemployment and nonemployment", *American Economic Review Papers and Proceedings*, **87** (2), 295–300.

Neumark, David and William Wascher (1995), "Minimum-wage effects on school and work transitions of teenagers", *American Economic Review*, **85** (2), May, 244–249.

Nickell, Stephen K. (1995), *The performance of companies*, Oxford: Blackwell.

Olson, M. (1995), "The secualr increase in European unemployment rates", *European Economic Review*, **39** (3–4).

Organization for Economic Cooperation and Development (OECD) (1994), *Jobs study, Evidence and Explanations*, Paris: OECD.

Organization for Economic Cooperation and Development (OECD) (1997), *Employment Outlook*, Paris: OECD.

Osterman, Paul (1995), "Skill, training, and the work organization in American establishments", *Industrial Relations*, **34** (2), April, 125–146.

Portales, C. and J. Gual (1997), "Firm strategy, organizational structure and the changing nature of jobs", Paper presented at 17th Meeting of the Strategic Management Society, Barcelona.

Reich, R.B. (1991), *The Work of Nations*, London: Simon & Schuster.

Revenga, A. (1992), "Exporting jobs: the impact of import competition on employment and wages in US manufacturing", *Quarterly Journal of Economics,* **92**, February, 225–286.

Rodrik, D. (1997), "Has globalization gone too far?" Institute for International Economics, Washington, DC, March.

Romer, Paul M. (1986), "Increasing returns and long-run growth", *Journal of Political Economy*, **94**, 1002–1037.

Sachs, J. and H.J. Shatz (1994), "Trade and jobs in U.S. manufacturing", *Brookings Papers on Economic Activity*, **1**, 1–84.

Saint-Paul, Gilles (1996), "Exploring the political economy of labor market institutions", *Economic Policy,* **23**, October, 263–315.

Segal, L.M. and D.G. Sullivan (1997), "The growth of temporary services work", *Journal of Economic Perspectives*, **11**, (2), Spring, 117–136.

Shackleton, J.R. (1995), *Training for Employment in Western Europe and the United States*, Cheltenham, UK: Edward Elgar.

Slaughter, M.J. (1995), "Multinational corporations, outsourcing, and American wage divergence", National Bureau of Economic Research Working Paper, No. 5253.

Whitley, R. (1996), "The institutional structuring of firm's strategies", in Jordi Gual, (ed.), *The Social Challenge of Job Creation*, Cheltenham, UK: Edward Elgar, 157–189.

Winston, C. (1993), "Economic deregulation: days of reckoning for microeconomists" *Journal of Economic Literature*, **XXXI** (3), September.

Womack, James, Daniel T. Jones and Daniel Roos (1990), *The Machine that Changed the World*, New York: Rawson Associates.

Wood, A. (1994), *North–South Trade, Employment and Inequality: Changing Fortunes in a Skill Driven World*, Oxford: Clarendon Press.

2.   Employment dynamics and labor market institutions

Stephen Nickell *

2:1.   SUMMARY

We provide a substantial body of evidence that institutional features of the labor market have an important impact on the degree of employment and unemployment persistence. In particular, we find that employment protection raises persistence, as does anything which tends to increase long-term unemployment or to reinforce the power of insiders. Important factors here include the duration of unemployment benefit and the degree to which unions coordinate their wage bargaining activities. Finally, we argue that unemployment persistence may not, of itself, be a bad thing but some of these factors, notably long benefit durations, will raise unemployment overall as well as the extent of its persistence.

2.2.   INTRODUCTION

In all OECD countries, one of the notable features of labor market behaviour is the degree of persistence in employment and unemployment following any kind of shock.[1] Thus the consequences of a particular shock seem to last for many years, although the extent of this persistence appears to vary substantially from one country to another. One should not conclude from this, however, that all individuals are stuck in whatever state they find themselves. In fact, there are enormous flows of individuals in and out of jobs. For example, in the United States, total annual separations in manufacturing were no less than 48 per cent of total employment in 1980.[2] And even in Italy, whose labor market is supposedly highly sclerotic, annual separations were equal to a third of the labor force between 1985 and 1991 (see Table 2.1, below). Not only are there large movements of individuals in and out of jobs, but there are also large movements of jobs

34

Table 2.1
Job and Worker Turnover

| | Job turnover[a] | | | | | | | Worker turnover[b] | | | |
| | | Total | | | Continuing establishments | | | | | | |
	Years	Creation	Destruction	Turnover	Creation	Destruction	Turnover	Years	Accessions	Separations	Turnover
Austria	(91–93)	7.7	7.5	15.2	5.7	6.2	11.9	(85)	21.9	19.9	41.8
Belgium	(83–85)	16.0	13.8	29.8	9.9	8.8	18.7	(84–91)*	29.0	29.0	58.0
Denmark	(83–89)	10.4	12.0	22.4	6.5	8.7	15.2	(84)	40.0	37.0	77.0
Finland	(86–91)	12.7	11.8	24.4	6.6	6.3	12.9	(87)	28.9	30.7	59.6
France	(84–91)	9.0	7.5	16.5	6.5	5.6	12.1	(84–90)	31.6	30.4	62.0
W. Germany	(83–90)	8.8	12.7	21.4	6.1	8.1	14.1				
Ireland	(84–85)	11.0	10.0	21.0	7.3	6.2	13.5	(85–91)	34.5	33.6	68.1
Italy	(87–92)						7.0	(90)**	11.9	10.1	22.0
Netherlands	(84–91)	8.2	7.2	15.4	6.0	7.5	13.5				
Norway	(85–92)	8.1	10.6	18.7	5.2	7.6	12.8				
Spain[c]	(93–94)				8.0	9.6	17.6	(93–94)*	26.6	28.5	55.1
Sweden	(85–92)	14.5	14.6	29.1	6.0	2.7	8.7	(77–81)*	16.8	17.8	34.6
UK	(85–91)	8.7	6.6	15.3				(67–85)	37.2	37.6	74.8
Canada	(83–91)	14.5	11.9	26.4	11.2	8.8	20.0	(88)	48.2	44.4	92.6
US	(84–91)	13.0	10.4	23.4	4.6	3.1	7.7	(85–93)			96.0
US (manu.)	(84–88)	8.2	10.4	18.6	6.7	7.7	14.4	(77–81)	45.2	46.0	91.2
Japan	(85–92)				8.6	5.3	13.9	(88–92)**	20.2	18.9	39.1
Australia (manu.)	(84–85)	16.1	13.2	29.3	7.1	4.6	11.7				
New Zealand	(87–92)	15.7	19.8	35.5	8.3	11.3	19.7				

NOTES:
(a) Job turnover (percent of total employment, yearly average) = job creation + job destruction. Worker turnover (percent of total employment, yearly average) = accessions + separations.
(b) Sources: (a) OECD Employment Outlook (1996), Table 5.1. (b) OECD Employment Outlook (1996), Table 5.2. Contini et al. (1995), Tables 7.1, 7.2. (c) Serrano (1996).
(*) Manufacturing.
(**) Continuing firms.

between firms (and even larger ones between establishments). Thus annual gross job losses in manufacturing in the United States are about 10 per cent, with comparable numbers in many other OECD countries (see Table 2.1).

Much of both person and job flows reflects idiosyncratic shocks, that is, shocks which are specific to firms and individuals and are not related to overall economic conditions. As a consequence of these shocks, individuals are continually separating from firms and, in so far as the individual flows pass through unemployment, they generate a background level of frictional unemployment which is relatively stable through time. Some idea of the extent of this frictional unemployment may be gleaned from Table 2.2, which reveals the inflow rate into unemployment for a number of OECD countries.

Table 2.2
Percentage Unemployment Rates and Inflows in Unemployment

| | Monthly inflow rate | | Unemployment rate |
	1985	1993	(1983–96)
Belgium	0.14	0.42	9.7
Denmark	–	1.75	9.9
Finland	1.49	2.83	9.1
France	0.32	0.34	10.4
W. Germany	0.25	0.57*	6.2
Ireland	0.35	0.55	15.1
Italy	0.14	0.41	7.6
Netherlands	0.28	0.24	8.4
Norway	0.32	0.45	4.2
Portugal	–	0.34	6.4
Spain	0.35	0.56	19.7
Sweden	0.66	1.25	4.3
UK	0.51	0.67	9.7
Canada	2.47	2.40	9.8
US	2.45	2.06	6.5
Japan	0.33	0.38	2.6
Australia	0.73	0.79	8.7
New Zealand	0.94	1.07	6.8

NOTES:
(i)   The inflow rate is defined as the monthly inflow into unemployment divided by employment. The monthly inflow is here measured by the number of unemployed who have durations of less than one month. This is an underestimate as it omits roughly half of those whose completed duration is less than one month. For further details see OECD (1995), Table 1.9. Unemployment refers to the OECD standardized rate in most cases. For full details, see Nickell (1997), Table 1.
(ii)   * Includes the former East Germany.

The fascinating thing about these numbers in the enormous range and the fact that there is no correlation between the inflow rate and the unemployment rate across the countries. This, of course, reflects the equally enormous range of unemployment durations across the countries, about which we shall have more to say later. Some effort has been devoted in recent years (following Lilien 1982) to investigating whether or not *autonomous* variations in these idiosyncratic, firm-level, shocks play an important role in explaining business-cycle fluctuations. The basic hypothesis is that business-cycle fluctuations arise from autonomous surges in industry structural change. While measures of structural turbulence are certainly correlated with unemployment fluctuations, it remains unclear as to whether or not the turbulence is generated ultimately by aggregate shocks as opposed to large numbers of micro-level disturbances (see, for example, Abraham and Katz 1986; Blanchard and Diamond 1989; Davis and Haltiwanger 1990; Abraham 1990). However, one thing is clear: the idiosyncratic disturbances do not appear to explain directly the high degree of unemployment persistence which we have already noted. For example, in the unemployment regressions reported in Davis and Haltiwanger (1990, Table 3), an enormous degree of unemployment persistence remains after controlling for current and lagged idiosyncratic shocks.[3]

Our main concern in this chapter, therefore, is with the persistence of the stocks of unemployment and employment in response to shocks. In particular we shall be concerned with how labor market institutions influence the extent of this persistence. In the next section we shall look more closely at employment behaviour and see how this relates to the issue of job creation and destruction. The following section is concerned with employment/unemployment dynamics and wage determination, and then we look at unemployment dynamics from a macroeconomic viewpoint. A final section concludes.

2.3.   EMPLOYMENT DYNAMICS FROM THE DEMAND SIDE

In this section we look first at employment determination at the firm level, focusing particularly on hires, quits and layoffs. Then we consider the implications for gross job creation and destruction, and finally we consider demand-side aggregate employment dynamics, looking at intercountry differences in demand-side persistence.

Employment determination at the firm level

By definition, the change in a firm's employment is given by the number of hires less quits and layoffs. Thus we have change in employment = hires – quits – layoffs   (2.1)

where quits include retirements. Each firm decides its employment in each period on the basis of labor costs and the demand for its products. However, it will also take note of the amount of hiring or firing required to attain the desired number of employees. Hiring and firing are costly activities and the more costly they are, the more the firm will take account of the extent to which its labor force must change (from the previous period) in order to get the number of employees it wants. If too much change is required, the firm will spread the employment adjustment over several periods by slowing down the hiring or firing rate. This will, of course, slow down the changes in employment and raise the degree of persistence. Bearing this in mind, we first look at cross-country differences in the turnover of jobs and workers and then see whether we can relate the costs of hiring and firing directly to the speed of employment adjustment in different countries.

Job and worker turnover

One measure of the speed with which firms make necessary adjustments is the extent of job turnover. This measures the rate at which firms destroy jobs which are unprofitable and create jobs which are profitable. The totals of job creation and job destruction are given as follows.

$$
\begin{aligned}
\text{job creation} \quad &= \text{(hires – quits – layoffs)} \ \textit{in expanding firms} \\
&= \text{hires(E) – quits(E) – layoffs(E)} &(2.2) \\
\text{job destruction} &= \text{(quits + layoffs – hires)} \ \textit{in contracting firms} \\
&= \text{quits(C) + layoffs(C) – hires(C).} &(2.3)
\end{aligned}
$$

(E) and (C) refer, respectively, to firms which are increasing their employment (expanding) or decreasing their employment (contracting). Of course, the number of layoffs in expanding firms may be rather low, but they can exist so long as workers are not homogeneous. Job turnover is simply defined:

job turnover = job creation + job destruction.   (2.4)

Thus it is a measure of the total rate at which jobs are created and destroyed in an economy. And since it is desirable for an economy to destroy unprofitable jobs and create profitable ones at a rapid rate, high job turnover is typically considered to be an indication of a well-functioning economy.

But job turnover clearly generates worker turnover. Every time a job is destroyed, a worker must leave, and every time a job is created, a worker is hired. However, workers can leave even if their job remains, so worker turnover is equal to job turnover *plus* the circulation of workers through existing jobs. More formally, worker turnover is defined as the sum of accessions and separations, the former simply being the number of hires and the latter being quits plus layoffs. Thus we have

worker turnover = hires + quits + layoffs   (2.5)

In Table 2.1, we see how job and worker turnover varies across countries. While there is substantial variation in job turnover across the OECD, there is no obvious contrast between Europe and North America. Of course, there are problems of comparability with data such as these (see Contini et al. 1995) but even so, there is no evidence here that jobs are created and destroyed at a more rapid rate in North America than in Europe. However, workers do appear to circulate faster through the existing jobs in North America, a feature which is consistent with their lower overall levels of employment protection. This suggests that we might look at how employment protection influences the dynamics of labor demand more generally.

Labor demand and employment protection

The speed at which firms adjust employment depends crucially on hiring and firing costs which, in their turn, will depend on employment protection legislation. In order to see whether this relationship is of any consequence in reality, we first note that we can measure the sluggishness of the adjustment of labor demand by the parameter λ in the equation

$$\mathbf{n_t} = \lambda \mathbf{n_{t-1}} + (1 - \lambda)\mathbf{n_t}^* \qquad (0 \leq \lambda < 1) \qquad (2.6)$$

where $\mathbf{n}$ = employment, $\mathbf{n}^*$ = target or "desired" employment and $\mathbf{t}$ = time period. Note that since (2.6) implies $\mathbf{n_t} - \mathbf{n_{t-1}} = (1 - \lambda)(\mathbf{n_t}^* - \mathbf{n_{t-1}})$, the parameter $(1 - \lambda)$ represents the proportion of the gap between target employment and actual employment which is filled in each period. If adjustment is more sluggish, λ is bigger and a smaller proportion of the gap gets filled in any one period.

In order to see whether the extent of sluggishness, as measured by λ, is indeed related to the size of hiring and firing costs and the extent of employment protection, we need measures of both λ and employment adjustment costs across a number of countries. In Table 2.3, we present three measures of sluggishness (λ), taken directly from three sets of employment equations in Layard et al. (1991), Bean et al. (1986), and Newell and Symons (1985). Along with these are four measures of adjustment costs, two indirect measures, an index of the tightness of employment protection legislation and the percentage of employees in manufacturing with job tenures of less than two years, which is, of course, inversely related to adjustment costs, and two direct measures, namely severance pay and periods of notice. These are both legal minima.

Table 2.3
Measures of the Sluggishness of Employment and of Adjustment Costs

	λ(LNJ)	λ(NS)	λ(BLN)	OECD ranking (EP)	% employees with tenure < 2years (PL2)	Severance pay (SEV)	Period of Notice (NOT)
Austria	0.85	0.84	0.56	16		12	0.5
Belgium	0.64	0.92	0.76	17	18	0	2
Denmark	0.48	–	0.26	5	27	0	0
Finland	0.45	0.91	0.32	10	26.3	0	6
France	0.74	0.90	0.72	14	22.2	1.5	2
W. Germany	0.86	0.88	0.36	15	21	0	3
Ireland	0.85	0.86	0.71	12	22	12.0	2
Italy	0.81	0.74	0.65	19	13	13.0	0
Netherlands	0.85	0.91	0.90	9	26.9	0	4
Norway	0.88	0	0.07	11	17	0	6
Spain	0.66	–	–	18	13.6	12	3
Sweden	0.60	0.78	0.16	13	–	0	6
Switzerland	0.81	0.83	0.12	6	29.3	8	6
UK	0.70	0.88	0.37	7	31	6	2
Canada	0.92	0.91	0.17	3	33.7	1	0.25
US	0.38	0.10	0	1	39.7	0	0
Japan	0.85	0.83	0.65	8	20	0	1
Australia	0.35	0.49	0.43	4	36.8	0	1
New Zealand	0.84	–	–	2	–	0	0.25
Expected effect on				(+)	(-)	(+)	(+)

The regressions reported in Table 2.3 indicate, first, that these measures are related to each other in the right sort of way. In particular high job tenure is strongly associated with strong employment protection legislation and high levels of severance pay. Second, two of the three measures of employment sluggishness (λ) are significantly related to job tenure and they generally bear a correctly signed relationship with our other measures of adjustment costs, with some of the coefficients being significant at the 10 per cent level. Overall, these results are consistent with our expectations concerning the underlying causes of sluggish adjustment in the demand for labor. But this is only one side of the story. Persistence overall is also generated by the process of wage determination, which is our next topic.

2.4.   EMPLOYMENT DYNAMICS AND WAGE SETTING

In general, company wages are influenced both by conditions in the external labor market and by how well the company is doing. Conditions in the external labor market impinge on employers via the ease with which they

REGRESSIONS			
PL2 = 28.9 − 0.65 SEV − 0.80 NOT, (2.0)　　　(0.9)	N = 16, R^2= 0.22	PL2 = 37.7 − 1.29 EP, (7.9)	N=16 R^2 = 0.82
λ(LNJ) = 0.99 −0.011 PL2, (2.1)	N = 16 R^2 = 0.23	λ(LNJ) = 0.68 + 0.010 SEV, (1.8)	N = 1 9 R^2 = 0.10
λ(LNJ) = 0.70 + 0.003 NOT, (0.2)	N = 19.0 R^2 = 0.0	λ(LNJ) = 0.63 + 0.0085 EP, (1.1)	N = 19 R^2 = 0.07
λ(NS) = 0.92 − 0.0081 PL2, (0.6)	N = 14 R^2 = 0.04	λ(NS) = 0.76 + 0.0059 SEV, (0.7)	N = 15 R^2 = 0.02
λ(NS) = 0.70 + 0.036 NOT, (1.5)	N = 15 R^2 = 0.13	λ(NS) = 0.54 +0.019 EP, (1.4)	N = 16 R^2 = 0.12
λ(BLN) = 0.89 − 0.01 PL2, (2.4)	N = 15 R^2 = 0.23	λ(BLN) = 0.50 + 0.014 SEV, (1.4)	N = 17 R^2= 0.06
λ(BLN) = 0.50 − 0.03 NOT, (1.1)	N=17 R^2 = 0.06	λ(BLN) = 0.15 + 0.028 EP, (2.4)	N = 17 R^2= 0.28

λ　Coefficient on lagged dependent variable in an employment equation, LNJ = Layard, Nickell and Jackman (1991, Ch. 9, Table A1, p. 450), NS = Newell and Symons (1985), BLN = Bean, Layard and Nickell (1986), both as reported in Alogoskoufis and Manning (1988, Table 6) and in Layard et al. (1991, Ch. 9, Table A3, pp. 454–466).

EP　OECD ranking of the strictness of employment protection legislation, with 19 as the most strictly regulated down to 1 as the most lax. OECD (1994, Part II, Table 6.7, Col. 5).

PL2　Percentage of manufacturing employees with tenure less than 2 years. It is based on Metcalf (1986, Table 4), and on OECD (1993, Table 4.1). Where information for a given country appears in both places, the average is reported. The figure for Spain is derived as follows. In OECD (1993), Table 4.1, it is reported that 31.6 per cent of employees had tenure less than 2 years. But much of this was a consequence of the introduction of fixed-term employment contracts in the mid-1980s. Since our sample period is mostly prior to this date, we must try and remove the impact of these fixed-term workers. In 1990, about 24 per cent of employees held fixed-term (≤ 3 year) contracts so, if we suppose that three-quarters of these have a job tenure under 2 years, removing these leaves 13.6 per cent as reported in the table.

SEV　Maximum legislated months of severance pay for blue-collar workers as reported in OECD (1993, Table 3.8).

NOT　Maximum legislated months of notice required for blue-collar workers, OECD (1993, Table 3.8).

can fill vacancies (negative effect on wages) and on employees via the ease with which they can obtain alternative employment if they lose their jobs (positive effect on wages). In fact, these are simply two sides of the same coin. Employers find it easy to fill vacancies if, and only if, employees find it hard to find alternative employment if they lose their jobs. So what makes it difficult to find another job? Obviously a larger number of unemployed will ensure increased competition for the available vacancies. But the situation is worse if a high proportion of the unemployed have only recently lost their jobs. These individuals are likely to compete more fiercely for work than longer-term unemployed and this generates a role for employment dynamics in wage setting. The proportion of short-term unemployed depends directly on the rate of flow into unemployment, so when unemployment is increasing, the short-term proportion tends to be high and additional downward pressure is exerted on wages. So this duration effect is one reason why changes in unemployment have an impact on wages additional to that generated by the level of unemployment. Turning to the effect of company performance on wage setting, the key factor here is the extent of job insecurity at given wages. Anything which raises job insecurity is likely to increase downward pressure on wages, because job insecurity is one of the major forces for wage moderation. And it is obvious that rising unemployment is associated directly with higher job insecurity. So this is another reason why *changes* in unemployment have an impact on wages.

To summarize, wages are influenced both by the level of unemployment in the outside labor market and by changes in that level. Given our interest in dynamics, it is these change effects which are of most interest here, and we have identified two reasons why increasing unemployment puts additional downward pressure on wages. These are the insider, job security effect – rising unemployment means increased job insecurity and downward pressure on wages, and the long-term unemployment effect – rising unemployment means proportionately more short-term and less long-term unemployment, more competition for jobs among the unemployed and hence downward pressure on wages. So what influences the size of these effects?

First, the job security effect depends on the power of insiders. Microeconometric evidence suggests that insiders tend to be weak in small firms (see Brunello and Wadhwani 1989). However, they are likely to be stronger if there is a high degree of employment protection. Furthermore, in unionized economies, if unions bargain wages in a coordinated fashion this would tend to enhance insider power although this would be offset by coordination on the part of the employers. The long-term unemployment effect is obviously going to be important in the presence of labor market institutions which encourage the growth of such unemployment. These include, in particular, easy availability of unemployment benefits for long periods and strong employment protection laws, which make employers very cautious about hiring. On the other hand, those countries which spend extensively on measures to encourage early exit from unemployment may be expected to have low levels of long-term unemployment. To investigate these issues, we use estimates for a number of countries of the unemployment change (Δu) effect on wages in a standard real wage equation of the form

$$w - p = \alpha_0 - \alpha_1 u - \alpha_2 \Delta u \ldots \qquad (7)$$

and relate these to the labor market factors discussed above. In Table 2.4, we present a set of estimates of the α_2 parameter as well as information on long-term unemployment, benefits, benefit duration, expenditure on labor market programmes, the size of the small-firm sector and measures of coordination on both the union and the employers' side. From the regressions, we see first that the Δu coefficient is positively influenced by the long-term unemployment rate, confirming the long-term unemployment effect discussed above. Furthermore, it is negatively affected by the proportion of employment in small firms and positively influenced by employment protection, which is consistent with the existence of insider-generated dynamics. Finally, the coordination effects are precisely as predicted, that is, negative for employer coordination and positive for union coordination. Overall, therefore, there is some evidence that both long-term unemployment effects and insider effects are at work in determining unemployment dynamics. The final regression then indicates the importance of benefit duration and employment protection in determining the extent of long-term unemployment, confirming the result reported in OECD (1993, p. 106).

2.5. UNEMPLOYMENT DYNAMICS IN THE AGGREGATE

Our purpose here is, first, to see how employment dynamics from both labor demand and wage setting interact to generate unemployment persistence in the macroeconomy. Second, we shall investigate patterns of unemployment dynamics across the OECD and relate them to the sort of institutional labor market factors which we have considered in the previous sections.

Unemployment persistence

The persistence of unemployment in an economy depends on the extent of sluggishness in labor demand and on the influence of employment dynamics on wage setting. To see this, we put together a labor demand equation based on (2.6) and a wage equation based on (2.7). Thus we have

labor demand: $n_t = \lambda n_{t-1} - \alpha(w - p) + z_n$ (8)
wage determination: $w - p = \alpha_0 - \alpha_1 u - \alpha_2 \Delta u + z_w$ (9)

where z_n, z_w are exogenous factors influencing labor demand and wages. The key dynamic parameters are the index of sluggishness in labor demand, λ, and the unemployment change effect on wages, α_2.

Table 2.4
Unemployment Change Effects in the Wage Equation

	α2(LNJ)	Long-term unemployed (LTU)%	Union coordination (UNCD)	Employer coordination (EMCD)	% Employees in small firms (PSF)	Expenditure on labor market programmes (LMP)	Benefit replacement ratio (RR)	Benefit duration (BD)
Belgium	0	35.9	2	2	32.8	7.4	60	48
Denmark	0	36.2	3	3	36.1	7.9	90	30
France	0.73	30.3	2	2	27.7	3.9	57	45
W. Germany	0	21.2	2	3	20.0	10.4	63	48
Ireland	0	31.8	1	1	34.6	5.0	50	48
Italy	2.51	35.8	2	1	32.8	0.8	2	6
Netherlands	0.36	27.1	2	2	34.6	2.7	70	48
Spain	0	27.5	2	1	–	2.1	80	42
UK	0.75	24.5	1	1	20.3	4.6	36	48
Australia	0	21.1	2	1	30.0	2.8	39	48
New Zealand	0	14.7	2	1	–	13.1	38	48
Canada	0.17	3.5	1	1	–	4.3	60	6
US	0.09	4.2	1	1	15.2	2.4	50	6
Japan	-3.69	18.8	2	2	47.1	5.6	60	6
Austria	0	13.3	3	3	37.0	11.3	60	48
Finland	0.33	12.0	3	3	23.9	12.9	75	48
Norway	2.74	10.8	3	3	–	9.8	65	18
Sweden	0	6.8	3	3	26.0	34.6	80	14
Switzerland	0	–	1	3	–	3.7	70	12
Expected Effect		+	+	–				

REGRESSIONS

α_2(LNJ) = 1.28 + 0.056 LTU – 0.14 PSF + 1.64 UNCD – 1.29 EMCD + 0.081 EP: $R^2 = 0.82$
            (2.5)   (5.1)   (3.2)   (1.3)   (2.0)   N = 14

LTU = 11.57 + 0.16 BD – 0.63 LMP + 0.85 EP: $R^2 = 0.49$
            (1.5)   (2.3)   (2.3)   N = 18

Data: Variables refer to the 1980s.

α_2	Coefficient on – Δu in a wage equation. LNJ = Layard, Nickell and Jackman (1991; Ch. 9, Table A2, p. 452).
LTU	Percentage of unemployed with a duration of unemployment of more than 1 year. Where possible, this is measured for each country when the aggregate unemployment rate is between 5 and 7 per cent (OECD, *Employment Outlook*, various issues).
UNCD (EMCD)	Extent of inter-union (inter-firm) coordination, both formal and informal, in the process of wage bargaining (3 = high, 2 = middle, 1 = low) (Layard et al. 1991, Annex 1.4).
PSF	Percentage of employees in manufacturing who work in firms that employ fewer than 100 persons (OECD, *Employment Outlook*, 1985, Table 26).
LMP	Expenditure on active labor market programmes per unemployed person as a percentage of output per person (OECD, *Employment Outlook*, September 1988, Table 3.1).
RR	Percentage unemployment benefit replacement ratio. Gross benefits for a single person under 50 as a percentage of the gross wage (except in W. Germany) in 1985 (Mainly US Deptartment of Health and Social Services, *Social Security Programs Throughout the World 1985* (Reserve Report No. 60) and Eurostat, Definition of Registered Unemployed, 1987, Theme 3, Series E).
BD	Duration of eligibility in months to some form of benefit paying more than $120 per month in 1985. Indefinite is set at 48 months. (Same as RR.)
EP	Employment protection, defined in Table 2.3.

Eliminating wages from (2.8) and (2.9), and rearranging, we obtain a dynamic unemployment equation of the form[4]

$$u_t = \{(\lambda+\alpha\alpha_2)/[1+\alpha(\alpha_1+\alpha_2)]\}u_{t-1} + \ldots \tag{10}$$

So the extent of persistence (the coefficient on lagged unemployment) is increasing in both α_2 and λ. Thus the features of the economy that influence α_2 and λ, which we have discussed in the previous two sections, should influence unemployment persistence.

To confirm that this is indeed the case, we can report the results of an analysis of unemployment persistence presented in Nickell (1995, Table 5). In an analysis of 19 OECD countries, unemployment dynamics were estimated to have the form

$$u_{it} = (0.84 – 0.081PL2_i + 0.041BD_i + 0.096UNCD_i – 0.073EMCD_i)u_{it-1} + \ldots$$
$$\quad (2.5) \qquad\qquad (7.4) \qquad (7.1) \qquad\qquad (8.4)$$

where **u** = unemployment rate, PL2 = percent age of employees with less than two years of job tenure (see Table 2.3), BD = benefit duration (see Table 2.4), UNCD (EMCD) = union (employer) coordination in wage bargaining (see Table 2.4), **i** = country, **t** = time, **t**-ratios are in brackets.[5]

The percentage of low-tenure employees is inversely related to employment protection (see Table 2.3) which therefore directly raises unemployment persistence. Longer benefit duration generates long-term unemployment which produces an unemployment change effect in wage setting, as does union coordination in wage setting, by strengthening the power of insiders. Employer coordination, on the other hand, has the opposite effect.

The impact of all these effects is quite substantial. For example, we find that the mean lag (in years) for countries with low persistence is about two to three times shorter than that for countries with high persistence. Thus we have mean lags of 2.5 years for Switzerland, 3.2 years for the United States and 3.8 years for Japan whereas the United Kingdom, Ireland, Belgium and the Netherlands all have mean lags between 7.1 and 9.1 years. Of course, all these numbers are the result of a very crude exercise. They are, however, indicative of the potential importance of institutional characteristics in explaining the different patterns of unemployment dynamics across the OECD.

2.6.   CONCLUSIONS

We have provided a substantial body of evidence that institutional features of the labor market have an important impact on the degree of employment and unemployment persistence. In particular, we find that employment protection raises persistence and anything which tends to increase long-term unemployment or reinforces the power of insiders will do the same. Does this mean that all these things are bad and should be eliminated?

The first question to ask here is whether unemployment persistence is, itself, a bad thing. If there is a high degree of persistence, the unemployment consequences of a negative shock last for a long time. But the same applies to a good shock. So the welfare consequences of this are not clearcut. In some respects rapid adjustment seems desirable. But if the adjustment is spread out over a longer period, individuals have more time to get used to the consequences.

What about the institutional features which generate high levels of persistence? Employment protection exists to protect employees from arbitrary or discriminatory decisions on the part of employers. In the process, however, it may reduce the ability of employers to adjust the level of employment in response to economic conditions. The consequences of this can be overstated, for it must be recognized that employers can typically reduce employment by 10 per cent per annum without cost, simply by not replacing employees who leave voluntarily. Nevertheless, employment protection can generate inefficiencies, particularly for small employers who cannot rely on the law of large numbers to generate a steady flow of natural wastage or if the laws are weighted too heavily in favour of preserving the jobs of incompetent employees. Obviously a balance must be struck but the macroeconomic arguments here do not seem very strong.

The same cannot be said of benefit duration. Long periods of eligibility for generous unemployment benefit will not only raise persistence, by generating long-term unemployment, but will also raise average unemployment by discouraging the acceptance of jobs of any duration. Alternative methods of protecting the unemployed from poverty are desirable.

Finally, the results on the coordination of unions and employers during wage bargaining indicate that employer coordination can help to offset the negative consequences of union power. This is particularly important for countries with strong unions, since it might be much easier to generate employer cooperation than to weaken the unions.

NOTES

*   This chapter was presented at the conference, "Job Creation: the Role of Labor Market Institutions", on 19-20 June 1997 at IESE, Barcelona. I am most grateful to Tracy Jones for help with this research and to the Leverhulme Trust (Programme on the Labor Market Consequences of Technological and Structural Change) for financial assistance. I must also thank Jordi Gual for his valuable comments on an earlier draft.

1   Direct information on this is provided in Layard et al. (1991, Ch. 9, Table 4), using a simple reduced-form regression of unemployment on its own lag and a series of variables to capture longer-term shifts in the equilibrium unemployment rate. It is important to recognize that if such variables are omitted and a simple univariate analysis of unemployment is used (for example, Alogoskoufis and Manning 1988, Table 4), then persistence is systematically overstated and the results are not informative about genuine levels of persistence.

2   See Employment and Training Report of the President (1982, Table C.13).

3   This can be seen in the very small DW statistics associated with the OLS regressions, ranging from 0.46 to 0.63.

4   We first rewrite (2.8) as $\mathbf{u_t} = \lambda \mathbf{u_{t-1}} + \alpha(\mathbf{w} - \mathbf{p}) - \mathbf{z_n} + \mathbf{l_t} - \lambda \mathbf{l_{t-1}}$ where $\mathbf{l}$ is the log labor force, assumed exogenous. (2.10) follows immediately from the elimination of $(\mathbf{w} - \mathbf{p})$ from this equation using (2.9).

5   We are forced to omit the variable relating to small firms because of insufficient data.

REFERENCES

Abraham, K.G. (1990), "Comment on Davis and Haltiwanger", National Bureau of Economic Research, *Macroeconomics Annual 1990*, Cambridge, MA: MIT Press, pp. 169–77.

Abraham, K.G. and L.F. Katz (1986), "Cyclical unemployment: sectoral shifts or aggregate disturbances", *Journal of Political Economy*, **94** (3), pt. 1; 507–22.

Alogoskoufis, G. and A. Manning (1988), "On the persistence of unemployment", *Economic Policy*, **7**, 42–69.

Bean, C.R., R. Layard and S.J. Nickell (1986), "The rise in unemployment: a multi country study", *Economica*, **53**, S1–S22.

Blanchard, O.J. and P.A. Diamond (1989), "The Beveridge Curve", *Brookings Papers on Economic Activity*, **1**, 1–60.

Brunello, G. and S. Wadhwani (1989), "The determinants of wage flexibility in Japan: some lessons from a comparison with the UK using micro data", Centre for Labor Economics, Discussion Paper No. 362, London School of Economics.

Contini, B., L. Pacelli, M. Filippi, G. Lioni and R. Revelli (1995), *A Study of Job Creation and Job Destruction in Europe*, A Study for the European Commission (D.G.V.), Turin: R. & P.

Davis, S.J. and J. Haltiwanger (1990), "Gross job creation and destruction: microeconomic evidence and macroeconomic implications", National Bureau of Economic Research, *Macroeconomics Annual 1990*, Cambridge, MA: MIT Press, 123–68.

Layard, R., S. Nickell and R. Jackman (1991) *Unemployment Macroeaconomic Performance and the Labour Market*, Oxford: Oxfor University Press.

Lilien, David M. (1982), "Sectorial Shifts and Cyclical Unemployment", *Journal of Political Economy*, **90**, (4) 777–803.

Metcalf, D. (1986), "Labor market flexibility and jobs: a survey of evidence from OECD countries with special reference to Great Britain and Europe", Centre for Labor Economics, Working Paper No. 870, London School of Economics.

Newell, A. and J.S.V. Symons (1985), "Wages and Unemployment in OECD Countries", Centre for Labor Economics, Discussion Paper No. 219, London School of Economics.

Nickell, S. (1995), "Labor market dynamics in OECD countries", Centre for Economic Performance, Discussion Paper No. 258, London School of Economics.

Nickell, S. (1997), "Labor market rigidities and unemployment: Europe versus North America", *Journal of Economic Perspectives*, Summer, **11** (3), 55–74.

Organization for Economic Cooperation and Development (OECD) (various years), *Employment Outlook*, Paris: OECD.

Serrano, C.G. (1996), "On employment adjustment, worker turnover and job reallocation", Madrid, mimeo.

3.   The organizational revolution and its implications for job creation*

Dennis J. Snower

3.1.   ABSTRACT

This chapter describes the ongoing "organizational revolution", a broad-based transformation of how production, work, and decision-making are organized within business enterprises. It argues that the organizational revolution, like the Industrial Revolution that preceded it, promises great increases in productivity, provided that the organization of economic activity is transformed accordingly. Four major forces are identified as driving the organizational revolution: changes in physical capital towards flexible, programmable equipment and computer-aided design and manufacture, change in information technology permitting greater decentralization of work, changes in human capital towards greater versatility, and changes in people's preferences regarding employment and consumption. The upshot of these changes is multi-faceted: flatter organizational structures, changes in the organization of production and product development, changes in the nature of products and in seller–customer relations, the gradual breakdown of occupational barriers, and changes in the nature of firms. The chapter examines the implications of these changes for labor market institutions, in particular, for the future of centralized bargaining, unemployment benefit systems, and job security legislation. It also explores the implications for labor market policies.

3.2.   INTRODUCTION

Over the past decade and a half, the distribution of employment prospects has become more unequal in many continental European countries; at the same time, the distribution of wage incomes has become more unequal in the UK and the US. These phenomena carry two growing social problems in their wake: unemployment and the plight of the working poor, falling ever more heavily on the poorly skilled and poorly educated people.

Beyond that, employees in many sectors of the UK and US economies, as well as some continental European countries, are reporting that their jobs have become markedly more insecure. This insecurity has perhaps been mirrored in the rise in temporary and part-time employment, and in the proliferation of flexible pay schemes. Expectations of lifetime employment are foundering. Occupational barriers are breaking down, as employees take responsibility for growing networks of tasks. As a result, skilled work is becoming increasingly idiosyncratic and, in response, employment contracts are becoming increasingly individualized.

Meanwhile, business managers and executives around the industrialized world have witnessed revolutionary changes in the characteristics of global competition and the nature of the customer–seller relationship. Customers are demanding increasingly differentiated treatment. In response, sellers are placing unprecedented emphasis on broad product lines, customer participation in the design of goods and services, and customer services associated with sale of goods. Competition for customers extends far beyond pricing and advertising factory-produced commodities; it now focuses increasingly on responsiveness to changing customer needs, flexibility, and quality control.

With growing frequency, managers report that they have had to discard the established notions of how businesses are to be run. The recent management, business administration and sociology literatures are replete with case studies that show, over and over again, that the new economic environment requires a new way of organizing production, product development, marketing and finance. The big increases in productivity seem to come not from inducing people to work harder, but from providing new institutional frameworks that enable them to work differently.

We are witnessing a vast transformation of how production, work and decision-making are organized within their business enterprises. Broad swaths of the manufacturing and service industries are being restructured, corporations reengineered. Lean production, computer-integrated manufacturing, and the delayering of middle management are symptoms of deep-seated change.

Although this phenomenon is among the hottest topics in the management literature, it has received surprisingly little attention from mainstream economists thus far. Although its implications for labor markets are profound and far-reaching, they have yet to receive explicit micro- and macroeconomic examination. The aim of this chapter is to take a step towards filling this gap.

I wish to present a fresh outlook on this phenomenon, one that isolates some major driving forces that underlie the constellation of changes above and that investigates how these forces affect labor market activity. I also wish to examine what are the implications of these labor market developments for the formulation of employment policy. As we shall see, the restructuring process is altering the motives for creating jobs and thus requires, in countries where unemployment is high and labor force participation is low, a new set of institutions and economic policies to stimulate job creation.

The fresh outlook to be summarized here shows the disparate experiences of executives, middle managers, workers and consumers all to be pieces in a single jigsaw puzzle. I shall argue that the changes which these various groups of people are experiencing all complement and reinforce one another. The upshot is that many of the inherited methods of producing, working and managing – based on the insights gained from more than a century of division of labor, standardization and mass production – are now widely obsolete.

I shall claim that once we see how the diverse pieces of the jigsaw puzzle fit together, we shall gain a new understanding of a wide variety of important, and seemingly disparate, economic phenomena, such as

- the breakdown of occupational barriers,
- the widening dispersion of wages within and across occupation, educational and job tenure groups in the UK and the US,
- the widening dispersion of employment prospects within and across these groups in many continental European countries,

accompanied, however, by

- a narrowing of the male–female wage differentials, in most OECD countries,
- the rising resistance to centralized bargaining in various European countries,
- the delayering of middle management,
- the success of various Japanese firms in exploiting technological advances over the past two decades, and
- the rise of federalist structures of decision–making within firms.

To my mind, the critical developments driving economic transformation are not just, as is often claimed, some combination of technological progress and the expansion of international trade. The critical developments, rather, are organizational: changes in the organization of production, the organization of work and the organization of authority within firms. These organizational shifts are all interdependent and mutually reinforcing. For this reason, I have called the resulting phenomenon the organizational revolution.[1]

I shall argue that one particularly important implication of the organizational revolution is that it magnifies existing market failures responsible for unemployment, inequality, and deficient training. Specifically, I shall contend that the forces driving organizational revolution are trapping many EC countries in a tightening web of labor market problems, and that these problems can be averted only if governments adopt a new generation of employment policies.

3.3.   HISTORICAL BACKGROUND

To understand the constellation of changes occurring now, we need a clear picture of where we have come from.

The critical organizational insight that permitted society to move from small-scale craft production to the mass production that characterized the Industrial Revolution was, quite simply, the division of labor. Back in 1776, Adam Smith described this insight in his well-known account of a small pin factory, employing just ten people, each devoted to a small number of specialized tasks in the making of a pin:

> One man draws out the wire, another straightens it, a third cuts it, a fourth points it, a fifth grinds it at the top for receive the head ... These ten persons could make among them upwards of 48,000 pins in a day. But if they had all wrought separately and independently, and without any of them having been educated to this peculiar business, they certainly could not each of them have made 20, perhaps not one pin in a day.

(Wealth of Nations)

Adam Smith was witnessing the beginning of a technological revolution that would enable people to achieve vast increases in productivity, provided that the organization of work was restructured appropriately. The division of labor into highly fragmented tasks permitted an efficient interaction between labor and the types of capital equipment – large single-purpose machines, rigid factory layouts, rail transport – that were generated by the Industrial Revolution. Furthermore, the emerging organization of work reduced the need for training, for it was clearly not necessary to have years of experience in order to perform a small number of well-defined tasks.

This insight was developed by Henry Ford, who confined each worker's job to the performance of a single operation along an assembly line. It was elaborated in Frederick Taylor's *Principles of Scientific Management*, and continued to be refined in the time-and-motion studies and the method time measurement (MTM) of the early postwar period.

Although the principle of the division of labor released unprecedented economies of scale, it posed an important management problem. As production processes were divided into ever smaller sets of tasks, the process of coordinating these tasks became incomparably more difficult. The technological economies, in other words, generated managerial diseconomies. Henry Ford never managed to master the complex organizational network – covering engineering, production, assembly and sales – spawned by his organization of production.

This problem was first mastered on a large scale by Alfred Sloan, who succeeded William Durant, the founder of General Motors. Sloan's insight was to apply the division of labor to management. The process of coordinating, managing and planning production tasks could itself be divided into fragmented tasks. Different managerial tasks could be performed in different functional departments, such as production, marketing, administration, finance and product development departments. This idea gave rise to the managerial pyramids – topped by a small number of senior executives and extending through layers of middle management. The middle managers were the avenues whereby the senior executives implemented their strategic decisions, coordinated the activities of the departments, and gained information about the firm's economic environment.

This combined division of labor in production and management is the main organizational legacy of the Industrial Revolution.

3.4.   THE UNDERLYING FORCES

We now find ourselves at the beginning of another revolution and, like the previous one, it promises great increases in productivity, provided that the organization of economic activity is transformed appropriately. This time round, however, the driving forces are not just technological; they are a network of complementary changes, occurring simultaneously in seemingly unrelated areas of economic life. It is perhaps this feature that has made them so difficult to recognize and their repercussions so difficult to assess.

There are at least four major underlying forces at work:

1.   Changes in physical capital

In the manufacturing sector, mass production techniques are in many cases giving way to programmable, multi-task equipment. The first part of this century witnessed the big technological breakthroughs that supported the processes of mass production, mass marketing and mass management: assembly lines; large, specialized manufacturing equipment; and large organizational networks within firms. The recent advances in capital equipment – multi-purpose machine tools; flexible, programmable manufacturing equipment; computer-aided design (CAD) and computer-aided manufacture (CAM) – favour a quite different genre of organization. Instead of increasing the returns to scale from combining labor with the newest vintages of capital goods, they reduce them. Instead of demanding workers to devote themselves to minute, repetitive tasks, the new advances facilitate the exercise of multiple skills through rotation among wide ranges of tasks. Instead of calling for centralization of decision-making, the introduction of computerized production, design and information-gathering processes permits decentralized decision-making among small teams of employees.

2.   Changes in information technologies

The flow of information within firms has been revolutionized through the introduction of computerized data systems. The management and workers now have at their disposal up-to-date information about inventories, order backlogs, production bottlenecks, customer requests, marketing problems and innovations – all on a virtually continuous basis. Through today's computer systems, it is now possible to create working teams comprising people situated in different parts of the globe. For example, designers at Ford Motor Company, located in different countries, communicate their ideas by manipulating a common set of images through interactive computers.

3.   Changes in human capital

Throughout the industrialized world there has been a steady increase in the supply of educated employees capable of performing multiple tasks. The human capital of these employees, generated through the systems of education and vocational training, permits organizations to integrate tasks along new organizational lines.

4.   Changes in preferences regarding employment and consumption

The above changes in human capital have been accompanied by changes in the employees' tastes away from monotonous, fragmented jobs and in favour of more varied, creative and challenging work. In addition, as human capital has risen, raising living standards in the process, consumer preferences have changed in favour of greater product variety.

3.5.   THE ORGANIZATIONAL UPSHOT

The upshot of these diverse changes is that they call for a new organizational framework within which to conduct our economic activities.[2] The framework we have inherited from the Industrial Revolution – based on the division of labor in production as well as management, the mass production standardized products, and centralization of decision-making within companies – is no longer appropriate to the physical and human capital, the information technology, and the consumer and worker preferences that we confront today.

In the old economic world, production processes involved transforming standardized inputs into standardized outputs. Machines and other capital equipment were specialized to perform single tasks. Consequently employers required their employees to be specialized to perform single tasks as well. Henry Ford is reputed to have said, "How come when I want a pair of hands I get a human being as well?"

In the new world, the capital equipment has become more versatile, and so the labor is required to be more versatile as well. The old occupational distinctions and job titles are becoming progressively less important. For entrepreneurs to succeed in this new environment, they cannot rely on incremental improvements within conventional institutional structures. Instead, they need to change the structures themselves, to organize their enterprises along new lines.

The simplest way to understand what this transformation involves is to look at a case study.[3] IBM Credit, a wholly owned subsidiary of IBM that finances the goods and services of the IBM corporation, provides a clear illustration. Hammer and Champy (1993, pp. 36–39), write that

> In its early years, IBM Credit's operation was positively Dickensian. When an IBM field salesperson called in with a request for financing, ... the person taking the call logged the request for a deal on a piece of paper. Then a specialist in the credit department "entered the information into a computer system and checked the potential borrower's creditworthiness." Then the business practices department "modified the standard loan covenant in response to customer request... Next, the request went to a pricer ... who keyed the data into a personal computer spreadsheet to determine the appropriate interest rate to charge the customer." Then an administrator in a clerical group "turned all this information into a quote letter that could be delivered to the field sales representative ... The entire process consumed six days on average ... [and] this turnaround was too long, since it gave the customer six days to find another source of financing ... In the end, IBM Credit replaced its specialists – the credit checkers, pricers, and so on – with generalists. Now, instead of sending an application from office to office, one person called a deal structurer processes the entire application from beginning to end ... IBM Credit also developed a new, sophisticated computer system to support the deal structurers" and in difficult situations they could "can get help from a small pool or real specialists – experts in credit checking, pricing, and so forth." As result, "IBM Credit slashed its ... turnaround to four hours. It did so without an increase in the head count ... [and] the number of deals that it handles has increased a hundredfold.

Needless to say, the reams of available case studies vary with regard to the organizational details, but it is unmistakable that most of them have some salient features in common. These are central characteristics of the organizational revolution.

First, the command-and-control style of management – where authority flows from the senior executives down through middle management to the workers in the functional departments – is replaced by a *flatter organizational structure*, with a large number of teams reporting directly to the central management with few, if any, intermediaries.

The specialization of the traditional firms tends to be reversed: each of the small teams performs many of the separate tasks that used to be divided among separate departments. The teams are now often organized with reference to particular sets of customers rather than tasks. It is the "integration" of tasks that permits the teams to give customers more individual attention. For example, Louis Gerstner, the chairman of IBM, moved from a country-based organizational structure towards one in which 14 groups deal with all aspects of a relationship with individual global customers.

These developments also mean that much of the middle management is no longer needed. For example, when Jack Smith became the head of General Motors in 1992, the number of middle managers was reduced from 13,000 to 2,000.

Second, there are radical, interrelated *changes in the organization of production and product development*. In both the manufacturing and service sectors, returns to scale in production are drastically reduced, with the introduction of flexible machine tools and programmable equipment and the use of computer-aided customization of goods and services. Setup and retooling costs have come down, and this permits production in smaller batch sizes, shorter production cycles, smaller delivery lags, and – with the help of computer-aided design – quicker product development.

These changes have enabled producers to adopt ideas such as "lean production" (keeping inventories low) and "just-in-time production" (delivering supplies only when they are required). These developments are not simply cost-cutting devices. They are also a method of decentralizing the production and associated learning process, since they expose bottlenecks where they arise and give the front-line workers the opportunity to overcome them on their own.

These innovations also permit an increasing degree of integration between design, engineering and manufacturing.

Third, there have been dramatic *changes in the nature of products and in seller–customer relations*. The new generation of companies offers broader product lines in smaller quantities. There is also greater emphasis on product quality and sensitivity to purchasers' requirements: products are developed and improved over progressively shorter periods of time, methods of quality control are becoming steadily more stringent, and more product adjustments are made in response to customer demand. There is also increasing scope for customer participation in the design of new products. These include not only information and repairs, but also prompt processing of orders and individualized marketing.

These developments have been spurred by changes in the nature of competition. The increased availability of information about alternative suppliers – through newspapers, television and the computer – has put companies under ever greater pressure to respond flexibly to their customers' changing needs, in terms of product specifications, delivery schedules, or payment terms. In addition, the advances in information technology have allowed sellers to give their customers more individualized treatment of their customers, and this differentiation of services has become an important aspect of competition nowadays.[4]

Fourth, in the new types of business organizations, *occupational barriers are breaking down*, as employees are given multiple responsibilities, often spanning production, development, finance, accounting, administration, training and customer relations.

The new, smaller, customer-oriented teams require versatility, cognitive and social competence, as well as judgement. What matters is not only the competence in a particular activity of production, organization, development and marketing, but also all-round knowledge, potential to acquire multiple skills, and ability to learn how the experience gained from one skill enhances another skill. In this context, traditional occupational distinctions begin to lose their significance and what we mean by *skilled* versus *unskilled* workers becomes radically changed.

And finally, we are witnessing profound *changes in the nature of firms*. The Nobel laureate Ronald Coase described firms as "islands of central planning in an ocean of market forces". This description is becoming less and less apt, as the boundaries between firms and their suppliers and between firms and consumers is becoming increasingly blurred. The improvements in information technology, the increased flexibility of modern production processes, and progressive differentiation of products offered, have given firms the incentive to exchange sensitive information with their suppliers, in order to respond more effectively to customer demands. For example, Nissan and Toyota teach their UK component suppliers the relevant manufacturing skills. It is becoming increasingly common for suppliers to place their own employees on their customers' factory floors in order to resolve production and delivery problems.

Beyond that, alliances and joint ventures are being created between airlines and hotel chains and automobile rental companies, between producers of computer hardware and software, and so on.

At the same time, as companies decentralize their activities in customer-oriented teams and associated profit centres, the relations between these centres tend to be governed by market incentives rather than central planning directives.

3.6.   IMPLICATIONS FOR LABOR MARKET INSTITUTIONS

The organizational changes outlined above are broad and diverse. The features that have been highlighted – the emphasis on customer-oriented teams, the use of flexible, programmable capital equipment in order to respond promptly to changing customer demands, the use of computer technology to decentralize information within firms and achieve closer relations with customers, the demand for versatile employees who are capable of using the experience acquired at one set of tasks to enhance their performance at other tasks, and the change in the boundaries of the firms, as they create independent profit centres within themselves and establish networks with other firms – these all appear to be typical of the overall restructuring process, but they are by no means universal among the restructured organizations. The restructuring strategies invariably differ from firm to firm and sector to sector – emphasizing some of the above features more than (and perhaps to the exclusion of) others – depending on the nature of the existing physical capital, the susceptibility of customer preferences and product specification to storage in computerized information systems, the availability of versatile workers, and the speed of customers' preference changes.

But although the new organizations resulting from the restructuring process are highly heterogeneous, it is nevertheless useful to have a name for them. In what follows, they will be called "holistic" organizations, to highlight the integration of tasks and the breaking of functional barriers taking place within them. These organizations will be contrasted with the traditional organizations, relying on the progressive division of labor within each firm and the progressive exploitation of economics of employee specialization and of scale. These latter organizations will be called "Tayloristic", in honour of Taylor's pioneering work on the scientific management of firms.

We now examine what the transformation of Tayloristic organizations into holistic ones means for the performance of some major labor market institutions.

3.6.1.   Centralized Bargaining

There are good reasons to believe that the restructuring process outlined above is likely to make centralized bargaining less efficient than heretofore, and thus lead to a decline in the importance of this form of wage determination relative to firm- and plant-level bargaining.[5] The hallmark of centralized bargaining is "equal pay for equal work", meaning that workers performing the same occupational roles should receive similar remuneration in return. In a world where most firms are Tayloristic and where employees perform reasonably uniform tasks within well-defined occupational groupings, the practice of giving people equal wages for equal work within each occupation may not be particularly inefficient. It may in fact come close to offering people wages in relation to their marginal products at the individual tasks that they perform. But once firms become holistic, their employees often do not perform tasks that are restricted to single occupational categories. Rather, their roles often span a variety of complementary tasks, cutting across several of the traditional occupational boundaries. Under these circumstances, centralized bargaining has quite different efficiency properties.

In order for the practice of "equal pay for equal work" to apply within holistic organizations, it is necessary to establish what the primary occupational role of each employee is and to impose some uniformity of pay within each primary occupation. In that event, however, centralized bargaining may often prevent remunerating workers in accordance with their marginal products. The reason is that when workers perform sets of complementary tasks, then their marginal products at one task depends on the other tasks they do. Now, there is no reason to expect that the restructuring process should lead to workers performing the *same* sets of complementary tasks at different firms. Quite on the contrary, as firms produce increasingly differentiated products and concentrate on increasingly idiosyncratic customer niches, it is reasonable to expect that the composition of complementary tasks of individual employees will become increasingly heterogeneous.

Then the marginal product of one employee at a particular task may be quite different from the marginal product of another employee at that same task, since the two employees perform that task in conjunction with different sets of other tasks. For example, the marginal product from selling a good may be quite different for an employee who is also engaged in product design than for one who is also engaged in the formulation of accounting procedures.

Consequently, in order for holistic organizations to reward workers in relation to their marginal products, it is necessary for them to offer different workers different remuneration for the same task, depending on what other tasks they do. But this practice would be in clear conflict with the main feature of centralized bargaining.

Beyond that, holistic organizations have incentives to offer different wages to workers in the same occupational, education or job tenure groups, since these workers may differ in terms of their degree of versatility or their social and cognitive skills – characteristics which become particularly important in the new organizations, where workers are given substantial autonomy in combining tasks and responding to customer preferences. Once again, the need to differentiate wages on the basis of the latter characteristics is in conflict with the prevailing rules of centralized bargaining.

Nor is it conceivable that the centralized bargaining principle of "equal pay for equal work" could be amended by redefining work along holistic lines. Since the combinations of tasks performed by holistic firms within a particular industry are often exceedingly heterogeneous, such a redefinition would require vast amounts of information to be available to the central wage bargainers – information on the constellations of tasks performed jointly in individual enterprises. This information is just as unlikely to be in the reach of central wage bargainers as information about production technologies is to be in the possession of the traditional, communist central planners.

By implication, as organizations transform themselves along holistic lines, centralized bargaining may be expected to become increasingly inefficient. In so doing, it creates opportunities for both employers and employees to make themselves better off by abandoning the principle of "equal pay for equal work" and, instead, letting remuneration depend on the composition of employees' bundles of complementary tasks. This means that employers and employees may be expected to gain growing incentives to replace centralized bargaining procedures by more decentralized arrangements. Such considerations may help explain the declining importance of centralized bargaining institutions for wage determination in numerous European and other OECD countries.

3.6.2. Unemployment Benefit Systems

Unemployment benefits are generally awarded on an all-or-nothing basis: only workers who have no jobs at all (or who work merely an insignificant number of hours per week) are eligible for unemployment benefits; the rest are not. This feature of unemployment benefit systems need not be particularly inefficient in a world where most people work either full time or not at all. But the restructuring process from Tayloristic to holistic organizations may be expected to increase the number of employees working part time.

The structure of holistic organizations often requires that they have a limited core of full-time employees engaged in managerial tasks central to the organizations as a whole, and that many of their more peripheral functions be performed by outside experts who are hired on a part-time basis and who may provide their services to a range of other companies. Business consultants, financial accounting experts, computer programmers, and many other types of professionals often fit this mould. These people are often able to enhance their capabilities at any particular organization by drawing on their experiences gained at similar companies elsewhere. Much of this work is by nature part-time, and part-timers, as noted, are usually excluded from receiving unemployment benefits.

For part-timers – particularly in times of recession, when their portfolio of jobs is relatively small and their services are thus underutilized – the marginal effective tax rate for moving from unemployment to employment can be very high. For when a part-timer finds work, he or she must give up all his or her unemployment benefits and associated welfare state entitlements in return for income from a small number of hours of work per week. Here the all-or-nothing basis for awarding unemployment benefits may play a major role in discouraging people from finding work. Under these circumstances, the ongoing organizational change creates a growing need for unemployment benefit reform, in particular, for awarding unemployment benefits on a pro-rata basis (that is, the size of the benefits depending on the number of hours worked per week). In order to keep government spending on such a "passive" labor market policy under control, it may be desirable for pro-rata unemployment benefits to be means-tested.

The unemployment benefit systems prevailing in most European countries are characterized by substantial inertia, in the sense that a significant amount of jobless time must elapse before people are able to qualify for unemployment benefits and the associated welfare state entitlements (such as housing and medical benefits from the state). In this respect, the systems penalize temporary employment, for when a person becomes temporarily employed, he or she gains not only the prospect of income for a limited period of time, but also the prospect of subsequent exclusion from unemployment benefits and other entitlements for a significant period.

The organizational restructuring process augments this difficulty by increasing the demand for temporary employment. We have seen how the advances in information technologies and the increased flexibility of physical capital has enabled firms to respond more readily to changes in customer demands. And such enhanced responsiveness also frequently requires firms to employ workers on a temporary basis while the demand for a particular product lasts and to relinquish them once that demand has shifted. Given the inertial features of many current unemployment benefit systems, workers often have a severe disincentive to accept such temporary jobs. To alleviate this difficulty, it may be necessary to make unemployment benefits and other entitlements more readily available to the jobless, with means-testing provisions used to limit the associated government budgetary outlay.

Another common feature of European unemployment benefit systems is that they are defined on a family basis rather than an individual basis. The major implication of this feature is that it prevents a person from receiving unemployment benefits if his or her spouse has a job. In practice, this means that if the main breadwinner in a family – usually a prime-age male – loses his job, it often becomes worthwhile for his wife (who frequently has a part-time or temporary job) to relinquish her position as well, in order to qualify for unemployment benefits and associated entitlements. In this sense, many current unemployment benefit systems discriminate against female employment.

This implication is particularly troublesome since the organizational revolution may be expected to promote the job prospects of women. Because of child-bearing and child-rearing considerations, women often have a greater demand for the temporary and part-time jobs that the holistic organizations are creating. In so far as women specialize less than men in terms of occupational skills, they might be better suited for the versatile positions in holistic organizations. The family-basis nature of unemployment benefit entitlements may, however, effectively restrict women's access to holistic jobs. To address this problem, it may be necessary to distribute unemployment benefits on an individual basis, perhaps using far stricter job search criteria as qualification for unemployment benefits in order to control the resulting government budgetary outlay.

3.6.3.   Job Security Legislation

The organizational revolution may be expected to have two major implications for job security legislation. On the one hand, it could reduce the coverage of such legislation by stimulating the creation of temporary jobs, along the lines outlined above. The greater the proportion of temporary employment in aggregate employment, the smaller the percentage of the working population who remain employed for long enough to become entitled to severance pay and legal protection from dismissal. In this respect, the restructuring process may make the existing job security legislation in many European countries increasingly irrelevant to labor market performance.

On the other hand, for those employees whose positions remain legally protected, the restructuring process may be expected to increase the inefficiency of existing job security legislation. The reason is that holistic organizations often require their employees to be flexible in changing the nature of jobs in response to the ever-changing product demands. However, job security legislation may induce employees to resist such flexibility, for employees who are costly to fire are able to stick to rigid work patterns with relatively little fear of dismissal.

The underlying problem here is that job security legislation is often specified in terms of the traditional occupational categories relevant to Tayloristic firms, but increasingly irrelevant to holistic firms. There is a straightforward policy response to this problem: it is to dismantle those job security provisions that are strongly tied to occupational lines, possibly replacing them with provisions that secure employees' jobs, but not job contents, within their firms.

3.7.   IMPLICATIONS FOR LABOR MARKET POLICIES

3.7.1.   Market Failures

The organizational revolution has potentially far-reaching implications for labor market policies since it may be expected to augment some important market failures in employment creation and training provision.

The efficiency wage literature[6] has highlighted some important market failures that prevent the free market mechanism from creating sufficient employment opportunities. In particular, the theory shows that the free market labor demand is inefficiently low when firms use wages as an incentive to promote productivity and reduce labor turnover costs. The underlying idea is that firms are unable to observe the productivities of their individual employees and thus unable to make their remunerations dependent on these productivities; nor are they able to observe the likelihood that individual employees will quit their current jobs, thereby imposing costs of hiring and training on their employers. However, the firms are able to influence productivity and labor turnover costs indirectly via the wage. The greater a firm's wage offer, the higher will be its average labor productivity in the firm (for the more able will be its job applicants and the more effort will its current incumbent employees put into their jobs, on average) and the lower will be its average expenditures on hiring and training per worker (for the lower will be its employees' incentives to quit). Thus the firm's profit-maximizing wage is the one at which the firm's marginal cost (the labor cost minus the labor turnover cost) from a wage increase is just equal to its marginal revenue (via the influence on productivity). This profit-maximizing wage may exceed the market-clearing wage, so that there is unemployment. This unemployment is generally inefficient since workers can impose harm on the firm (for example, by shirking or quitting) without having to pay for this harm. On account of this uncompensated cost, labor demand tends to be inefficiently low.

The organizational revolution is likely to augment this market failure. The decentralization of information within the holistic firm, the increasing complexity of the combinations of tasks that employees are required to perform, the greater responsibility of front-line employees to adjust their task combinations to meet customer demands – these features all make it more difficult for employers to monitor the productivity of their employees. Furthermore, the versatility that is required of employees in holistic firms is a characteristic that usually makes it easier for them to transfer their skills to other firms. The resulting quit propensity will be exceedingly difficult for employers to monitor. And these monitoring difficulties, as noted above, underlie the market failure that gives rise to deficient employment in the efficiency wage context.

Furthermore, the organizational revolution may be expected to make the free market mechanism progressively less capable of providing adequate incentives for the provision and acquisition of the appropriate skills. It is a common belief among neoclassical economists that, in a free market, people pay all the costs and get all the benefits from their training. If the training is "general" (useful to all firms), then the worker will be rewarded for this training via the subsequent wage income (which the competition among firms will raise to the associated marginal product of labor) and thus the worker is also in a position to pay all the costs of the training. If the training is "specific" (useful only to one particular firm), then the benefits from training fall exclusively on the trainer and trainee. Thus if they share the costs of training in proportion to the benefits they each receive, then an efficient amount of training will be provided. If that were the whole story, then it would be no efficiency case for government support of training.

There is, however, a fundamental flaw in this argument;[7] it is that training is either general or specific. In practice, however, most training is useful to a limited number of firms. These firms are imperfect competitors in the labor market and use their market power to drive their employees' wages beneath their productivity. Thus the employees cannot appropriate all the returns from their training. But since workers are mobile between firms, the potential benefits from training accrue not only to the firm providing it and the worker acquiring it, but also to other firms that could make use of it. Since some of the benefit from training falls on firms that employ workers after they have been trained elsewhere, it is impossible for the trainer and trainee to capture all the benefits from training. And whenever people do not get paid fully for the services they provide, the free market mechanism will generate too few of these services. This is the essence of the "poaching externality".[8]

This externality is amplified through complementarities between labor and capital.[9] In the presence of such complementarities, deficient investment in human capital reduces the productivity of physical capital and thereby leads to deficient investment in physical capital which, in turn, reinforces the deficient investment in human capital. In addition, free markets can get stuck in a "low-skill, bad-job trap".[10] This trap occurs when firms create few skilled vacancies because there are few skilled workers available, and when few workers acquire skills because there are few skilled vacancies.

The organizational revolution magnifies these various market failures because it enhances the transferability of human and physical capital among firms. The improved information flows that characterize the organizational revolution also make it easier for low-skill, bad-job traps to arise. It is on this account that we may expect a steadily growing need for government policies that address the existing market failures in training.

The organizational revolution calls for a new approach to education in various European countries. Some European educational systems, such as that of the UK, require students to specialize at relatively early ages. For example, the UK secondary school qualifications and most UK university syllabuses pull in this direction. This approach appears particularly unsuited to the requirements of the new economic order. A more holistic approach to education – such as the liberal arts degrees common in the US – may prove to be more in keeping with the changing times.

With regard to on-the-job training, the Japanese practice of encouraging job rotation as a prerequisite for promotion and giving employers a free hand in making job reassignments may well give employees valuable experience to exploit the recent breakthroughs in production and information technologies. It may well deserve policy support.

If the analysis above is correct, then, as time goes on, it will become increasingly important for a country to have a skilled, versatile and adaptable workforce. The current policy of some EC countries of subsidizing low-paying jobs – whether through tax breaks or in-work benefits – reduces people's monetary incentives to acquire skills. Unless this policy is combined with an enlightened training policy that puts these incentives back in place, it could seriously injure this country's ability to fill the skilled, versatile jobs that are being created through the organizational revolution.

Furthermore, as noted, many existing European labor market institutions – especially the centralized wage bargaining institutions, unemployment benefit systems, and job security legislation – are likely to inhibit many of the sorts of jobs created through holistic organizations. A new approach to employment policy is required to bring the institutions into harmony with organizational developments.

I now turn to a policy proposal which, in my judgement, exemplifies the required policy approach to employment and training

3.7.2.   A Policy Proposal

The proposal is to create *unemployment and training accounts* (UTAs).[11] Under this programme, every employable person would have an unemployment account to provide support against job loss and a training account to provide funding to acquire new skills. Instead of paying taxes to finance unemployment support, further education and training, employed people would be required to make regular contributions to their UTAs. The mandatory contributions would rise with their incomes. To maintain the living standards of the poor, the government would pay contributions of the lowest-income groups, and tax the contributions of the higher-income groups. People could also make voluntary contributions in excess of these amounts.

If people became unemployed, they could make limited withdrawals from their unemployment accounts instead of receiving unemployment benefits. If they wished to acquire skills, they could draw on their training accounts instead of receiving government grants, subsidies, and loans. If their UTA balances fell below a specified limit, they would receive public assistance on the same basis as under our current system. If their UTA balances became sufficiently high, they could use the surplus funds for other purposes. At the end of their working lives, their remaining UTA balances could be used to top up their pensions.

People would be able to borrow money on favourable terms for their training accounts, enabling them to finance their training through their future incomes. Unemployed people who developed promising job market skills could receive government loan guarantees when they borrowed training account money. Employers' contributions to training accounts would receive favourable tax treatment.

People would be free to make withdrawals from their training accounts at any point in their working lifetimes. Those who identified their preferred careers early in their working lives could draw substantially on their accounts soon after leaving secondary school. Those who took longer to find their niche in the labor market, or those who required retraining upon changing occupations, would make significant withdrawals much later in their careers. In this way, the training accounts would enable people to remain employable and adaptable throughout their working lives.

The UTAs would initially be managed largely on a pay-as-you-go basis (similar to savings accounts, from which people can make withdrawals even though the banks use most of the money for other purposes). With the passage of time, the UTAs would eventually be turned into a fully funded system, in which individuals would have discretion over who could manage their UTAs. To guard against bankruptcy, the financial activities of the private-sector UTA fund managers would be regulated, along lines similar to the regulation of commercial banks.

Adopting the UTA system could substantially reduce the level of long-term unemployment and promote skills. In particular, moving from unemployment benefits to unemployment accounts would give people greater incentives to avoid long periods of unemployment. For the longer people remain unemployed, the lower will be their unemployment account balances and consequently the smaller the funds available to them later on. And since the unemployment accounts generate more employment than unemployment benefits, the unemployment account contributions necessary to finance a given level of unemployment support will be lower than the taxes necessary to finance the same level of unemployment benefits.

Furthermore, the training accounts would be better suited than the current education and training programmes to ensure people's lifetime employability, since the accounts could be accessed whenever employees and their employers found it maximally worthwhile. In this way, employers and employees stand to gain from the switch to UTAs. Retired people would gain through their ability to use their UTA balances to augment their pensions. And the government would gain, since the removal of the distortions from the unemployment benefit system would promote new economic activity and thereby generate increased tax revenue. Beyond that, the UTAs would be more efficient than the current system at redistributing income from rich to poor, since unemployment benefits and training schemes are not targeted exclusively at the poor, whereas government contributions to UTAs would be.

In order to provide additional incentives to find work and acquire the relevant skills, the government would provide subsidies for long-term unemployed people who used their UTAs to provide recruitment vouchers or training vouchers for firms that hired them. The size of each person's voucher would depend on his or her wages earned over next two years of subsequent employment. The recruitment vouchers would reduce firms' cost of employing the long-term unemployed; the training vouchers would reduce the cost of training them. The subsidies would be set so that they could be financed through the tax revenues from people's first two years of subsequent employment and through the abolition of in-work benefits.

In short, replacing the current system of unemployment benefits and government-run training programmes with the UTA system would reduce unemployment and simultaneously promote equality. While people are generally resentful of their tax burden and often demeaned by the existing unemployment benefits and training programmes, they would be more willing to contribute to personalized accounts for their own purposes. The UTAs would give people more freedom to use unemployment support and training funds to meet their diverse individual needs. It would give them greater latitude to respond to changing job opportunities, finance periods of job search, acquire skills and provide for retirement. And all this could be done without creating greater inequality or increasing government expenditure.

This policy proposal is merely exemplary of a more general policy approach.[12] The approach is to identify the disincentives for employment and training that are created by existing labor market policies and then to redirect the funds that finance these policies towards new measures that replace the disincentives by incentives for job creation and skill acquisition. Given the market failures in employment and training outlined above, such incentives are required to reduce existing labor market distortions.

The organizational revolution is creating radically new labor market conditions throughout the advanced industrialized countries. It is vital to develop a new set of labor market policies to suit these conditions.

NOTES

*   Many of the ideas in this chapter are the outgrowth of earlier collaboration with Assar Lindbeck. Our joint work in this area is listed in the references.

1   Examples of studies where this constellation of organizational changes is described are Hammer and Champy (1993), Milgrom and Roberts (1990), NUTEK (1996), Pfeiffer (1994), Wikström and Norman (1994). See also Appelbaum and Bott (1994), Kremer and Maskin (1995), Mitchell et al. (1990) and Piore and Sabel (1984).

2   For some formal analyses of the organizational implications, see Lindbeck and Snower (1996 a and b, 1997).

3   The business literature is replete with case studies along these general lines. A few further examples where this process has been pursued particularly thoroughly are ABB, the producer of heavy capital goods, Bell Atlantic, Motorola, and the airline SAS.

4   Hammer and Champy (1993) write that "In Houston, if a customer calls Pizza Hut to order a pepperoni and mushroom pie, the same kind of pizza that the customer ordered last week, the clerk asks if the caller would like to try a new combination. If the person says "yes", the clerk mails him or her discount coupons with offerings   customized to the individual's tastes. When a consumer calls Whirlpool's service line, the call is automatically routed to the same service representative with whom the consumer spoke last time, creating a sense of personal relationship." (p. 19).

5   For a formal analysis of the argument that follows, see Lindbeck and Snower (1996b).

6   See, for example, Malcomson (1981), Shapiro and Stiglitz (1984), and Weiss (1980).

7   See, for example, Stevens (1996).

8   Since the poaching externality (like other externalities) refers to a failure of the market to remunerate an economic activity, it is intrinsically difficult to measure it directly, although studies by Haskell and Martin (1993) and Greenhalgh and Mavrotas (1993) suggest that observed skill shortages may be a manifestation of the poaching externality. Furthermore, some studies indicate that certain forms of employer-provided training are transferable across employers (for example, Booth 1991, 1993 and Blanchflower and Lynch 1994).

9   See Acemoglou (1996).

10   See Snower (1996).

11   See Snower (1997) and Orszag and Snower (1997a,b).

12   For another proposal lying within this general approach, see Snower (1994).

REFERENCES

Acemoglou, Daren (1996), "Credit constraints, investment externalities and growth", in Alison Booth and Dennis J. Snower (eds), *Acquiring Skills,* Cambridge; Cambridge University Press, 41–62.

Appelbaum, Eileen and Rosemary Bott (1994), *The New American Workplace*, Ithaca, NY: Industrial and Labor Relations Press.

Blanchflower, Danny and Lisa M. Lynch (1994), "Training at work: a comparison of US and British youths", in L.M. Lynch (ed.), *International Comparisons of Private Sector Training*, Chicago: Chicago University Press and National Bureau of Economic Research.

Booth, Alison L. (1991), "Job-related formal training: who receives it and what is it worth?", *Oxford Bulletin of Economics and Statistics*, **53**, 281–294.

Booth, Alison L. (1993), "Private sector training and graduate earnings", *Review of Economics and Statistics*, **76**, 164–170.

Greenhalgh, Christine and G. Mavrotas (1993), "The role of career aspirations and financial constraints in individual access to vocational training", *Oxford Economic Papers*, **46** (4).

Hammer, Michael and James Champy (1993), *Reengineering the Corporations*, New York: Harper Business.

Haskell, Jonathan and Chris Martin (1993), "The causes of skill shortages in Britain", *Oxford Economic Papers*, **45**, 573–588.

Kremer, Michael and Eric Maskin (1995), "Segregation and the rise in inequality", mimeo.

Lindbeck, Assar and Dennis J. Snower (1996a), "Restructuring production and work", Discussion Paper No. 1323, Centre for Economic Policy Research, London.

Lindbeck, Assar and Dennis J. Snower (1996b), "Centralized bargaining, multi-tasking and work incentives", Seminar Paper No. 620, Institute for International Economic Studies, University of Stockholm.

Lindbeck, Assar and Dennis J. Snower (1997), "The division of labor within firms", Discussion Paper, Institute for International Economic Studies, University of Stockholm.

Malcomson, J.M. (1981), "Unemployment and the efficiency wage hypothesis", *Economic Journal*, **91**, 848–866.

Milgrom, Paul and John Roberts (1990), "The economics of modern manufacturing. technology, strategy and organization", *American Economic Review*, 511–528.

Mitchell, Daniel J.B., David Lewin and Edward E. Lawler III (1990), "Alternative pay systems, firm performance, and productivity", in Alan S. Blinder (ed.), *Paying for Productivity: A Look at the Evidence*, Washington, DC: The Brookings Institution,

NUTEK (1996), *Towards Flexible Organizations*, Stockholm: Swedish National Board for Industrial and Technical Development.

Orszag, Mike and Dennis J. Snower (1997a), "Expanding the welfare system", *European Economy*, forthcoming.

Orszag, Mike and Dennis J. Snower (1997b), "From unemployment benefits to unemployment accounts", mimeo.

Pfeiffer, Jeffrey (1994), *Competitive Advantage Through People*, Boston, MA: Harvard Business School Press.

Piore, Michael J. and F. Sabel (1984), *The Second Industrial Divide, Possibilities for Prosperity*, New York: Basic Books.

Shapiro, C. and J.E. Stiglitz (1984), "Equilibrium unemployment as a worker discipline device", *American Economic Review*, **74** (3), 433–444.

Snower, Dennis J. (1994), "Converting unemployment benefits into employment subsidies", *American Economic Review*, **84** (2), May, 65–70.

Snower, Dennis J. (1996), "The low-skill, bad-job trap", in Alison Booth and Dennis J. Snower (eds), *Acquiring Skills*, Cambridge: Cambridge University Press, 109–124.

Snower, Dennis J. (1997), "Achieving prosperity and social cohesion in the 21st century: the reform-oriented approach", in W. Michalski (ed.), *Prosperity and Cohesion*, Paris: OECD, forthcoming.

Stevens, Margaret (1996), "Transferable training and poaching externalities", in Alison Booth and Dennis J. Snower (eds), *Acquiring Skills*, Cambridge: Cambridge University Press, 19–40.

Weiss, A. (1980), "Job queues and layoffs in labor markets with flexible wages", *Journal of Political Economy*, **88**, 526–538.

Wikström, Solveig and Richard Norman (1994), *Knowledge and Value*, London: Routledge.

4. The shifting structure of the American labor market

Paul Osterman

4.1. INTRODUCTION

The American economy is paradoxical. On the one hand, it has generated millions of new jobs, on the other hand insecurity has increased. When we move beyond macro statistics, the paradoxes are even more striking. Firms are rapidly introducing new work systems, such as teams and quality programmes, which promise not only greater productivity but also more interesting and rewarding work. However, employees' sense of insecurity has grown, the fraction of work which might be called contingent or temporary has increased, and wages have stagnated. The labor market is evidently facing in two directions and this ambiguity is the source of considerable confusion about just how to interpret recent trends.

In this chapter I shall concentrate on what is happening to the quality of work in America. Job creation *per se* is not the problem and only a brief amount of time will be spent on it. The interesting issues revolve around the two-faced nature of the jobs which are being created.

4.2. WHAT IS HAPPENING IN THE AMERICAN LABOR MARKET

4.2.1. Job Growth

Job growth in the American economy has been the envy of the world. Between the peak year of 1979 and 1996 total employment grew from about 98 million to 126 million, a net addition of 28 million jobs in 17 years. This is obviously an impressive record, particularly compared to Europe. Currently the unemployment rate is at its lowest level in many years. There are some shadings to these facts: the employment to population ratio for men

71

actually fell (from 0.73 to 0.70) between 1979 and 1996 while that for women increased sharply (0.47 to 0.56). None the less, on balance the American "job machine" is the proudest achievement of the economy.

4.2.2.   Wage Stagnation and Inequality

The facts regarding wage trends in the American economy are very well known and do not bear much repetition. Since the last peak year of 1979 median earnings have grown very slowly if at all and inequality has increased sharply.

Between the years 1989 and 1995, median family income fell in real terms by $1,400. Over the same period, hourly wages increased in total by two-tenths of 1 per cent. Clearly the average American employee is barely better off today than he or she was at the end of the last business-cycle peak (Mishel et al., pp. 24, 44).

In terms of inequality, there are numerous alternative ways of presenting the basic facts, but the following is as good as any. In 1979 among 25-to 34-year-old full-time male workers those in the top decile earned 65 per cent more than the median worker. In 1995 the top 10 per cent earned 93 per cent more than the median. Another fact: between 1979 and 1995 the share of total money income going to all households increased for the top 20 per cent of households and declined for all of the remaining 80 per cent of households. That is, over this period only the top 20 per cent of households were better off in 1995 than they were in 1979.[1]

4.2.3.   Insecurity and Layoffs

Despite the impressive job growth and low unemployment rate there is a widespread feeling among many informed observers that the current labor market is much more insecure and dangerous than in the past. Constant reports of the numerous layoffs and restructuring of recent years explain this feeling and it has been given additional credibility by media stories such as the *New York Times* series on dislocation or the *Newsweek* cover story which featured pictures of chief executive officers responsible for layoffs and characterized them as "Corporate Killers".

Despite this popular perception, economists have been much more sceptical. Long ingrained, and reasonable, academic instincts are, first, to discount evidence based on a few examples or anecdotes no matter how dramatic and, second, to resist the idea that something fundamental has changed. After all, this is a very big economy and even a few very large layoffs are insignificant in the larger picture. Second, dramatic changes are very rare. As a result, researchers have taken to their data sets in search of confirming or disconfirming data and the results have been less clear than the newspaper stories might lead one to expect. The results have, none the less, tended to show some worsening in the degree of security in the labor market.

In one important sense the academic critics have missed the point. Imagine that one hundred people worked together steadily for a number of years. One day I walk in and summarily fire one person and then walk out. It is true, as the researcher would point out, that only 1 per cent of the group have lost their job. However, the world has been turned upside down for everyone. Henceforth the remaining 99 employees will come to work every day wondering when their turn will come and this worry will inevitably alter a wide range of labor market behaviours. The lesson is that even statistically small changes can have very substantial ramifications.

This being said, it is still important to learn what the data have to say. However, this is easier said than done. There is a variety of ways to ask and answer the question of whether economic insecurity has increased in recent years and each approach has its own peculiar strengths and weaknesses. We shall work our way through the different data sources and analytical approaches.

4.2.4. Employment Tenure

The term "employment tenure" refers to the number of years a person has worked for a given employer. A natural implication of the notion that jobs have become less secure is that if we could collect data on the distribution of employment tenure in the labor force – the percentage of employees who have long and short tenure – we would see that the distribution would shift over time as people lost previously secure jobs. Hypothetically (if other factors such as entry and exit rates remained constant), one might expect that the fraction of the labor force with job tenure over, say, ten years, would be smaller now than it was 15 years ago. If this were true it could be taken as evidence that job security has truly worsened.

The Bureau of Labor Statistics has, as part of the Current Population Survey, periodically asked people about the number of years they have worked for their employer and hence it is indeed possible to see how these distributions have shifted over time. Unfortunately, there is a series of technical problems with these data which complicate their use. People tend to round off their answers, they tend to heap their answers in five-year intervals, and in some years the wording of the question shifts slightly but with potentially important consequences. As a result, researchers working with these data have had to make a series of adjustments which mean that any results need to be interpreted as rough estimates, not exact answers.

In Table 4.1, I report the findings of Neumark et al. (1997), who have done some of the most careful work with these data. Each entry in the table represents the probability that a person with whatever characteristics are stated will be working for the same employer four years after the survey year. So, for example, in the top panel the number 0.561 means that 56.1 per cent of all people who were employed in 1983 worked for the same employer four years later in 1987.[2]

Table 4.1 Four–year retention rates			
	1983–87	**1987–91**	**1991–95**
All Workers	0.561	0.539	0.538
9 to 15 Years' Tenure	0.861	0.821	0.746
Source: Neumark et al. (1997)			

Comparing the two end-points, 1983–87 and 1991–95, it appears that there has been a slight worsening of employment stability. For all employees, and for those in what might be termed the middle of their career, the chances of holding the same job for a four-year period are worse in the 1990s than early in the 1980s and this is despite the very robust economy of recent years.

A problem with these data, however, is that what they capture is whether someone has stayed with his or her employer. Job stability in this sense is determined by two events, whether the person has lost their job involuntarily (a layoff) or whether he or she quit. It is quite possible that the chances of being laid off have increased but that quits have declined as people choose to avoid risk by remaining with their employer. In this scenario, economic insecurity has become worse but this is not reflected in data which are based upon job tenure.

The solution to this problem lies in studying the pattern of quits and layoffs over time. However, these data are not available for the entire workforce. What is available are data on why people who are unemployed lost their job, and Table 4.2 displays these data. This table includes data for three years, two business-cycle peaks (1979 and 1989) and 1996, a year which, while not an official peak, is surely near one. In this table the data are limited to people who are unemployed because they left jobs. New labor market entrants and re-entrants are excluded.

Table 4.2 Distribution of reasons for unemployment, age 20 and over						
	Men			**Women**		
	1979	**1989**	**1996**	**1979**	**1989**	**1996**
Quits	0.180	0.175	0.135	0.302	0.313	0.239
Temporary Layoffs	0.267	0.237	0.260	0.244	0.198	0.224
Permanent Layoffs	0.551	0.586	0.603	0.452	0.488	0.536
Source: Employment and Earnings.						

These data show that over time, and controlling for the business cycle, the pool of unemployed is increasingly made up of those who were laid off and, correspondingly, decreasingly made up of those who quit their jobs. Furthermore, among those who had experienced layoffs, a growing fraction were victims of permanent, as opposed to temporary layoffs.

4.2.5. Evidence from the Dislocated Worker Data

An additional source of evidence comes from the Dislocated Worker Surveys conducted as a supplement to the monthly Current Population Surveys. Every two years since 1984 one of the monthly surveys (either in January or February) has asked respondents whether they had lost their job over the past three or five years due to a plant closing, large-scale layoff, insufficient work, or other reasons. Because these data have been collected regularly over time and because of the large sample sizes, they are an excellent source of information on job loss. There are also some complicated technical issues regarding these data, which I relegate to a footnote.[3]

The key trends are summarized in Table 4.3. The Table shows dislocation rates (the number of people dislocated as a percentage of employment of the relevant group at the beginning of the period) over time for various subgroups. It is apparent that the rate of dislocation has benn rising for both men and women has been rising and that this has occurred even though the unemployment rate has declined in recent years. It is also apparent that while non-college workers continue to suffer substantially higher rates of dislocation than those with college, the gap has been narrowing. Both sets of facts – increasing dislocation and a shifting occupational mix – point to structural changes in the labor market.

	All	College	No college	Unemployment rate
1996	0.12	0.09	0.13	6.1
1994	0.11	0.08	0.12	7.5
1992	0.11	0.08	0.13	5.6
1990	0.08	0.05	0.09	5.5
1988	0.09	0.05	0.10	7.0
1986	0.09	0.05	0.10	7.5
1984	0.12	0.06	0.13	9.7

Table 4.3
Dislocation rates for ages 20–64

Note: Dislocated Worker Survey Tapes. The dislocation rate is a total for the three years prior to each survey (for example, the 1996 rate is the number of people aged 20–64 dislocated in the years 1993, 1994 and 1995 divided by the number of people aged 20–64 working in 1996). The unemployment rate is for two years prior to each survey (for example, the rate for 1996 is for the year 1994).

4.2.6.   Contingent Employment

One of the most widely noted trends in the American labor market has been the emergence of what many commentators have come to call "contingent" work. This is a term which is meant to contrast with what we used to think of as a "standard" job: a stable relationship with one employer with whom the worker built a career. Many of the regulations governing the American labor market are built around this image: for example, unemployment insurance is based upon time accumulated at work with a specific employer. In addition, because benefits such as health insurance are typically provided by employers, the characteristics of the employer/employee link is crucial.

The term "contingent employment" covers diverse forms and it will be important to distinguish among these. However, some preliminary broad data are useful. The government classifies employment into industry codes, so-called SICs (Standard Industrial Classifications). In the period 1991 to 1996, the fastest-growing SIC code in terms of employment was number 736, Personnel Supply Services, that is, temporary help agencies. In the years 1994 to 1996, the revenue growth of publicly traded staffing firms averaged an annual increase of 24.5 per cent (Baird Company). Another indicator is that in 1996, 34 of *Inc. Magazine*'s list of the 500 fastest-growing private companies were staffing firms.

Two images dominate popular interpretations of this kind of employment. One image is largely negative. In the words of the *San Jose Mercury News*, the paper serving the Silicon Valley where the use of temps is probably more intense than anywhere else in the nation, these workers are "America's new migrant labourers", moving from job to job without security and without benefits. Set against this is the image of the independent contractor choosing temporary work because of the freedom and flexibility it offers. It is easy to find anecdotes which support both interpretations; the question is in what proportions the temporary labor force is split. Additional central issues regard the long-term impact of temporary employment upon people, what drives firms to use temporary workers, and what are the consequences of this type of employment for productivity and quality.

4.2.7.   The Organization of Contingent Employment

How many contingent employees are there and where do they work? Contingent employment takes many forms, not simply job placement via temporary agencies. Other typical configurations include on-call employees who work in pools put together by the host employer and independent contractors who establish direct relationships with the employer. In February 1995, a special supplement to the monthly Current Population Survey (a very large nationally representative survey of the labor force which is managed by the Department of Labor's Bureau of Labor Statistics) asked about these forms of work. The fraction of the labor force reporting various contingent relationships is shown in Table 4.4.

Table 4.4	
Distribution of the workforce by employment type	
Agency Temporaries	1.1%
On-Call or Day Labourers	1.9%
Contract Workers	1.3%
Independent Contractors	1.0%
Short-Term Hires	3.4%
Regular Part-Time	15.2%
Regular Full-Time	76.1%

Source: February, 1995 Current Population Survey as analysed by Houseman (1997).

As is apparent, only 8.7 per cent of all employees report themselves as being "non-regular" in some sense of that term. Given that so much attention has been devoted to temporary agency employment, it is striking that only barely over 1 per cent of employees report themselves working for agencies. These numbers are consistent with the results from my 1992 National Survey of Establishments. In that survey I asked about two categories of contingent work, employees hired through a temporary help agency and employees who are part of the host firm's on-call pool. In these data (which were limited to private for-profit establishments with 50 or more employees) an average of 2.7 per cent of employment came from temporary help agencies and 1.9 per cent consisted of in-house temporary help pools. Given that the 1992 survey was limited to private sector establishments with 50 or more employees, the numbers are roughly consistent. They are also consistent with a 1996 survey by Susan Houseman of 550 establishments, public and private, with five or more employees. She found that 1.5 per cent of total employment came from temporary agencies and short-term hires accounted for 2.3 per cent of employment (Houseman 1997).

Although these numbers may seem small, it is important to recognize that they represent point-in-time estimates. Over the course of a year the number of people who flow through temporary help employment at some point is much larger. Houseman collected duration of job data which enabled her to make an estimate of the relationship of these stocks and flows and her data suggest that the number of people who work for temporary agencies over the course of a year is seven to eight times more than the number who are reported as employed at any given point. Hence the phenomenon is much more important than the modest slice-in-time employment numbers would suggest. In addition, as we have just observed, this form of employment is growing rapidly and, we shall see, is becoming an integral element in firms' human resource strategies.

One of the striking aspects of contingent employment is its penetration into a wide range of occupational categories. The old image of temporary office work is no longer accurate. Table 4.5, which is taken from a leading industry publication, provides a good sense of this diversity. Industrial work is essentially as important as clerical/office work and there is also a strong representation in relatively higher-skill areas.

Table 4.5 Revenue by type of sector in staffing industry (Billions of dollars)	
Medical	4.0
Professional	4.8
Technical/computer	11.4
Office/clerical	13.7
Industrial	11.2

Source: *Staffing Industry Review*, Staffing Industry Analysts, Los Altos, CA.

There is a variety of other ways in which the industry has matured and become more central to a wider range of employer activities. Increasingly, temporary help firms take responsibility for an entire work function, for example call centres which handle customer relations. Indicative of this trend is a recent agreement between Manpower Inc. and Ameritech. They plan jointly to seek call-centre business, with Manpower supplying the people and Ameritech providing the technology. Call-centre outsourcing is growing at a rate of between 20 and 40 per cent a year (*Staffing Industry Review*, December, 1997, p. 8) and, according to one source, all types of Vendor on Premise agreements have grown from 2 per cent of total temporary help agency revenues in 1992 to 11 per cent in 1996 (ibid., p. 11).

Another innovation of growing importance are national contracts in which a large employer with branches across the nation signs a master agreement with one agency, for example, Manpower, Olsten, or Kelly Services, to provide temporary workers throughout the firm's operations wherever it is located. Examples of these accounts are agreements between Manpower Inc. and EDS and Hewlett-Packard, Olsten with Lexmark and Chase Manhattan, and Kelly Services with Johnson & Johnson. These agreements also underwrite another emerging tendency in the industry: the development of subcontractor networks and supplier tiers within the temporary help industry. Increasingly large temporary help firms are establishing subcontracting relationships with local agencies to provide speciality employees when the larger firm cannot meet the demand.

4.2.8. Who Are Contingent Employees?

Table 4.6 uses the February 1995 Current Population Survey data to describe the characteristics of the people who work in various forms of non-standard employment as well regular or "traditional" employment. People who work for temporary agencies or in "on-call" situations are slightly more likely to be women, more likely to be black, and are somewhat less well educated than people in standard arrangements. However, by contrast, contract workers appear to be slightly more educated and substantially more male than regular workers. These patterns serve to emphasize the point that it is important to distinguish among various types of contingent work.

	Traditional arrangements	Temp agencies	On-call	Contract firms
	Table 4.6			
	Demographic characteristics of contingent employees			
Men (%)	52.8	47.2	50.1	71.5
Age 40 (%)	28.0	25.0	20.5	15.2
HS degree or less	42.2	47.6	48.5	39.3
College graduate	28.9	20.3	20.8	30.6
Black (%)	10.9	21.8	11.0	11.7

Source: Bureau of Labor Statistics Report 900, August 1995.

4.2.9. What Drives the Growth of Contingent Employment?

Why are firms making growing use of contingent employment? There are several explanations which seem plausible. The first is the most traditional: in the past, temporary help was used to handle peak load problems, temporary increases in the need for labor. This may still be the story but without some additional argument it cannot explain the growth in temporary usage. Either demand is becoming more variable or alternatively firms are lowering their threshold for defining the portion of demand which is variable and the portion which is stable. Evidence suggests that both explanations are viable. The business press is full of stories about the shortening product life cycle and the research literature supports this view. In addition, anecdotal evidence also suggests that the hurdle has risen for justifying the addition of permanent employment.

Other explanations for the growth in contingent employment look to deeper changes in how firms view their organizations. At its most general level, the rhetoric of "core competencies" has led firms to take responsibility only for those activities in which they have a comparative advantage and which contribute directly to profits. Just as firms have out-sourced activities ranging from the lowest skilled such as cleaning (to cleaning companies) to the highest skilled such as information technology (to firms such as EDS or Anderson Consulting), so they are increasingly willing to outsource their labor force. Everything is up for question, the only issue is how deeply into the organization will this new way of thinking bite.

One step along the continuum is the core–periphery model. In this formulation, companies remain committed to providing a reasonable degree of employment security to a core labor force but in order to do so they need to shield those employees from market forces. They accomplish this by buffering the core workforce with contingent employees whose comings and goings absorb market flux. In this set-up the world has changed for the temps but for the lucky people in the core life goes on much as before. However, the reality may be even more dramatic. Taken to its logical conclusion the new state of mind leads the firm to ask continually which groups of employees are "core" and which are not and so everyone is ultimately at risk.

A third explanation for the rise of contingent employment views temporary help firms as new labor market institutions which enable firms to perform more efficiently the traditional functions of screening and hiring employees. In this view, the use of temporary employment is a way to outsource the initial recruitment function and then to bring workers on to the premises in order to observe their performance prior to making an offer. This leads to what, in the jargon of the staffing industry, is called "temp to perm" employment. In interviews in the Silicon Valley I found that this was a very common pattern. For example, Selection, a maker of circuit boards, employs about 4,500 regular employees and about 1,000 temporary workers. The only way to get hired as a regular employee is to first work as a temp. Many other firms reported a similar practice.

Finally, supply-side explanations must be given their due. Perhaps a growing number of employees want the freedom and control which is associated with contingent employment. In this formulation, firms are responding by increasing this form of employment in order to attract people with the skills they need.

There are several strategies for distinguishing among these explanations, one of which is simply to ask employers why they use contingent employment. In the 1992 National Survey of Establishments I asked respondents to indicate the most important reason for utilizing contingent employment, and Table 4.7 describes the responses. The responses were open-ended and were coded into the four categories in the table. It is apparent that what might be thought of as the most traditional explanation, dealing with peak load problems, dominates. If we consider together the two cost-related rationales, lower wages and savings in benefits, then cost becomes the second most important explanation.

Table 4.7
Five most common advantages
Percentage of establishments citing each

Peak load	60.7%
Obtain scarce skills	21.1%
Save benefit costs	18.0%
Enable you to shed labor more easily	18.9%
Costs in general are less	16.3%

Five most common disadvantages
Percentage of establishments citing each

Not enough skilled people available	30.4%
These workers not committed to the firm's success	32.0%
Too expensive	20.6%
Turnover too high to build a skilled labor force	20.5%
Inadequate control over these workers	16.7%

Source: National Survey of Establishments, 1992.

There are, however, several problems with simple questions of this kind. First, respondents may vary in what they mean by the explanations they give. Second, one would like to be able to understand more systematically what are the characteristics of firms which make more or less intensive use of contingent employees. The 1992 National Survey of Establishments contained a variety of variables which in principle might explain variation across workplaces in the use of contingent employment. In order to explore the importance of these considerations, I estimated a statistical relationship in which the dependent variable was an indicator of whether or not the establishment made use of contingent employees and the explanatory variables described various potentially relevant characteristics of the establishment.[4]

In this model, several variables prove to be statistically significant predictors of the use of contingent employment. Establishments which have collective bargaining relationships with at least some of their employees are much less intensive users of contingent workers than are establishments which are "union free". This role of unions is very much in the expected direction since unions would be expected to resist employment arrangements which reduce the number of regular workers. Larger establishments (measured by employment size) and establishments which are part of a larger organization are also more likely to use contingent employment. This makes sense given that contingent employment is likely to flow from a formalized personnel policy which in turn is associated with size and connections to a larger organization.

Indeed, a variable measuring whether or not the establishment has a human resources department also proves statistically significant.

In addition to these considerations, the greater emphasis the establishment places upon competing on the basis of quality, variety and service (versus low cost) the less likely is it to use contingent employment. This makes sense if we believe that contingent workers are less committed to the long-run success of the enterprise and less willing to put in extra effort to satisfy customers than are regular workers. Establishments which have job rotation schemes in place are less likely to use contingent employees, presumably because their regular workforce is more flexible and can more easily fill in.

4.2.10. The Impact of Contingent Employment upon Employee Welfare

Public concern about the growth of contingent employment is driven by the implicit assumption that these jobs are not as good as regular employment and that, in addition, people who are "stuck" in contingent jobs may suffer long-term adverse consequences.

In her survey, Houseman found that the actual wage paid to temporary employees was not typically below that of regular employees but that when benefits were considered total compensation is much less. This is supported in the Current Population Survey, data from which are reported in Table 4.8. It is apparent that contingent workers are in much worse shape than regular employees both with regard to benefits and in terms of the fraction of employees at the very low end of the pay distribution. It is worth noting that while some contingent employees receive health insurance from a source other than their employer (for example, a spouse who is working), this is not typical and does not compensate sufficiently to bring contingent employees to the level of regular workers.

Table 4.8 Well-being indicators for contingent employees (%)			
	No employer health insurance	**No health insurance any source**	**Below poverty line**
Agency temps	80.1	54.0	25.3
On-call	74.0	33.5	17.0
Short-term hires	59.8	27.4	16.9
Regular FT	15.9	12.2	7.1

Source: Current Population Survey, February 1995, as analysed in Houseman (1997).

4.2.11. Changing Forms of Work Organization

Whereas increased insecurity and the spread of contingent employment can be seen as negative trends in the labor market, there are other developments within firms which are much more positive. In particular, a growing number of firms are adopting new forms of work organization which are not only more productive but which entail advantages for the labor force. These new work systems are often termed "high-performance work organizations".

The nature of high-performance work organizations

Up until a decade or so ago, the US industrial relations system and work organization could be characterized by what might be termed a traditional model. In the traditional system the workplace was organized around tight divisions of labor and narrowly designed specialized jobs. Decision-making was in the hands of supervisors who decided how the jobs were to be performed, how work was scheduled, and how workers were judged. Employee participation was limited and clear detailed rules specified either in a personnel policy or a collective bargaining contract determined the criteria governing career progression from one job to another and the compensation associated with each individual job. Grievance procedures were the dominant voice mechanism for employees if they believed that their job rights had been violated in some way by the supervisor or by some other management decision. Finally, in the traditional model, employers were free to adjust employment levels as they wished and hence hire–fire was the rule.

This system is under attack because it is increasingly perceived as less productive than the alternatives. The central problem lies in the internal rigidities associated with the traditional model. Consider, for example, the situation at General Motors under the traditional system. Among the job titles were "install front seats", "install rear seats", "install garnish moldings", and "install door trim panels". A "front seat installer" would not install rear seats (Katz 1985).

It is important to see that this system was not irrational. In a world in which employers hire and fire at will, rigid job classifications will emerge with the intention of providing at least some level of protection to the labor force. Hence the system made some sense given the constraints under which it was created.

Although not irrational in its own terms, the traditional system has increasingly been seen as failing to meet the needs of firms and employees. The sources of failure are several. The efforts by firms to improve quality and to better meet customer needs have both required a reorganization of production which puts more power in the hands of employees further down the organizational hierarchy. This tendency is given further impetus by efforts to cut costs which also lead to elimination of bureaucratic layers and greater responsibility at lower levels. In order to "empower" these employees, their job definitions need to be flexible, they require greater levels of discretion, they often find themselves working in teams, and they require higher levels of skill and training. All of these imply a transformation in how work is organized.

In more specific terms, what do these reforms consist of? How might a reader concretely envisage the content of these changes? The beginning to any answer to this question is to recognize (as the data presented below will demonstrate) that there is no single model which is being adopted everywhere. In some settings, such as the General Motors Saturn plant, joint union/employee/manager activities extend from work teams on the shop floor to joint "management" committees at every level of the plant and in every area, from product design to supplier relations. This, however, is only one model and an unusual one at that. In other firms, change is being driven by the quality movement and the transformation consists of a combination of work teams and of-line problem-solving groups.

A useful way of envisaging the nature of the new systems is to break them down into their component parts and examine the options for each component. As we work our way through these elements it should become clear that the central principle is increased employee power and responsibility. However, the extent to which this occurs is not uniform across all employers who introduce elements of the new systems.

The organization of work

At the core of the new systems are changes in how employees do their job. Perhaps the most typical innovation is the introduction of work teams. In many instances these teams are led by a management employee, but that person's role has changed to one of a "coach" or "facilitator". In other instances the teams are self-directed. In both instances, at the core of the idea of teams is that the employees take responsibility for a group of tasks, that there is a sense of responsibility for the team's product, that the workers are broadly skilled, and that there is an element of job rotation.

In many cases the teams can decide how best to do their job but this is not always the case. For example, at the General Motors–Toyota joint venture, NUMMI, each task is rigidly prescribed. However, employees have considerable power to make suggestions as to how to alter these prescriptions. This brings us to the second point.

Involvement in off-line activities

In many "transformed" firms employees are involved in aspects other than direct work activities. The most common example is problem-solving groups in which employees work in groups, often consisting of a cross-section of employees and hence to some extent obviating traditional managerial/non-managerial distinctions. These groups address problems such as production techniques, quality issues, and health and safety. In the most extreme form these groups can take up topics which in the past have been seen as clearly "managerial", for example, outsourcing and supplier policy.

Link to broader objectives

It is frequently the case that organizations which implement the innovations described above do so as part of broader efforts to transform the firm. These efforts include flattening of organizational hierarchies and renewed emphasis on quality and customer satisfaction. Both of these objectives are consistent with empowering workers.

Link to other human resource policies

Organizations which implement these changes in work organization typically also transform other aspects of their human resource systems. The two most consistent changes are increased use of performance-based compensation and higher levels of training. The importance of increased training is straightforward: to the extent that employees have more responsibilities and to the extent that they exercise greater discretion, they need to be prepared.

Performance-based compensation shifts risk from the employer to the workers and in this sense can be interpreted as a degradation of employment conditions. On the other hand, it also gives workers and teams which have new powers the opportunity to reap rewards from their effort.

There is greater variation in other human resource policies. Some employers have linked work reorganization with higher levels of employment security. Examples include Saturn, NUMMI and Xerox. These employers pursue this policy because they understand that the traditional system provided security in the form of belief in rigid work rules and that in order to induce employees to provide greater flexibility they need to be compensated with some level of security commitment. However, the firms which undertake policies along these lines appear to be in the minority. A key question, to which we shall return, is whether it will be possible to sustain new work systems in an environment of fear.

Firms also vary in their approach towards unions. In some settings the new work systems are implemented in cooperation with unions. In other instances, however, the new systems are either part of a policy to avoid unionization or are implemented unilaterally without the cooperation of the existing union. Again, a difficult question is whether in the long run the more conflictual strategies are viable.

Documenting changes in work organization

How much work reorganization is occurring in America and what are the characteristics of employers who are undertaking these activities? To answer these questions I shall present data from my 1992 survey. The patterns in this survey are consistent with those found in other work on the same topic. In analysing that survey I shall focus on the four characteristics most often seen as most central to transformed organizations: self-directed work teams, job rotation, use of employee problem-solving groups (or quality circles, QC), and use of total quality management (TQM). (The core job family was defined as the largest group of non-supervisory workers directly involved in the production of the good or service. These could be either blue or white collar.)

For each, the respondent was asked whether or not the practice was employed in the establishment and if so what percentage of core employees were involved (the percentage involved is termed the "penetration rate").

Table 4.9 shows the distribution of each practice for two levels of penetration: whether the practice is used at all and whether at least 50 per cent of *core* employees are involved. It is clear that if we simply ask whether or not a given practice is used among any fraction of *core* employees then we would conclude that the elements of flexible work are quite widespread. For example, more than half of the establishments use teams and 33.5 per cent of the establishments employ TQM. The story becomes different, however, when we examine penetration. Looking at the intermediate category of 50 percent or more employees involved, the rates fall sharply. Each practice falls by roughly 15 percentage points.

Table 4.9
Distribution of practice at different levels of penetration

| | Any percentage level of penetration | |
	All (%)	Manufacturing (%)
Teams	54.5%	50.1%
Rotation	43.4%	55.6%
TQM	33.5%	44.9%
QC	40.8%	45.6%
Nothing	21.8%	16.0%
	50 percent level of penetration	
	All (%)	Manufacturing (%)
Teams	40.5%	32.3%
Rotation	26.6%	37.4%
TQM	24.5%	32.1%
QC	27.4%	29.7%
Nothing	36.0%	33.2%

Source: National Survey of Establishments, 1992.

Even so, the distribution of self-directed workteams is surprisingly widespread. There is clearly some discontinuity between the extent of usage of this practice and the others.

The manufacturing/blue-collar patterns are similar in that there is a substantial diffusion of the practices at any usage level and there is a drop-off when one sets a 50 per cent threshold for participation. Self-directed teams appear less widespread in manufacturing than elsewhere in the economy but the other practices are more common.

These data lead to the natural question of whether the practices form groups from which emerge identifiable patterns which might be thought of as the new systems discussed in the literature. Table 4.10 shows how the practices cluster together when a 50 per cent penetration threshold is set (no conclusions are changed when other thresholds are imposed). It appears that there is no single major dominant cluster of practices. There is some representation for each of the possible combinations and in most of the cases the distribution of clusters seems rather even.

Table 4.10
Clustering of work practices (50 per cent or more penetration, in %)

	Entire sample	Manufacturing/blue collar
Nothing	36.0	33.2
All	4.8	5.0
Teams only	14.4	5.5
Rotation only	7.0	11.7
QC only	3.1	2.4
TQM only	2.6	4.5
Team/Rotation	4.8	4.6
Team/QC	4.3	3.3
Team/TQM	4.6	4.2
Rotation/QC	3.0	3.3
Rotation/TQM	1.5	4.5
TQM/QC	4.4	4.9
Team/TQM/QC	3.6	4.2
Team/Rotation/TQM	1.2	1.6
Team/Rotation/QC	2.3	3.4
Rotation/TQM/QC	1.4	2.9

Source: National Survey of Establishments, 1992.

Supportive human resource practices

Many students of human resources believe that reform in work organization needs to be accompanied by supportive human resource policies. For example, with respect to compensation, observers believe that many firms which have moved towards more flexible work organization have accompanied the shifts in work systems with comparable changes in wage systems. This is on the theory that when employees are given more power to determine outcomes they should have a financial stake in enterprise success.

A second area concerns training. The implementation of flexible work systems would seem to require higher levels of skills than are typically afforded employees in traditional mass production systems. One would therefore expect that investments in training would be higher in transformed work systems.

As already noted, there are strong reasons to believe that firms engaged in work reform must be prepared to provide enhanced levels of job security. On the other hand, there have been widespread recent layoffs even in firms such as IBM or DEC, which are thought to exemplify flexible work organization.

The National Survey of Establishments asked a series of questions regarding these human resource practices and the results are displayed in Table 4.11. The patterns do support the idea that sustainable work reforms need to be underwritten by broader shifts in human resource systems. Enhanced training and innovative compensation policies are linked to sustained workplace reform. However, as might be suggested by the widespread wave of layoffs and restructuring, employment security does not seem linked to work reorganization.

Table 4.11
Supporting human resource practices

	All	Establishment has at least one flexible work practice with 50% penetration	Establishment has no flexible work practice with 50% penetration	t-statistic
Gainsharing	0.137	0.144	0.126	0.946
Pay for Skill	0.304	0.364	0.197	**4.676
Profit-Sharing /Bonus	0.447	0.478	0.393	*2.008
Percent in off-the-job training	0.320	0.375	0.219	**4.838
Percent in Cross- Training	0.451	0.529	0.314	**7.456
Employment Security Policy	0.398	0.394	0.404	0.179

Notes: The t-statistics are based upon equations which include core occupation and industry controls.
*   Significant different at 5% level
**   Significant difference at 1% level
Source: National Survey of Establishments, 1992.

What explains variation in work innovation?

The goal of this section is to understand why some firms do and others do not engage in work reorganization. This is a question of more than just academic interest. We cannot predict the rate or extent of diffusion of high-performance work systems without first understanding what considerations underwrite its adoption. In this section we shall review some of the key findings from the National Survey of Establishments. The patterns described here have been analysed in greater statistical detail in Osterman (1994).

Before beginning with the survey, however, it is important to understand that broad contextual considerations, which cannot be captured in a survey, can influence adoption of work systems. One set of such factors includes laws and regulations affecting the workplace. For example, in Germany most employers are required to establish works councils which provide formal employee voice mechanisms. These institutions are likely in turn to lead to a variety of work practices which we would consider to fall under the high-performance label. In a similar vein, the reluctance of Japanese firms to poach labor from each other leads to low turnover which in turn permits considerable investments in the human capital of the incumbent workforce and work systems designed to take advantage of that investment.

Another contextual factor is the nature of the product and the production process. Presumably the gains from high-performance work systems are weaker, if not non-existent, when the work is relatively simple and can be standardized. That this is true is suggested by Milkman's study of Japanese transplants in California's electronics assembly industry. The Japanese managers of these firms were certainly knowledgeable about high-performance work practices and faced no constraints from their home offices in establishing them. Yet Milkman found in her survey of 50 Japanese-owned electronic assembly plants that

> the Japanese owned plants in California bear little resemblance to the Japanese management model. Relatively few have quality circles or the equivalent; flexible teams are even more exceptional; and most of the managers we interviewed laughed outright when asked about just-in-time delivery or the like.
>
> One "Japanese practice" is more typical of these plants, however; most are committed, in principle, to avoiding layoffs. However, even this is tempered by the fact that these plants typically have high turnover rates ...

(Milkman 1991, pp. 79–80)

This general point about context is supported by the National Survey of Establishments, which found that the skill level of the production process was an important determinant of whether transformed work systems were adopted (Osterman 1994). Putting the matter most starkly, even the most enthusiastic advocate of high-performance work systems should agree that they are not appropriate under all circumstances.

Turning now to other findings from the survey, an important place to start is with the competitive strategy of the firm. The National Survey of Establishments assigned 100 points to the strategy of competing on cost and then asked respondents to indicate how many points their establishment would assign, relative to this, to competing on the basis of quality, of variety, and of service. Many commentators believe that enterprises which emphasize these latter three strategies are following what might be termed the "high road" and it is important to see, first, how widespread such strategies are and, second, whether they are related to adoption of new work practices.

Table 4.12 shows the average score of the respondents with respect to each of the strategies. Evidently, product variety is not central to the strategy of most establishments but, relative to cost, quality and service rank quite highly. It is worth noting, in passing, that the weak support given to product variety somewhat undercuts the emphasis in the literature on what has been termed "flexible specialization" (Piore and Sabel 1984).

Table 4.12
Competitive strategies of firms
(points to quality, variety, service relative to 100 points given to cost-based competition)

	All	Manufacturing
Quality	168	177
Variety	88	88
Service	227	182

Source: National Survey of Establishments, 1992.

Table 4.13 shows the relationship between each of the strategic elements and the establishment's use of innovative work systems. It is apparent that firms which place a high value on quality as a competitive strategy make much greater use of all four new work systems than do other enterprises. By contrast, there is essentially no relationship between stress on variety and work organization and the relationship with respect to service is very mixed. The conclusion, then, is that a key determinant of whether firms engage in work reform is whether their competitive strategy emphasizes quality.

An additional aspect of the establishment's competitive position which proves to be important is whether the establishment was among the 32 per cent in the sample which competes in international markets. For example, the average penetration (percentage of core employees involved) in TQM was 38 per cent for establishments which compete internationally and 19 per cent for those which did not. This is a not unexpected finding given that these establishments are more likely to face competition from other firms which employ various forms of high-performance work systems and given the fact that international exposure provides learning opportunities.

Table 4.13
Product market strategy and flexible work organization
(percentage of core employees involved in each practice by whether score
on product market strategy is above or below average)

	Variety		Quality		Service	
	Above	**Below**	**Above**	**Below**	**Above**	**Below**
Teams	0.39	0.39	0.45	0.35	0.54	0.36
QC	0.29	0.26	0.40	0.28	0.19	0.29
TQM	0.24	0.26	0.44	0.21	0.22	0.26
Rotation	0.28	0.25	0.42	0.23	0.36	0.24

Source: National Survey of Establishments, 1992.

Among the most interesting findings is the strong role that employer values play in influencing adoption of flexible work systems. It is well known from anecdotal evidence that firms which appear to observers to be similar with respect to markets, technology, and other structural characteristics none the less differ considerably in their human resource practices. One possibility is that the values of the firm – for example the extent to which the enterprise is seen as a community or a "family" – might be important. This consideration is given weight by the observation that Japanese employers have more of a community or stakeholder view of their enterprise than do Americans and that this helps explain various work practices.

It is difficult to measure directly the entire range of possibly relevant values. However, the National Survey of Establishments did seek to measure one particular set of values, attitudes towards helping employee families, and this can be seen as a proxy for more general employees-friendly values.

About 50 per cent of the survey instrument contained a long series of questions about benefits, particularly work family benefits, and about enterprise values regarding these benefits. This portion of the questionnaire was administered prior to the work organization questions and hence the respondent's reply on values was unrelated to any suggestion which might have been implanted by the work organization section. In the context of asking about benefits the respondent was asked

"In general, what is your establishment's philosophy about how appropriate it is to help increase the wellbeing of employees with respect to their personal or family situations?" The distribution of responses on the five point scale was: 1.7 per cent, "not appropriate"; 9.4 per cent, "a little appropriate"; 33.0 per cent, "moderately appropriate"; 42.8 per cent, "very appropriate"; and 12.8 per cent "extremely appropriate".

Table 4.14 shows the how the penetration of the work practices varies with whether or not the establishment replied that it was "very" or "extremely" appropriate to help with the personal family situation of employees. It is apparent that the relationship is very strong.

Table 4.14 Relationship of establishment values and work practices		
	It is "very" or "extremely" appropriate	Other reply
Percentage Teams	47	29
Percentage QC	36	16
Percentage TQM	29	19
Percentage Rotation	31	20
Source: National Survey of Establishments, 1992.		

There are several commonly discussed factors which prove *not* to be important in influencing whether or not establishments adopt flexible work systems. Notable among these are establishment size and union status. With respect to size, many observers would have predicted that small firms are less likely to implement high-performance work systems because they lack resources for training and implementation as well as, often, knowledge concerning the best way to proceed. However, it is also important to recall that the sample is limited to establishments with 50 of more employees and hence the smallest firms are not included. The failure of the union status variable to prove important probably reflects the fact that we lack a measure of the nature of the bargaining relationship. It is clear from many of the examples presented here, Saturn, Xerox and Corning, that when the relationship is healthy, unions can play an important role in supporting and sustaining the transition to high-performance work organizations.

Perhaps the most fundamental lesson to be taken from this section is the close relationship between the firm's business strategy and its approach towards work organization. Both international competition and a "high road" competitive strategy drive the adoption of new forms of work organization. This clearly places human resources at the core of the firm's competitive strategy but it also means that it is difficult to conceive of altering work organization without first addressing the issue of product market strategy.

4.3.   SUMMARY

I conclude the chapter by presenting an overall interpretation of the material presented above. The data point to two opposite trends. On the one hand, jobs are improving in that there has been a widespread dissemination of so-called high-performance work systems (a trend which more recent surveys show is continuing). On the other hand, jobs are getting worse in that they are more insecure and pay is not increasing. How can these two seemingly opposite tendencies be reconciled?

Division of labor guides not just production but also intellectual work and hence when we think about current developments we tend to divide up the problem into manageable questions. There is an enormous, and still growing, literature on wage stagnation and increased earnings inequality. Whether jobs are more insecure now than in the past is another topic hotly debated in both the popular and academic literature. Similarly, contingent work is a research theme of growing popularity.

There are obvious advantages to identifying discrete trends and studying them in depth. The risk is that we lose sight of the forest. In this case the forest is that the real story about the past two decades is that the postwar institutional structure of the labor market has been destroyed and that we are living in a period in which a new institutional structure is being erected. The destruction of the old rules and the difficult search for new ones creates both economic outcomes (stagnating wages) and psychological outcomes (uncertainty and insecurity) which are disturbing.

The institutional structure of the labor market operates at two levels. At the more abstract level the term refers to "shared rules, which can be laws or collective understandings, held in place by custom, explicit agreement, or tacit agreement". These shared understandings or norms can, as we shall see, have a powerful impact on behaviour and when the norms change, behaviour can change dramatically. At a more concrete level the idea refers to more tangible institutions – unions, job training programmes, temporary help firms – whose activities influence labor market outcomes. The transformation of these concrete institutions is often intimately related to changing norms and shared understandings about the labor market. Taken as a whole the institutional structure provides a coherent set of practices, norms and rules of thumb which shaped our expectations and which guided the behaviour of both firms and workers.

Looking back we can discern what were the norms which undergirded the old structure. One example is that while blue-collar workers might be laid off, white-collar employees and managers were treated as fixed factors of production. Related to this was the long-standing view that layoffs take place in periods of economic decline but that a firm which is doing well will share this good fortune with its employees. In the field of labor relations, despite a 1938 Supreme Court opinion which permitted the permanent replacement of strikers, "good" employers did not do this. When it came to wage setting, more attention was paid to maintaining constant relative wages across occupations and industries than to adjusting wages to the supply and demand conditions of the external labor market.

These rules and norms were so widely accepted that much of the best-known academic research of the 1950s, 1960s and even 1970s was devoted to documenting their existence, studying their consequences, and generating theories to explain their emergence and even their "optimality". Yet just listing these norms makes it clear how dramatically the labor market has shifted. Healthy employers lay off workers, including managers. Unions have declined and strikers are routinely replaced. The wage structure has been blown apart.

If the old institutional structure is gone, what is replacing it? One natural conclusion, to which many people jump, is that the old system constituted a set of "unnatural" constraints on market forces and we are moving into an era in which market forces are unfettered.

There are strong views pushing towards this conclusion. CEOs, even those whose firms are laying off employees and losing sales, justify their compensation as did Gilbert Amelio of Apple who explained his $2.5 million dollar salary with the comment that "It is a market determined figure".[5]

There is much which supports this broad interpretation. The power of the market seems evident in the impact of newly energized stockholders as they seek higher performance from firms in their portfolio. This quest for better returns has led to some of the layoffs and restructuring which has undermined the old system. The image of an irresistible market is reinforced as firms in nations such as Germany and Japan increasingly behave like American companies as they shed employees and move to regions with cheaper labor.

There is no question that market forces are one of the prime movers behind the changes we observe. It does not follow, however, that the labor market will settle down into the bourse celebrated in both elementary and advanced economic theory. The fundamental fact is that a truly unbridled market is not politically or socially acceptable. The market is not irresistible. It will be resisted; the question is what form this resistance will take and how different interests will be weighed.

The ultimate unacceptability of the unbridled market was established in the social science literature in Polanyi's classic book *The Great Transformation*. He showed how the spread of the market destroyed the structure of traditional society and then described the constant efforts by society to reconstruct itself and to push back against the market. In the end, people do not want their lives governed by impersonal and atomistic forces and they eventually seek to limit the scope and power of those forces. Sometimes the market may have the upper hand and other times it is in retreat. However, in no circumstances is the triumph of the market complete or permanent, nor should we expect it to be or desire it to be. This constant tension takes on special force in the arena which most directly touches people, the labor market.

The choices facing us are, however, far from clear. There are several reasons why it is very difficult to understand where we want to go. First, although the language of the market is used as a rhetorical weapon in the ongoing struggle over the shape of the new institutional structure, it is none the less true that new economic realities do constrain our choices in novel ways. Many firms, particularly those normally regarded as leaders, unquestionably face fierce overseas competition which constrains what is possible with respect to wages and costs. Information technology and other production innovations enable firms to produce with less labor and to shift production in response to relatively small differences in wages and other costs. Aggressive institutional investors have a point when they argue that American firms have become top heavy with management and that "reengineering" could indeed shave costs.

The second reason why it is hard to picture our destination is that some of the alternatives which have traditionally attracted reformers have lost their sheen. What has happened in Germany is paradigmatic. Until recently the standard interpretation of Germany was that in the postwar period an institutional structure had been created which forced firms on to the so-called "high road" of high wages and job security. That institutional structure consisted of strong unions, works councils within firms, high levels of worker training administered jointly by government, unions and firms, and cooperative behaviour among erstwhile competitors. In effect, market forces had been channelled in particular directions and the success of the German economy in terms of wages, job security and economic growth seemed to ratify this strategy.

The third reason why the future seems so uncertain is that new institutional forms have emerged whose current function and future possibilities we do not fully understand. We do not, however, have a real grip on the meaning of this development. Early writing about temporary workers tended to view the phenomenon as uniformly bad, a degradation of "normal" wages, hours and benefits. There is considerable truth to this view but we also now understand that some employees prefer the flexibility inherent in a temporary job. More to the present point, however, is that temporary help firms are playing an increasingly important role in shaping the operation of the labor market. They are becoming an important labor market institution. For example, they recruit and screen potential regular employees for firms (hence performing a "labor exchange" function), they staff the human resource departments of some firms (they are an outsourcer), and they have linked up with outplacement firms to help find jobs for laid-off workers (a function in principle performed by the public employment and training system). Where all of this will go is unclear and the uncertainty adds to the difficulty of understanding the choices which confront us.

NOTES

1 These statistics are taken from the *Economic Report of the President*, 1996.
2 These figures are based on synthetic cohorts obtained by linking together successive surveys.
3 Some surveys asked about dislocation over the past three years while others asked about the past five years. An adjustment is necessary to ensure that the data are comparable across years and that no biases are introduced by different recall periods. In addition, the dislocation rates for all men and women refer to dislocation for any reason while the dislocation rates by occupation are limited to those who were dislocated due to plant closings, large-scale layoffs, or the elimination of jobs. This is due to the skip patterns in the questionnaire.
4 I estimated a logit model. On the right hand side were measures of whether or not the establishment was unionized, the size (measured by employment) of the establishment, whether or not the establishment was part of a larger organization, the presence of a human resources department, an index of the establishment's commitment to competing on the basis of quality, variety, and service versus pure cost competition, and the extent of use of work practices including teams, job rotation, quality circles, and total quality management. A fuller description of how these variables are defined and constructed can be found in Osterman (1994).
5 *Business Week*, 26 February 1996, p. 47.

REFERENCES

Houseman, Susan (1997), "Temporary, Part-Time, and Contract Employment in the United States: New Evidence From An Employer Survey", W.E. Upjohn Institute.
Katz, Harry (1985), *Shifting Gears: Changing Labor Relations in the U.S. Auto Industry*, Cambridge, MA: MIT Press.
Milkman, Ruth (1991), *California's Japanese Factories; Labor Relations and Economic Globalization*, Los Angeles: UCLA Institute of Industrial Relations.
Mishel, Lawrence R., John Schmitt and Jared Bernstein (1997), *State of Working America, 1996-1997*, Armonk: M.E. Sharpe Incorporated.

Neumark, David, Daniel Polsky and Daniel Hansen (1997), "Has job stability declined yet? New evidence for the 1990s'. mimeo, February.

Osterman, Paul (1994), "How Common Is Workplace Transformation and How Can We Explain Who Does It?" *Industrial and Labor Relations Review*, **47**, January, 173–188.

Piore, Michael and Charles Sabel (1984), *The Second Industrial Divide*, New York: Basic Books.

Polanyi, Karl (1994), "The Great Transformation", New York: Farrar & Rinehart.

Staffing Industry Review, Staffing Industry Analysts, Los Altos, California.

5   External and internal labor markets in Spain: a relational contracts perpective

Vicente Salas*

5.1.   INTRODUCTION

The aim of this chapter is to provide an overview of the current and future situation of the Spanish labor market. The approach reflects the peculiar features of the employment relation and points to the need to account for internal as well as external labor market considerations, in order to obtain a more accurate view of labor relations in Spain. Our point of departure establishes a relationship between the competition strategy and the organizational structure of the firms, and the nature of the dominant form of employment relation. Therefore, the current legal and institutional framework that shapes and regulates labor relations in Spain is evaluated from the point of view of its contribution to facilitating or complicating the strategic and organizational choice of Spanish firms in the near future.

Many analysts, especially those from the management field, have emphasized the strategic value of human resources in modern market competition. Specific human capital is encouraged, as is the sense of loyalty and commitment of the workers towards the firm. Leading world firms, such as IBM or HP, have offered stability, training, higher wages and job empowerment to their workers, in exchange for a more active participation on the part of their employees in problem solving and the continuous improvement of production and sales activities. Firms that are well established in world markets, but which have their headquarters in the US, a country considered as a paradigm in labor market deregulation, are adopting human resources policies that have been dominant in firms belonging to other advanced countries, such as Germany or Japan, where labor markets are a long way from being competitive.[1]

Management-led changes in human resources policies raise a number of new issues and questions: do we actually need strict labor market regulations (apart from safety standards) when firms already implement practices that contribute to socially desirable standards of well-being for the labor force (stability, training, participation, a share in productivity gains)? Is it time for countries such as Spain, where labor markets and employment relations are highly regulated, to deregulate extensively in order to facilitate the free choices of workers and managers?

In order to offer some answers to these questions, this chapter adopts a conceptual perspective where the employment relation is viewed as a *relational contract* between workers and firms. This type of contract is preferred when complete contingent contracts have very high transaction costs (due to bounded rationality reasons), or when short-term spot contracting is inefficient (due to high resource specificity). The relational contract is incomplete and covers a long period of time, which means that a governance system is required in order to arrive at a decision when unanticipated contingencies arise. In general, more incomplete contracts will allow for more flexibility *ex post* but, at the same time, more incompleteness makes the choice of the governance system particularly important, since it has to induce efficient decisions *ex ante* before the employment relation begins.[2]

I conjecture that, in recent years, technological innovations and the intensification of product market competition have increased the economic value of specific human capital and, at the same time, the value of more flexibility in meeting consumers' changing demands. Therefore, both *ex ante* efficiency (incentives to invest in specific human capital) and *ex post* flexibility are required. The governance of the employment relation has to take into account both aims and, for this reason, an evolution is detected from hierarchical governance (where decision rights are centralized in the employers) towards bilateral governance (where decision rights are shared with the employees). The current situation in labor markets and employment relations in Spain appears to be far away from what may be considered as desirable, given the observed trends in strategy, organization and governance. Therefore, this chapter examines the possible obstacles to change and adaptation.

5.2. THE RECENT EVOLUTION OF LABOR MARKETS IN SPAIN

The performance of the Spanish labor markets has been an active field of research in recent years.[3] However, most of this research has dealt with aggregate data, searching for answers to the question of why Spanish unemployment is more than twice the average rate of unemployment in other European countries. In other words, the focus of interest has been mainly the external labor market, but little research is available on the actual characteristics of the internal labor markets. In this section I present some observations on the recent behaviour of the external labor market in Spain, as well as some empirical evidence on the determinants of the employment of non-permanent workers by manufacturing firms; this evidence will allow us to detect some patterns in the internal labor markets among Spanish firms.

5.2.1.   Employment and the Competitiveness of Spanish Firms

Spain joined the European Economic Community (EEC) in 1986 and from this moment the Spanish economy began to take the final steps towards full external economic integration. From the date of entry until 1989, Spanish firms enjoyed a very favourable situation, with prices adjusting to international levels and labor costs rising less than product prices. Profits were high and growth was stimulated by high levels of investment and the creation of new jobs.

From 1989 onwards, the prices of tradable goods continued to be determined by international markets, but non-tradable goods, mainly firm and consumer services, suffered increases in prices that were much higher than those of tradable goods, causing a dual inflationary situation which resulted in increases in the consumer price index significantly above those experienced in other developed countries. Wages started to increase in order to maintain purchasing power, while international competitiveness, measured in terms of the effective real exchange rate defined over unit labor costs, began to fall. Spanish firms lost market share in both internal and external product markets. Productive resources, labor and capital were underemployed and profits shrank to a level of return on investment well below the cost of capital. Private investment fell and several hundred thousand manufacturing jobs were destroyed.

The situation changed in 1994 when, after several devaluations, a new parity was established for the peseta in the European Monetary System, and when firms recovered productivity levels after adjustments in their labor force. For many analysts, this recovery in the Spanish economy was clear evidence that the exchange rate is a key adjusting variable for the country's economy, with a very inflexible labor market unable to respond to the actual competitive position of firms when pressure was exerted for salary increases.

One important feature of the Spanish economy during this 1989–94 period was that Spain lost its position in the race towards real convergence to European levels of output per capita. With the prospect of monetary union the exchange rate will no longer be available to compensate for losses in competitiveness due to higher labor costs. If the level of employment has to be maintained and, if possible increased, then labor costs will have to follow closely the path of total factor productivity. Therefore, a more detailed look at the determinants of this productivity is required. The internal organization of the firm, together with more effective labor relations, are often regarded as sources of competitive advantage, in that they foster increases in productivity. This is why I believe that more knowledge about the internal labor markets in Spanish firms is required in order to measure the competitive prospects for the Spanish economy.

5.2.2. Non-permanent Employment in Spanish Manufacturing Firms as Evidence of the Functioning of Internal LABOR Markets[4]

Apart from the high rate of unemployment, another destructive feature of the Spanish labor market has been the substitution, in recent years, of permanent workers for non-permanent or temporary ones. Presumably, firing costs are too high for permanent employees and, therefore, firms prefer to hire workers on fixed-term contracts in order to save such costs if the employment relation has to be discontinued. However, little is known about how non-permanent employment varies across firms and what determines its changes over time. In this section empirical evidence on this aspect, on the basis of individual-firm data, is provided and some tentative conclusions on the characteristics of the internal labor markets among Spanish manufacturing firms in the early 1990s are drawn.

The first descriptive information is contained in Table 5.1, which shows the proportion of non-permanent workers by sectors of activity (NACE) and firm size in 1991 and 1994. As can be seen, the proportion of non-permanent workers is higher in firms employing more than 200 workers, a difference that is maintained almost unchanged over time and which is reflected in practically all the manufacturing sub-sectors. Within each class, size differences can be perceived in the importance of these non-permanent workers in some sub-sectors as compared to others, and a close association between the sectoral averages of the two size classes can also be noted. In this sense, the proportion of non-permanent workers tends to be higher in more labor-intensive sectors, such as food, timber and furniture, leather goods and footwear, and textiles and clothing, while it tends to be lower in more capital-intensive sectors, such as chemicals, machinery, motor vehicles and engines, and beverages.

In both the large- and the small-firm groups, the proportion of non-permanent workers is lower in 1994 than in 1991, although it was the large firms that reduced their levels of non-permanent workers to the greatest extent. It is probably the case that a substantial part of the adjustment in industrial employment which took place between 1991 and 1995 (with the loss of some 550,000 jobs) was achieved by the firing of a high number of non-permanent workers employed until that time by large firms. With respect to small firms, the loss of employment appears to have affected permanent and non-permanent workers more equally.

	Table 5.1			
	Non-permanent employment in the Spanish manufacturing sector			
	Non-permanent employment, 1991 (%) Size		Non-permanent employment, 1994 (%) Size	
	≤ 200	> 200	≤ 200	> 200
NACE91				
Ferrous and non-ferrous metals	39.6	7.0	23.2	6.2
Non-metallic mineral products	29.0	14.2	23.4	15.2
Chemical products	18.7	9.3	15.1	8.8
Metallic products	26.6	14.7	25.5	16.0
Agricultural and industrial machinery	21.5	12.9	16.9	8.6
Office machinery, data processing, opticals	18.9	11.9	24.9	16.6
Electrical materials and accessories	34.1	16.3	28.7	12.3
Motor vehicles and engines	15.1	15.9	20.0	11.2
Other transport material	24.8	6.6	31.9	4.4
Meat, meat products	33.7	37.4	34.9	33.3
Food and tobacco	29.7	29.8	30.3	27.7
Beverages	13.3	14.9	14.0	11.8
Textiles and clothing	28.7	17.6	33.1	14.0
Leather goods and footwear	38.1	24.0	34.7	8.8
Timber and furniture	34.9	26.9	33.6	40.2
Paper, paper products and printing	22.5	15.2	21.9	11.1
Rubber and plastic products	24.7	21.0	27.8	27.8
Other manufactured products	24.5	25.7	25.1	13.3
Total	**27.9**	**16.6**	**27.1**	**14.5**

Source: Encuesta Sobre Estrategias Empresariales, ESEE (Business Strategies Survey), 1992, 1995; see note 4.

The information provided by the ESEE also allows us to determine which of the individual-firm characteristics explain the differences in the proportion of non-permanent workers in a given time period, as well as changes in this proportion between 1991 and 1994 (see Table 5.2). In 1991, from among those firms employing more than 200 workers, the proportion of non-permanent workers was greater in younger firms, in firms that advertise their products, in private firms (in comparison with state-owned ones), in national firms (in comparison with those with foreign ownership), in family-owned firms, in firms that produce goods for final consumption (in comparison with firms producing intermediate products), in firms operating in markets where demand is expanding (in comparison with firms in low-growth markets) and in firms with a higher proportion of R&D employees. Within the group of firms employing fewer than 200 workers, the proportion of non-permanent workers increased with size, with the expansive character of the market and with the proportion of laborers over the total labor force, and reduced with the age of the firm.

Table 5.2
Determinants of the proportion of non-permanent workers in the Spanish manufacturing sector

| | 1991 | | 1994 | |
	Large firms (> 200)	Small firms (≤ 200)	Large firms (> 200)	Small firms (≤ 200)
Constant	−2.856	2.865	−2.998	−19.554
Proportion of laborers	0.032	0.160**	0.088*	0.203**
Proportion of employees with university degree	−0.066	0.086	0.014	−0.214
Proportion of personnel in R&D	28.440*	24.41	8.956	1.858
Total personnel	1.30 E−05	0.051**	−5.00 E−04	0.048**
Exporting firm[a]	1.96	−1.804	2.35	0.073
Number of products	−1.268	−1.292	−2.535*	−3.626*
Carrying out publicity[a]	4.300*	4.190**	5.361*	−0.498**
Carrying out R+D[a]	−0.744	−2.881	−3.329*	−1.258
Age	−0.148**	−0.479**	-0.135**	−0.498**
Mass production[a]	0.268	−0.168	1.706	1.751
Flexible assembly system[a]	−1.309	−3.562	−2.091	−1.859
Consumer products [a]	8.460**	2.637	7.350**	5.342**
National [a]	3.22	6.347	3.003*	11.593**
Privately owned [a]	10.610**	12.614	8.095**	20.591*
Family owned [a]	7.910**	−1.05	3.479	6.365**
Expanding market [a]	4.940**	6.610**	4.348**	8.030**
Likelihood function	−2.448.58**	−4.563.05**	−2.078.70**	−4591.26**

Notes
*   **p ≥ 10%**   ** **p ≥ 5%**   a   Dummy variables.
Source: Own calculations based on ESEE, see note 4. Tobit estimations.

In 1994, the determinants of the proportion of non-permanent workers at individual-firm level were more similar as between small and large firms than in 1991. The differences are now that in the group of largest firms, the proportion of non-permanent workers is higher in firms that advertised their products and lower in firms that carried out R&D

activities. Furthermore, from among the firms with 200 or fewer employees, the proportion of non-permanent workers increases with the size of the firm, that is to say, it was higher among medium-sized firms than among smaller firms.

The variation in the proportion of non-permanent workers between 1991 and 1994 is linked, both for large and small firms, with the variation in employment, in such a way that firms which increased their level of employment also increased the proportion of non-permanent workers to the greatest extent (see Table 5.3). In other words, during the crisis of the early 1990s, a significant part of new employment in manufacturing firms corresponded to non-permanent workers. Specifically, it should be noted that the variation in non-permanent workers was positively associated with the variation in employees with a university degree, indicating that advantage was taken of non-permanent hiring during this period in order to incorporate individuals with higher levels of education into the labor force.

Table 5.3
Determinants of the variation in the proportion of non-permanent workers in the Spanish manufacturing sector: 1991–1994

	Large Firms	**Small Firms**
Constant	5.317*	1.622
Δ Proportion of laborers	0.069	-0.015
Δ Proportion of employees with university degree	0.254*	0.552**
Δ Proportion of personnel in R&D	37.265**	24.900
Total personnel	0.0149**	0.231**
Standarized product x Δ total personnel	-0.0130**	0.132
Δ Number of products	0.128	-0.036
Moves to carry out publicity	2.587	3.207*
Moves to carry out R&D	-1.271	0.179
Δ Intermediate consumptions over production	0.102*	0.0585**
Mass production 1991	-3.56**	3.458**
Flexible assembly systems 1991	0.259	-0.396
Consumer products 1991	-1.897	2.077
National 1991	-0.477	-1.513
Privately owned 1991	-4.259*	-6.56
Family owned 1991	-3.119*	1.612
Expansive market 1991	-2.757*	-0.850
F-statistic	2.65**	5.619**

Notes
* $p \le 10\%$ ** $p \le 5\%$ Δ indicates absolute variation.
Source: Own calculations based on ESEE; see note 4. Estimation by OLS.

In the group of firms with more than 200 employees, the variation in the proportion of non-permanent workers between 1991 and 1994 was lower among firms that, in 1991, used mass production systems, compared with firms that used other production systems; in private firms, compared with state-owned ones; in family firms compared with non-family ones; in firms that operate in expanding markets, compared with firms in low-growth markets. Within the small firms group, the proportion of non-permanent employees increased among firms that started to advertise their products and amongst firms that used mass production systems in 1991. That proportion was reduced among firms that decided to carry out R&D activities during the period 1991–94. In both large and small-sized firms, the proportion of non-permanent workers was positively associated with increases in the proportion of intermediate consumption over total production.

Discussion

The wide range of information available in Spain on external labor markets contrasts with the little we know about internal markets and practices in human capital management. Questions such as the diffusion of organizational innovations (a broad definition which covers jobs enrichment, the use of workteams, quality circles, encouraging the participation of employees in problem solving and so on) and the introduction of personnel management models that encourage flexible wages, profit sharing, health and security at work (as general policies of the firm), investment in training and so on, which have been the subject of extensive study in other countries, remain largely unknown areas in Spain.[5]

A better understanding of the business determinants in the use of non-permanent workers in Spanish firms could well provide relevant information on the functioning of internal labor markets in Spain. The unequal proportion of non-permanent workers according to the size of the firm and the sector of activity suggests that there are organizational and technological-type factors and market conditions which exert an influence over the decision by Spanish firms to use non-permanent workers in production and sale, although in the case of firms with 200 or fewer employees, the proportion of non-permanent workers among the different sectors is more homogeneous than in the case of the large-sized firms. Firms that have been subject to the same labor market regulations have chosen different proportions of non-permanent workers in their labor force. This means that the preferences for non-permanent workers are not determined solely by regulatory changes.

Consequently, the recent reforms intended to encourage permanent employment and discourage temporary employment by Spanish firms will have different costs and benefits, depending upon the internal and external characteristics of the firms.

Non-permanent workers can provide firms with greater flexibility, while at the same time giving greater security of employment to employees considered as "core", that is to say, those who carry with them the essential capacities of the organization.[6] Alternatively, non-permanent workers can be a medium by which to reduce production costs, in that they negotiate the conditions of employment from a weaker position than that of permanent workers. On the basis of the available data, it is not possible to distinguish from among the permanent workers those who enjoy this status because the policy of the firm guarantees them stability, and those who do so because they are linked to the firm with an indefinite contract that carries higher firing costs for the employer. Therefore, the above-mentioned data make it difficult to determine whether the non-permanent status reflects an attempt to protect core employees or to reduce costs as compared to those of indefinite contracting.

In any event, the evidence tells us that the increase in non-permanent workers is linked to increases in the labor force and that younger firms have a higher proportion of non-permanent workers than older ones. Therefore, the situation of non-permanence has clearly been the "entrance" to Spanish firms during the last few years; at the same time, it has been the "exit" from them, especially for the largest firms, given that it is in this group that a reduction in the proportion of non-permanent workers can be found in 1994, as compared to 1991. Among the largest firms, those with a higher proportion of temporary employees in 1991 (private, family-owned and operating in expanding markets), are also those which reduce more intensively the proportion of such employees between 1991 and 1994; this suggests that some of these non-permanent workers acquired the status of permanent over time.

One result particularly worthy of note is that the evolution of the firms towards a greater specialization (the proportion of intermediate consumption over the value of the production rises) increases the proportion of non-permanent workers, both in large and in small firms. This evidence might support the thesis that non-permanent workers provide a safety net for core employees, in that the tendency towards specialization presupposes a concentration in the distinctive skills of the firm. The evidence that increases in employment carry with them higher increases in non-permanent workers in firms producing non-standardized products also indicates that giving protection to core employees is a priority among firms with differentiated products, where the human capital will, in general, be more specific. The negative association between the proportion of non-permanent workers and the number of products in 1994 suggests that the most diversified firms could provide greater stability to their essential employees without recourse to non-permanent employment.

It is possible to conclude that the employment of non-permanent or temporary workers by Spanish manufacturing firms cannot be explained solely by the regulation of the labor markets and the high firing costs, since they are the same for all firms and the employment of these workers seems to be affected by competitive, technological and organizational factors. Moreover, the costs and benefits of non-permanent workers seem to vary with the age and the size of the firm. This means that market regulation, if it exists, should provide enough flexibility to firms in order for them to adjust their employment policies to the differentiated costs and benefits of temporary employment.

5.3. THE EMPLOYMENT RELATION: A CONCEPTUAL FRAMEWORK

If we are interested in explaining certain features of employment relations in Spain, examining the internal labor markets as well as the external ones, it is important to have a conceptual framework on how internal markets work. Generally, the economics of labor markets considers labor as a standardized commodity that can be purchased at a given price. Unemployment is explained in terms of market frictions which force wages up to a level above the marginal opportunity cost of the workers: limited substitutability between internal and external workers, transitory imbalances between job vacancies and workers' skills, imperfect supervision and the payment of efficiency wages, and so on.[7] However, the literature pays hardly any attention to the actual course of the employment relation while the worker is inside the firm. To overcome this limitation a richer conceptualization is required, such as the one rooted in early papers by Coase (1937) and Simon (1951), and extended by Williamson et al. (1975), within the framework of rational contracting, and by Kreps (1990, 1996), under the concept of incomplete contracting with hierarchical governance. More generally, this framework is also known as the theory of internal labor markets: Doeringer and Piore (1971), Osterman (1992).

Transaction cost economies induce workers and firms to engage in long-term or permanent relations, with repeated transactions regulated by a general contract, instead of a continuous renegotiation of the contract for the different labor services to be provided. Bounded rationality makes it impossible to anticipate all future contingencies that may modify the conditions under which labor services will be provided at the moment at which the contract is signed. Moreover, if such anticipation of contingencies was feasible, in many cases the contract could not be signed because it is impossible for the two parties to verify *ex post* which contingency actually occurred. Therefore, exhaustive contingent contracts cannot be used to regulate the long-term relationship. Finally, it is likely that the repeated transaction will generate a specific knowledge and co-specialization of the human and other physical capital involved in the production process, so that the labor relation is conducted under the conditions of idiosyncratic exchange. In most cases, the permanent relation can be viewed as a way to stimulate and increase specific human capital, in the search for competitive advantages.

For all these reasons, the labor contract is necessarily incomplete, in the sense that it establishes a general framework under which the labor services are provided; however, it is ambiguous and empty on what to do under the many specific circumstances that will appear in the future as the relationship takes place. Therefore, the contract has to provide for a governance structure which is responsible for making decisions when non-anticipated events occur in the transaction. In what follows we present the illustration developed by Kreps (1996) as an update of the first insights into the special features of the employment relation suggested by Simon (1951). The illustration brings together incomplete contracting, regulation concerns and specific investments, and shows the relevance of the correct choice of governance structure.

Consider the situation described in Figure 5.1 where, in the first step one person, the employee, decides whether to accept or reject entering into an employment relation; subsequently, the state of nature will be revealed and another person, the employer, will decide which task has to be performed, with the respective pay-offs.

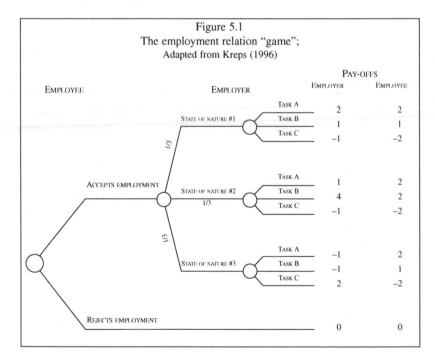

Figure 5.1
The employment relation "game";
Adapted from Kreps (1996)

Assume first that the information in Figure 5.1 is common knowledge for both the employer and the employee.[8] In this case, the employee will accept the contract and the employment relation will be completed since its expected utility is positive: under state of nature #1 the employer will assign task A, under state #2, task B and under state #3, task C; therefore, the expected employee utility will be 1/3 [1/3 (2 + 1 − 2)], greater than 0, the normalized utility when the contract is rejected.[9] The employer, on the other hand, obtains a positive expected utility of 8/3, so that the total wealth created is 3 (1/3 + 8/3). If the variability of possible results for the employee under the discretionary decisions of the employer is narrow, in the sense that there are no extreme negative values or they are very unlikely, then it may be in the interest of the employee to accept the discretion (authority in the terms of Simon) of the employer.

Notice that the above situation is preferred to a second in which the discretion of the employer is null and the employment relation is conducted as a standardized sales contract. This contract would specify a task to be performed under any possible state of nature to be revealed in the future. In our illustration, the employer will choose task B, since this is the one with higher expected utility of 4/3 [(1 + 4 − 1) 1/3], and the employee will accept, since the utility if he performs task B is 1. The total wealth created is now 7/3, less than 3, the wealth under the incomplete contract.

The situation under the incomplete contract could be different if the employee does not know precisely what states of nature may occur or, for example, attaches a high subjective probability to state #3, which implies a negative utility of −3. In this case, if the probability attached to state #3 is greater than 0.5, then the expected utility for the employee of the incomplete contract is negative and, therefore, no transaction will take place. Thus, in this case, the employment relation can only take place under a sales contract that specifies a particular job to be performed under any circumstances.

Reputational equilibria

When explicit contracts are not feasible (because information is not verifiable, for example), then the employment relation governed by the hierarchical authority of the employer may still be viable if the employer can credibly commit him- or herself to avoid assigning tasks that are harmful to the employee. In the above example, the employee will accept employment, even if there is a high probability that state #3 occurs, if the employer can credibly commit him- or herself not to ask for task C. If the assignment is limited to tasks A or B, then the utility of the employee is always positive and, therefore, the employment will be acceptable.

Under the implicit contracting framework, the promise of not asking for task C will be credible if reputational concerns induce the employer to choose to comply with the promise. This will happen if, in a repeated transactional environment, the discounted future pay-off when the promise is maintained is higher than the pay-off of abusing the trust and losing future trade opportunities as a penalty for breaking the promise. In our example, the employer has a short-term gain of 3 if state #3 occurs and he or she decides to assign task C. However, this gain has to be weighted against future losses if no other employee wants to enter into a transaction with the "abusive" employer. The interest of the employer in protecting his or her reputation may induce the employee to trust the promise that actions and tasks assignments will be made taking into account the interests of all affected parties.

The above analysis is simply the result of applying the theory of repeated games to implicit contracting. This theory established that implicit contracts *may be* viable and efficient under certain conditions. These conditions relate to:

   a) the distribution of benefits and losses over time and how much they are weighted;
   b) the past history of the relationship; and
   c) the observability of the actions.

The benefits of short-term opportunities may be so high (due, for example, to the importance of quasi-rents in a relation specific investment) as to compensate the losses due to surrendering a reputation for honesty and the credibility of the promises; if this is the case, the incentives for the other parties to trust the promises will fail. The same is true if the discount factor is very low, so that future losses hardly count when compared with the short-term gains of abusing trust, or if the parties anticipate that the frequency of future transactions will be too low.

Second, the efficiency of a repeated relationship may depend on the history: most often, repeated games have multiple equilibria with one of them being short-term optimization with no promises or trust. Thus, an institution is required, one that helps to choose the most efficient equilibria and coordinates the action needed to implement them. If the history of the relation has witnessed a sequence of unattended promises and mutual lies, then the most likely equilibrium to be selected will be the (inefficient) short-term optimization. The building of trust in the relation will be very difficult and will require a high coordination effort.

Third, cooperation and trust may be infeasible. The arguments of the repeated games framework establish that those who act opportunistically and fail to comply with their promises will be penalized by the others, who will avoid trading with them. The penalty process will be effective only if the actions of those who make promises can be observable by those who will transact with them in the future. If the actions are not observable, then reputation is no longer an issue of concern.

The implicit and incomplete contract must determine which party to the transaction will hold the residual decision rights, for example, the rights to decide when unforeseen circumstances occur. The above exposition suggests two criteria to be taken into account in this assignment:

    a) the information available to make decisions on the assignment of persons to tasks, and

    b) the conditions that will make possible efficient reputational equilibria (Kreps 1996).

The employment relation described by Simon (1951) implicitly assumes that the employer has more information than the employee about the technology, job descriptions and environment and can therefore make more efficient decisions on the assignment of workers to jobs. The employer is also in a better position to make promises and to take reputational concerns into consideration, since he or she is likely to repeat more often the transaction that goes together with the employment relation, and his or her decisions are easier to observe by future potential transactors. All these factors suggest that the *hierarchical governance* structure is the most efficient when conducting the employment relation.

Recent changes in technological and demand conditions seem to have induced many firms to delegate decision rights on job assignment and the actual tasks to be performed to lower levels of the organizational hierarchy. Presumably, those who are actually performing the tasks are better informed than the central authority, or the knowledge is too specific to be efficiently transmitted to a distant decision maker, and/or the time available to respond to consumer demands is very short.

The decision to trust now moves from the employer to the employees (assuming that explicit incentive contracts are still very costly to write and enforce). Therefore, conditions have to be created in order to foster reputational concerns on the part of the employees. "To lengthen the duration of the employment relationship and/or to provide employees with increased costs of sundering the specific relationship" (Kreps 1996, p. 572) are steps in this direction. The hierarchical governance structure is now replaced by a *balanced bilateral* one.

Finally, there may also be a place for a *trilateral governance* in the employment relation, such as in cases where the appropriate actions of those holding the decision rights are unclear because of observability problems. If these instances arise infrequently in an ongoing relationship, then a role exists for an authority that is external to that relationship to make the decision.

5.4.   CURRENT SITUATION AND PERSPECTIVES FOR THE EMPLOYMENT RELATION IN SPAIN

5.4.1. Comparative Cases

The Spanish case

It is generally accepted that labor relations in Spain have been conditioned by a very detailed legal regulation that has placed enormous limits on the free contracting between employers and employees. Labor regulations have increased labor costs, thus reducing employment, and have introduced strong rigidities into the organization of production and sales activities.

Legal regulation covers areas ranging from the organization of work inside the firm to the conditions under which a worker can be fired by the employer. With respect to the organization of work, labor laws regulate functional and geographic mobility, the definition of employment categories, the fixing of the number of hours to be worked, changes to working conditions, and so on. Particular mention should be made of the *Ordenanzas Laborales* (Labor Statutes), introduced in the 1940s and in force until the 1990s, which established in great detail the tasks which each employment category could carry out in each and every one of the productive areas. The termination of the employment relationship on the part of the employer has been determined on the basis of causality principles, with those dismissals that do not fall within grounds specifically provided by law being the subject of economic penalties.

Within the proposed conceptual framework employed in this chapter, it can be confirmed that in Spain the employment relationship has been developed essentially under the governance of contracts having an almost complete character, where the payment of the wage grants the firm the right to decide unilaterally on the use of the services provided by the worker within an ambit of very limited discretion. In other words, it can be said that the regulation has infringed the "authority" of the employer which, in the context of our analysis, means that "hierarchical governance" gives the employer only a scant margin to exercise any initiative when deciding upon the use of the labor services that he or she has purchased. The significant fact is that the complete nature of the employment contract is not the result of a negotiation between the parties (employers and trade unions, for example), nor can it be said that the regulator has been guided in his or her decisions by criteria of economic efficiency; quite the opposite is the case, with Pérez-Díaz and Rodríguez (1996) attributing the strict regulation of the labor market and employment relations in Spain to "paternalistic" attitudes and the search for social legitimacy on the part of a politically authoritarian regime.

The rigidity which such a restrictive regulatory framework necessarily imposes is assimilated without too many difficulties by the Spanish economy when aggregate demand and the relative prices of the productive factors remain stable, as was the case during the 1960s and the beginning of the 1970s. However, it collapses when the economy is subjected to strong external shocks (for example, energy crises, the liberalization of foreign markets) which demand rapid and important adjustments in the productive structures and in the organization of work. The social response to the need for change has been, in the first place, regulatory and has consisted in developing a more extensive range of contractual modalities (for example, temporary, part-time, apprenticeship, specific project), with it being possible to choose the most appropriate for each particular employment situation. The spirit and the rule which underlie the use, above all, of complete contracts when regulating the employment relationship are not changed, in that while the range of contracts from which to choose has been extended, once the contract has been entered into, the discretion of the employer remains very limited. In a certain sense, it can be said that there is a change in the manner in which employment relationships are begun and ended in the external markets, but the internal markets remain unaltered.

The second response to the need to adapt to external changes during the course of the employment relationship has been, without doubt, the renegotiation between employees and employers within each firm, in function of the changing circumstances with respect to those previously provided for. It is to be expected that such a renegotiation would improve efficiency in the allocation of resources, as compared to the application of the solutions initially written in the contract. However, the results, in terms of the division of such improvements, would be affected by the nature of the contract which governs the employment relationship, as we have seen in the general discussion: were the employment relationship to be governed by a more incomplete contract, then the renegotiation would place the employer in a more favourable negotiating position than he or she would have occupied in reality under the existing contractual modalities, which are more favourable to the interests of the employees. In the final analysis, this means that achieving internal flexibility would imply firms having to support higher labor costs than those provided for in the collective wages agreement, although one can foresee that the conditions under which such renegotiations take place would be very different from one firm to another (particularly between large and small firms).[10]

The example used as illustration in the previous section may help to explain this point. Assume that state of nature #3 occurs and that employer and employee renegotiate the contract so that task A is performed in order to maximize total utility, which equals 1. The solution of the bargaining problem is assumed to be the Nash equilibrium, where each party receives the pay-off of the non-agreement solution plus a half of the incremental gain if the agreement is reached.

When the employment relation is regulated by a sales contract under which the worker will perform task B if there is no agreement in the renegotiation process, the pay-offs from the Nash bargaining equilibrium are:

$$\text{Employer} = -1 + 1/2\,(1 - 0) = -\,1/2$$
$$\text{Employee} = 1 + 1/2\,(1 - 0) = 11/2$$

since the non-agreement pay-offs are –1 for the employer and 1 for the employee, when task B is performed and the state of nature is #3.

On the other hand, if the contract were incomplete and the employer had decision rights, then, if no agreement were reached, the employer would choose task C if the state of nature is #3. Therefore, the pay-offs are:

$$\text{Employer} = 2 + 1/2\,(1 - 0) = 21/2$$
$$\text{Employee} = -\,2 + 1/2\,(1 - 0) = -\,11/2$$

since now the non-agreement pay-offs are 2 and –2.

It is clear that how the labor relation is governed has different effects on the *ex post* pay-offs of the parties. Therefore, governance will also affect the decision to enter into the relationship, as well as any specific investment to be made *ex ante*.

With highly regulated internal labor markets and a casuistry over the grounds for terminating the employment relationship that is highly determined by the type of contract chosen (for example, temporary, specific project, permanent), collective negotiations, which are carried out at three levels, namely national, sectoral–territorial and firm, have for many years concentrated exclusively on wages. Furthermore, the market is segmented between "internal" employees, protected by permanent contracts, and "external" employees, who have temporary or contingent contracts, with the representatives of the former group playing a more leading role in collective negotiations. Given that the internal employee perceives a relatively low probability of losing his or her employment, he or she gives priority in his or her negotiations to the level of wages, paying less attention to the level of employment. In summary, the contractual responses to the demands for internal flexibility have had a negative effect on the external labor markets.[11]

The situation in other countries

The very limited legal regulation of the external labor markets in countries such as the US places them in a situation that is apparently quite different from that of Spain. However, so far as the functioning of the internal labor markets is concerned, the effective differences are less, although these have been arrived at by a separate route.

The papers that have analysed the history of employment relations in the

US[12] place emphasis on the fact that the dominant pattern for the organization of work has been characterized by a very narrow definition being given to jobs that require a mid-level qualification, in this way seeking to optimize the mass production of large volumes of standardized goods. Trade unions and employers have accepted these employment categories and codified them into a job classification system, which has become a key element in the case law for industrial relations. The employers centralize information and decisions, but the discretional framework for internal mobility is limited. Furthermore, large firms adopt bureaucratic forms of internal organization with stable and rigid rules which remove any doubts over possible discretional abuses on the part of employers and determine the functioning of the internal labor market (for example, single entry door, internal promotion, the wage assigned to a job, respect for seniority, recognition of trade union rights in supervising the application of these rules). In summary, the aim is to achieve a "Taylorist"-inspired organization of work ("there is an ideal person for each job") directed by way of centralized information flows, with a low dependence on specific human resources (which allows the option of exit to be exercised as a control mechanism) and the search for the competitiveness of the firm through standardization and low product costs.

When considering the functioning of the internal labor markets, the true contrast with the Spanish case seems to be found in Japan and Germany, where labor organization is implemented on the basis of the decentralization of information and the encouragement of specificity in productive resources. A broad definition is given to jobs, while employees possess multi-functional skills which favour rotation between jobs and make possible a high level of internal flexibility; work teams are organized, enjoying a high degree of decision-making autonomy within the scope of their functions, and encouragement is given to the individual or collective resolution of problems and to organizational learning. In more technical terms, it is possible to speak of employment relations that are subject to long-term incomplete relational contracts. These are governed through a balanced bilateral system where reputational solutions guarantee mutual trust between employers and employees that no actions will be taken which imply the expropriation of incomes that are attributable to the specific investments made by each party. A certain degree of decision-vetoing power for each of the parties requires that consensus be reached on solutions relating to the maximization of joint net wealth. Information transparency, complemented in the German case by employee representation on the highest governing bodies of the firm, facilitates the necessary information *ex post* on the situation of the firm, essential for the viability of reputational equilibrium. The promise of stability and security of employment stimulates the creative contribution of the employees to improvements in productivity and product quality. This implies that the external markets will play a limited role in wage formation, but the intense competition faced in the products markets obliges the employers and the employees to take into account that if the situation of the firm deteriorates because of the loss of competitiveness, then jobs will be lost. For this reason, wage determination will also be sensitive to levels of employment and, in the final analysis, to the probability of being unemployed.

In recent years, a significant number of American firms have experienced a change in their internal labor markets, seeking to draw closer to the internal market model that is dominant among Japanese and German firms. The "lean production" model has substituted for the "mass production" model, and the Toyota production system for the Taylorist system. To a certain extent, the tendency to make good use of the advantages, in terms of flexibility and rapidity of response, that are provided by the decentralization of information and decision-making, as well as to counterattack the threat of cost competition posed by emerging countries by the use of more specific resources capable of improving product value for customers, seems to have been the most common response adopted by many firms in the more advanced countries. Furthermore, decentralization and flexibility have been achieved efficiently thanks to technological advances that reduce both information and communication costs and the costs of moving from one product to another in the manufacturing process. This means that the new forms of work organization and management of human resources which, for many firms, have meant drawing closer to the "Japanese model", are the result of changes in competitive strategy and organizational structure introduced by the volition of the management of these firms. We are not, therefore, considering a change that has been provoked by regulatory or institutional (trade union pressure) causes, but one that has been driven by expectations for higher profits in the long term.

This reflection leads us to the conclusion that firms have a vested interest in incorporating human resources into their competitive strategies, that is to say, giving a strategic value to these resources by considering them as a key factor in competitiveness.

Human resources should no longer be viewed as a source of costs which have to be minimized through achieving the desired effort with the lowest possible wages, and should be converted into a resource to be revalued through constant investments in training, increases in productivity and higher-wage incomes. In this way, compatibility would be achieved between employers' interests, orientated to the maximization of profits, and employees' interests, directed towards maximizing wages and personal fulfilment in a job that grants them initiative and a decision-making capacity.

However, a closer examination of these "work-enrichment" processes shows that they affect only a small part of the workforce, namely those recognized by firms as "core" employees. The balance may even have to support losses in the real value of their wages and more precarious employment conditions, necessary to ensure the protection of the advantages of the "privileged" employees. The final result would be a "duality" in the labor market, produced not only because legal regulation segments the market by providing for contracts which imply different effective costs for a similar result, but also because this very duality is required by the competitive strategy of the firm. In summary, some of the organization and employment changes introduced by firms could be increasing the wage differences in the workforce as a whole, with this running in parallel with a possible improvement in efficiency levels. Some analysts identify these moves towards greater inequality above all in countries such as the UK and the US, where trade unions have lost specific weight.

5.4.2.   The Transformation of Employment Relations in Spain

The globally negative evaluation of the functioning of the labor market in Spain, by virtue of its inability to generate sufficient quality employment, has led to a succession of reforms although, as we have mentioned earlier, these have always maintained the figure of the formal and explicit contract as the basic governance structure for employment relations. Furthermore, appeals have been made for restraint in direct and indirect (the termination of the employment contract on the part of the firm) wage costs as the only method to slow down the destruction of jobs, with this furthermore being in harmony with a competitive strategy on the part of Spanish firms which generically rests on low production costs.

The current unemployment situation undoubtedly requires that attention be given to unit labor costs as the critical variable when deciding exactly what has an impact on the conditions which lead to job creation. However, this should not prevent us from reflecting on the possibilities of beginning a job creation dynamic which is compatible with the improvement of the productive capacities of the employees and, therefore, with a sustained improvement in real wages. The idea that only the containment of unit labor costs can serve as the basis for the maintenance of employment in Spain should, I feel, be abandoned, and I say this for two reasons.

First, because the concentration of efforts exclusively towards the contention of costs could well generate a spiral in the Spanish economy of low wages→low levels of training and skill acquisition→low employee motivation→low productivity→low wages, leading to very negative consequences in the medium term if the ultimate objective is for Spanish society to progress towards real convergence with Europe while at the same time respecting certain limits in the equitable distribution of wealth. Second, because if it is argued that it will be the entrepreneurs and managers themselves who, in their own interests, introduce the strategic changes towards competitive differentiation and participatory organization which will improve the quality of human resources, we are undervaluing the difficulties of the changes and the impact of the institutional environment[13] on their viability, as well as the external effects of inequality and duality to which I have already alluded.

In the light of all this, I feel it is necessary to open a debate in Spain on how to move from employment relations that are sustained on the basis of complete contracts to others that rest on relational contracts, that is to say, incomplete long-term contracts, where there is sufficient adaptive flexibility to respond quickly to the changing circumstances of the environment and where it is possible for efficient reputational equilibria to emerge. This clearly means that we must distance ourselves from a situation, such as the current one, where the verification of contractual compliance lies principally with the ordinary Courts of Law (with the resultant difficulties for the resolution of disputes given that, in order to gain flexibility, the contract is completed with information that is increasingly more difficult to verify, such as "the competitiveness of the firm", as lawful grounds for dismissal), and move to a new situation where interested self-regulation predominates. Within this, the "trust" of one party in the delegation of decision-making to another rests on the expectation that account will be taken of general interests and that earlier promises will be complied with, given that the "reputation" of the party making the decisions will depend upon this and, further, that there will be a desire to preserve such a reputation because it has an economic value.[14]

This general approach requires certain qualifications when it is applied to the specific reality of Spain, in that the relational contract also demands a determined system of governance and the choice of such a contractual form opens more alternatives. One of the versions of the approach set out in this chapter is that defended by the employers' organizations in Spain, which can be summarized in terms of "the deregulation of employment relationships and the granting of greater authority to the employer". This approach, when couched in technical terms, is the equivalent of choosing the hierarchical relationship as the form of governance in the relational contract. Increasing the authority of the employer means making the employment contract more incomplete. The employee can choose to become a party to this contract without a higher salary to compensate for the uncertainty of the work to be carried out in the circumstances where there are favourable exit or abandonment conditions for the relationship (general human capital and relatively low rates of unemployment). Alternatively, the acceptance of a greater degree of authority for the employer without monetary compensations may be achieved if the conditions for the emergence of an efficient reputational equilibrium emerge, in the sense that the promise of the employer to use this additional authority in the search for greater collective efficiency is a credible one.

It is difficult, in abstract terms, to evaluate the consequences of this proposal, but the experience of what has taken place in the US, where the model of hierarchical governance has predominated, is illustrative. First, in order to achieve the trust of the employees, the large American firms had to adopt the rigid internal markets model supposed by the Taylorist organization of direct work, together with an administrative machine of a bureaucratic nature. Second, in these firms human capital of a general character predominates and the competitive advantage is reinforced in costs. Third, the level of employment is the main adjustment variable to the economic cycle, given that there is no explicit or implicit undertaking for stability of employment. Fourth, during the last few years many US firms have sought to evolve from this model towards another which encourages specific capital and decentralizes information and decision-making, alluding to the excessive rigidities posed by the hierarchical model. All this means that hierarchy has traditionally achieved external flexibility, but very limited internal flexibility, given that the latter has to be renounced in order to increase the trust of the employees when they are incorporated into the employment relationship and to restrain the wage increases that would be demanded in order to compensate for the uncertainty felt by these employees towards a very open contract.

As against hierarchical governance, we have the alternative of bilateral governance. However, this offers no advantages unless it is within the framework of an organization of work based on the decentralization of information and decision-making, that is to say, an evolving internal labor market in which encouragement is given to the participation and involvement of the employees in the resolution of problems and in continuous improvement. Once again, the experience of US firms in the introduction of new organizational models could be illustrative. It has been said that the move from the hierarchical to the bilateral relationship can be considered in the American case as an exchange, in which the employees accept greater internal flexibility in exchange for the promise of greater stability of employment. To some extent, this is what has been proposed in Spain under the terms of the recent *Acuerdo Interconfederal para la Estabilidad en el Empleo* (AIEE), which forms part of the more general Agreement for the Reform of the Labor Market, but with significant differences. In effect, the AIEE seeks above all to substitute non-permanent contracts for permanent ones, that is to say, its aim is external flexibility (by making the costs of dismissal cheaper, it is supposed that firms can adjust their workforce more easily, should they so desire), in exchange for greater stability of employment (it being understood that the permanent contract continues to have a sufficiently high cost of termination so as to give a greater sense of security to the employee that his or her job is stable).

An agreement that is more in accord with the desire to encourage the internal flexibility of firms is the *Acuerdo sobre Cobertura de Vacíos* (ACU), which also forms part of the earlier mentioned Agreement for the Reform of the Labor Market. The ACU purports to cover the regulatory lacunas that have appeared following the repeal of *Ordenanzas Laborales*, until these gaps are filled by the corresponding collective agreement. It is clear that it represents a significant advance towards the desired flexibility, but it falls some way short of confronting the challenge of improving stability of employment through the introduction of more flexible and participatory forms in the organization of production. The next step should be to analyse how the trade unions and employers' organizations could contribute to the spread of the new productive models among firms.

What bilateral governance proposes is that stability of employment is an undertaking on the part of the employer with respect to the workforce, in exchange for which he or she seeks greater loyalty from the employee towards the firm, a higher degree of participation and involvement in productive and organizational improvements and a willingness towards geographical and functional mobility when production and/or the market so demands. Stability of employment forms part of a transaction sustained by an implicit contract that the parties wish to enter into because they anticipate that the promises are credible and that it is in their particular interest to comply with the undertaking. It does not seek, therefore, to substitute one complete contract, protected by a claim for breach of contract before the ordinary Courts of Law, for another of a similar nature, but with other provisions for termination; but rather a change in the very nature of the contract, from one of a complete and explicit character to another which is incomplete and implicit.[15]

So far as the current Spanish situation is concerned, what is relevant is whether the dominant culture and practice in employment relations is impeding the spread of strategic (differentiation) and organizational (participation) innovations which will have the effect of distancing us from our traditional dependence on competitive advantages in costs and will create a positive social externality by improving the quality and productivity of our human resources. Taking this one step further, in the sense that strategic and organizational change is desirable, we should consider what institutions are necessary to implement this change and to make it viable, because bilateral governance also demands decentralization and specificity of the resources required by the strategy and organization that is chosen. Thus, for example, it is clear that the promise of stability of employment is an undertaking to be complied with so long as the company is viable and the management not fraudulent. It will correspond to the employees or their collective representative bodies (workers' councils, for example) to supervise and confirm that such conditions are being complied with, which will require a great deal of communication and informative transparency from the owners/management to the employees. If this transparency is denied, it is impossible for the mutual trust that is required by an implicit contract to emerge.

Apart from transparency, another way to give credibility to the undertaking of stability in employment on the part of the employers is by way of investment in a form of training which develops multiple skills in the employees so that if, as a consequence of their contributions to and suggestions for productive improvements, the current job disappears, the employee has the necessary skills to occupy a different one. Training in multiple skills generates other benefits beyond giving security in return for the collaboration of the employee in productivity improvements, in that it makes it possible to give more rapid and efficient responses to unforeseen circumstances in the job and facilitates the accumulation and processing of information.[16]

Investment in training which develops multi-functional skills in workers is similar to the initiative which seeks to encourage the "employability" of employees through continuous training which will help them to find another job if they lose their current one. These initiatives will contribute towards the development of a feeling of stability among the employees in the circumstances where the demand for workers falls for some jobs and, at the same time, increases for others. The efficiency of these initiatives will be lower when there is a fall in the aggregate demand for labor. Furthermore, care will have to be taken to avoid the appearance of conduct akin to "free riding" on the part of employers, that is to say, where those who do not invest in the employability of their employees take advantage of the investment made by others.

The institutionalization of the training of employees in multiple skills will demand initiatives that ensure the participation of *all* the firms in this training effort.

The discussion in the previous section showed that, in some instances, efficient reputational equilibrium is not feasible because the monetary gain of abusing trust outweighs the cost of lost reputation. An example of such a situation is when the employer may take the decision to move an entire manufacturing operation offshore (Kreps 1996, p. 573). When this is the case, a trilateral governance form with third party arbitration may be more efficient than hierarchical governance.

Therefore, arbitration, especially contractually provided, may become another important institution for the efficiency of internal labor markets in Spain.

In the scenario that I describe here, the collective bodies which represent employers and employees have a new role as contributors to the existence of efficient reputational equilibria. In effect, it is easier for these equilibria to exist when the holders of the reputation are organizations than when they are individuals, in that the time horizon of the former is longer and the relative benefits of short-term opportunistic conduct are lower. A separate matter is at what level (for example firm, sector, state, supranational) of the collective organization should the reputation be deposited in order to achieve the maximum efficiency, but this would require a more detailed analysis of the theme than I am in a position to provide in this chapter.

5.4.3. Implications for Job Creation

Up to now, we have spoken of changes in employment relations in Spain, that is to say, the point to which the internal labor markets should evolve in order to achieve internal flexibility in firms, within a framework that encourages the qualitative improvement of the available human resources. It is also important to evaluate the implications of this new tendency for the creation of employment, that is to say, for the functioning of the external markets.

Encouraging the participation and involvement of employees in the resolution of problems and in continuous improvement, if this is achieved, results in an improvement in productivity. In order for firms to maintain the level of employment, this improvement must be translated into an increase in production and sales in the market which, in turn, will foreseeably require a reduction in prices in order to stimulate demand. If the organizational innovations that favour increases in productivity are spread through the economy as a whole, then a reduction in prices and an increase in real wages will be achieved, with the resultant improvement in welfare. Depending on the price elasticity of demand, the increase in production that follows the fall in prices will, in certain markets, suppose a higher level of employment and, therefore, a positive aggregate effect over employment and real wages can be expected.

However, if the organizational innovation is limited to a reduced collective of firms and the general level of prices is not altered by the decisions of these firms, then the higher productivity will have to be compensated to the employees who have achieved it by way of an increase in their nominal wages, although this increase must be limited in order to allow for a simultaneous fall in prices to stimulate demand and contribute towards the maintenance of employment. In summary, organizational innovation will increase the income generated by those firms who practise it, and this increase will be divided among the employees, customers and employers, with a lower immediate repercussion over the level of employment.

Organizational innovation can have an additional positive effect over employment as a consequence of the change in the rewards system that it carries with it. In order for employee participation to improve productivity, it is necessary that the rewards of the workers are linked to the results (profits) of the firm.[17] Therefore, the spread of participatory forms of organization would suppose the generalization of reward systems of the "profit sharing" type which, in turn, implies a fall in the marginal costs of the labor resource. As a consequence of the reduction in the marginal labor costs, the demand for this factor will increase and net employment will be created.[18] One can foresee that the fall in marginal costs will allow for a reduction in prices, with the resultant increase in real (average) wages and in aggregated demand.

Reward systems with variable wages, depending on results, imply that the economic risks are shared between employees and employers. It is well known that the latter have greater opportunities to diversify risks than the former and, therefore, the solution of mixed, fixed and variable rewards might be inefficient from the point of view of the allocation of risks. In response to this argument, it can be said that the improvements in efficiency flowing from the incentives given to employees to make a greater productive effort, with the resultant repercussion in real wages, could compensate for the disutility for the assumption of risks. Second, the greater stability of employment that is made possible by flexibility in wages must be a stabilizing element in the growth of aggregate demand, reducing the volatility of that growth and, therefore, the level of risk for the economy as a whole.

Finally, certain changes in the institutions which accompany the organizational innovation could also contribute to the creation of employment. Our proposal for institutional change is based on an evolution from employment relations based upon explicit and relatively complete contracts towards a new situation where implicit incomplete contracts predominate, based upon reputational equilibria between individual (employers and employees) and collective (employers' organizations, trade unions, workers councils) agents. This implies a progressive deregulation of the labor market and greater self-regulation on the part of the agents involved. It is to be hoped that the new scenario would suppose a change in the utility function of the trade unions when negotiating the terms of the contracts. In effect, if current regulation leads to a situation whereby the employees with permanent contracts assume a negotiating position which gives limited weight to the level of employment and a high weight to the wage, then in the new situation the permanent character of the contract will depend on the viability of the firm and/or of the employment opportunities of each employee and will, in principle, be similar for everyone (or at least for all those with similar qualifications). Therefore, in this new situation, the trade union representative who negotiates is no longer biased in his or her preferences towards the situation of the employee with a permanent contract, but rather towards that of any employee. The final result will be a preferences function for the trade union representative in which equal weight is given to the wage and to the probability of employment and, in these cases, it is understood that employment is determined on the basis of the marginal or opportunity wage and not on the basis of the average wage, as is the case when the trade union negotiates taking only the wage into account.[19]

In this new scenario, employment is determined in a manner similar to that which would result in a competitive market. The presence of a trade union which negotiates does not interfere in the determination of efficient employment, always provided that the utility function takes into account both the wage and the probability of employment, although it may affect the distribution of organizational rents between employers and employees.

The situation would not be the same if the differences in the status of the employees were the result of strategic and organizational decisions on the part of the management of the firm, rather than the result of the legal regulation of the market, for example, if a distinction is drawn between "core" employees and "peripheral" or contingent employees. In this case, it would be the management of the firm who would exert pressure for the organizational rents to be divided with the core employees, in that it is they who have created it with their specific skills, with the contingent employees being excluded. It is difficult to imagine that during the course of negotiations the trade unions could reconcile the interests of employees with such different levels of employment status. However, if we do not wish to see these differences in employment status being transformed into external differences in wages and social status (as appears to have occurred in the US), then the trade unions must provide answers to the phenomenon of "contingency" that could be produced in the labor market.

5.5.   CONCLUSIONS

This chapter investigates the dominant features of employment relations in Spanish firms, on the basis of the insights provided by the theory of relational contracting. The empirical evidence of the second section shows that the employer's choice between permanent and temporary contracts for the governance of the employment relation is not only determined by regulatory constraints (such as firing costs), but also by technological and organizational constraints determined by the firm's strategy. The heterogeneity in the population of firms requires non-discriminatory conditions in their choice of the contract form. In this respect, the recent labor market reforms, penalizing temporary contracts relative to permanent ones, may be moving in the opposite direction if firms choose between permanent and temporary contracts according to their productive needs. The lesson to be learned from this analysis is that labor market reforms that emphasize only external flexibility, by broadening the range of complete contracts, will always be limited because of the high heterogeneity in the needs of the firms and their permanent change over time. A new paradigm is needed, centred around incomplete contracts and the choice of efficient governance structures.

The current situation of Spanish firms may be characterized as follows:
   a) a competitive advantage sustained by unit labor costs;
   b) employment relations governed by relatively complete contracts;
   c) a response to flexibility which has taken the form of a multiplicity of contracts, with the resultant duality of employees according to the type of employment contract which binds them to the firm; and

    d) internal labor markets conditioned by Taylorist (in the large firms) and paternalistic (in the small firms) forms for the organization of production.

Firms operating in other countries with employment relations not so very different from those prevalent in Spain, albeit for other reasons, especially firms in Anglo-Saxon countries, appear to have reacted to the pressures exerted by an environment where advances in information, communication and production technologies have increased the intensity of competition and, at the same time, the possibilities of internal organization. Competitive advantage is now looked for in product differentiation and in rapidity of service to the customer, which implies converting human capital into a strategic resource and increasing its opportunities for participation in problem solving and continuous improvement. Internal flexibility substitutes for external and, in order to achieve this, the internal labor markets cease to be regulated by bureaucratic rules and depend more on relational contracts, which are long term and under which encouragement is given to mutual trust between employers and employees through efficient reputational equilibria. For many, this change implies drawing closer to the model of strategic competition and internal organization that is dominant in countries such as Germany and Japan, although in the Anglo-Saxon countries a greater duality between "core" and "peripheral" employees appears to have been detected, with a rise in inequality in society as a whole.

Thus, Spanish firms are presented with two main options, that is to say, either to continue with their historical inertia or to evolve along the lines of those firms which strengthen their human resources as a competitive advantage and encourage participation as a source of productivity and quality. Given that society as a whole cannot be indifferent to these options, this merits a collective reflection on the conditions which influence the viability of change and transformation. It is to be supposed that, with current levels of unemployment, individual firms would find it advantageous to improve the productivity of employees by way of a total deregulation of the labor market, thereby converting the threat of dismissal into their main disciplinary instrument and reinforcing the "authority" of the employer. The question to be asked is whether this reasoning is correct or, by contrast, whether such a deregulation would allow for greater organizational innovation and a more rapid convergence on the part of the Spanish firm towards the models of "excellence" described in this chapter.

My view is that the deregulation of the labor market must be considered in a broader framework of institutional development which provides balancing elements and facilitates evolution in the desired direction. Within this institutional development, I propose:

    a) a strengthening of employee representational bodies, both in the firm and in society at large; the spread of information transparency from the employer to the employees;

b) to rely on third party arbitration, when reputation alone will leave one of the parties unprotected against the actions of the other, and

c) an undertaking on the part of employers to provide training in multiple qualifications and the enhanced employability of the employees.

Throughout this chapter I have tried to offer arguments which justify this proposal for institutional development on the basis of its contribution to the viability of efficient reputational equilibria and, at the same time, because they ensure a certain equity in the division of wealth which the new framework must contribute towards creating.

NOTES

*   I acknowledge the comments of Jordi Gual on a previous version of this chapter.

1   Locke et al. (1995) provide a reasonably complete and up-to-date panorama of the business and institutional changes detected in human resource policies and the functioning of the labor markets in advanced countries. Becker and Gerhart (1996) and Pheffer (1994) contain a business perspective on human resource policy and firm competitiveness.

2   See MacNeil (1974) and Williamson (1975, 1985) for a discussion on the types of contracts and their economic relevance. Williamson et al. (1975) apply these contractual relations to the study of the employment relation.

3   Viñals (1996) and Sebastián (1996), which contain an extensive literature on the external labor markets in Spain. The consequences of the segmentation of permanent and non-permanent employment are analysed in Bentolila and Dolado (1994) and Jimeno and Toharia (1993, 1996).

4   This section is based on the results of a project under the same title which I am carrying out jointly with Fernando Merino of the Fundación Empresa Pública.

5   There is some partial evidence. The ESADE study on the competitiveness of the industrial firm in Catalunia (1996) sought to determine the degree of diffusion of the new organizational forms among Catalan firms, but possible erroneous interpretations of the meaning of the questions posed has prevented an evaluation of the results obtained. In another part, the same study affirms that "among small and medium sized firms the paradigm of control centralized in the employer dominates, while in the large firms, which are generally subsidiaries of multinationals, the paradigm of bureaucratic control continues, with a low degree of decentralization", ESADE (1996, p. 365). Pérez-Díaz and Rodríguez (1995) reach similar conclusions.

6   See Osterman (1994, p. 184).

7   Blanchard and Katz (1997) analyse the relation between these imperfections and the natural rate of non-inflationary unemployment in the economy (NAIRU).

8   It is supposed, however, that the information is non-verifiable and that this prevents contracts being made that are contingent to the state of nature.

9   We suppose that the option of exiting from the relation and ensuring a utility of 0

is not feasible *ex post* because there are investments in specific human capital or opportunity costs that are higher than the losses that would be obtained by continuing in the relation.

10 Espina (1977, p. 11) contains the following phrase from the President of the Asociación Española de Directores de Personal (AEDIPE) which is illustrative of this point: "it is necessary to pay two or three points of wage increases each time that something new has to be introduced into the collective agreement". Also see Dolado et al. (1997).

11 Salas (1996) presents models of the external market and compares the results of employment and wages when the objective function of the employees' representational body is the difference between the perceived wage and the opportunity wage, and when the objective function includes the expected wage taking into account the probability of being unemployed. The analytical results make clear that in the first case the level of employment is inefficient, while in the second an efficient level of employment is achieved.

12 See Weinstein and Kochan (1995) and Kochan and Weinstein (1994).

13 Levine and Tyson (1990) and Kochan et al. (1992) provide detailed analyses of the institutional conditions which affect the introduction and diffusion of organizational innovations and human resource policies. Also see Salas (1993).

14 Concern for stability of employment, defended by employers and employees alike, illustrates the problem of trust in employment relations in Spain. Up to now, stability of employment has been based on contracting by way of a permanent contract, with it being thought that the high cost of firing was a guarantee that such an event would take place only in extreme cases. If this is the case, then at the time at which compensation for firing is reduced or even eliminated altogether, the permanent contract would be more or less stable depending on the credibility of the promise on the part of the employer to provide employment stability to the employees. Therefore, stability of employment would be based on the trust between employers and employees.

15 Ichniowski (1992) studies a practical case of the transformation of employment relations in a specific firm, from one of confrontation and lack of trust between employees and management towards a new situation of trust and collaboration.

16 Aoki (1988) formalizes the relationship between the development of multiple skills and security of employment.

17 See Levine and Tyson (1990).

18 We would be moving closer to the proposal of Weitzman (1984) on the so-called "share economy"; Weitzman (1995) offers an updated reflection on this theme.

19 See note 11 and Aoki (1988).

REFERENCES

Aoki, M. (1988), *Information, Incentives and Bargaining in the Japanese Economy*, New York: Cambridge University Press.

Becker, B. and B. Gerhart (1996), "The impact of human resource management on organizational performance: progress and prospects", *Academy of Management Journal*, **39** (4), August, 770–801.

Bentolila, S. and J.J. Dolado (1994), "Labor flexibility and wages: lessons from Spain", *Economic Policy*, **18**, 53–99.

Blanchard, O.and L. Kastz (1977), "What we know and do not know about the natural rate of unemployment", *Journal of Economic Perspectives*, Winter.

Coase, R. (1937), "The Nature of the Firm", *Economica*, **4**.

Doeringer, P. and P. Piore (1971), *Internal Labor Markets and Manpower Analysis*, Lexington, MA: D.C. Heath.

Dolado, J.J., F. Felgueroso and J.F. Jimeno (1997), "Los efectos de los salarios pactados en convenio sobre las ganancias salariales: La evidencia en España", FEDEA, D.T. No. 97–4.

ESADE (1996), *Competitivitat de l'Empresa Industrial a Catalunya*, Barcelona: ESADE.

Espina, A. (1997), "El Guadiana de la concertación neocorporativista en España: De la huelga general de 1988 a los acuerdos de 1977", in F. Minguelez and C. Prieto (eds), *Las Relaciones de Empleo en España*, Siglo XXI.

Hart, O. (1995), *Firms, Contracts and Financial Structure*, Oxford: Oxford University. Press.

Ichniowski, C. (1992), "Human resources practices and productive labor management relations", in D. Lewin, O. Mitchell and P. Sherer (eds), *Research Frontiers in Industrial Relations and Human Resources*, Industrial Relations Research Association.

Jimeno, J.F. and L. Toharia (1993), "The effects of fixed term employment on wages: theory and evidence from Spain", *Investigaciones Económicas*, **XVII**.

Jimeno, J.F. and L. Toharia (1996), "Effort, absenteeism and fixed term employment contracts", *Revista Española de Economía*.

Kochan, Th., L. Batt and L. Dyer (1992), "International human resources studies: a framework for future research", in D. Lewin, O. Mitchell and P. Sherer (eds), *Research Frontiers in Industrial Relations and Human Resources*, Industrial Relations Research Association.

Kochan, Th. and M. Weinstein (1994), "Recent developments in US industrial relations", *British Journal of Industrial Relations*, **32** (4), December, 483–504.

Kreps, D. (1996), "Corporate culture and economic theory", in P. Buckley and J. Michie (eds), *Firms, Organizations and Contracts*, Oxford: Oxford University Press.

Kreps, D. (1996), "Markets and hierarchies and (mathematical) economic theory", *Industrial and Corporate Change*, **4**.

Levine, R. and A. Tyson (1990), "Participation, productivity and the firm's environment" in A. Blinder (ed.), *Paying for Productivity*, Washington, DC: Brookings Institution.

Locke, R., Th. Kochan and M. Piore (1995), *Employment Relations in a Changing World Economy*, Cambridge, MA: MIT Press.

MacNeil, Y. (1974), "The many features of contracts", *Southern California Law Review*, **47**.

Osterman, P. (1992), "Internal labor markets in a changing environment: models and evidence", in D. Lewin, O. Mitchell and P. Sherer (eds), *Research Frontiers in Industrial Relations and Human Resources*, Industrial Relations Research Association.

Osterman, P. (1994), "How common is workplace transformation and who adopts it?" *Industrial and Labor Relations Review*, **47**, January, 173–188.

Pérez-Díaz, V and J.C. Rodríguez (1995), "Inertial choices: an overview of Spanish human resources", in R. Locke, Th. Kockan and M. Piore (eds), *Employment Relations in a Changing World Economy*, Cambridge, MA: MIT Press, 165–196.

Pheffer, J. (1994), *Competitive Advantage through People: Understanding the Power of the Work Force*, Cambridge, MA: Harvard Business School Press.

Salas, V. (1993), "La empresa en el análisis económico", *Papeles de Economía Española*, **57**, 126–148.

Salas, V. (1996), *Economía de la Empresa*, 2nd edn, Barcelona: Ariel.

Sebastián, C. (1996), "Creating employment in Spain: labor market imperfections", in J. Gual (ed.), *The Social Challenge of Job Creation*, Cheltenham, UK: Edward Elgar, 119–153.

Simón, H. (1951), "A formal theory of the employment relationship", *Econometrica*, **19**.

Viñals, J. (1996), "Job creation in Spain: a macroeconomic view", in J. Gual (ed.), *The Social Challenge of Job Creation*, Cheltenham, UK: Edward Elgar, 91–118.

Weinstein, M. and Th. Kochan (1995), "The limits of diffusion: recent developments in industrial relations and human resource practices", in R. Locke, Th. Kochan and M. Piore, *Employment Relations in a Changing World*, Cambridge, MA: MIT Press, 1–31.

Weitzman, M. (1984), *The Share Economy*, Cambridge, MA: Harvard University Press.

Weitzman, M. (1995), "Incentives effects of profit sharing", in H. Siebert (ed.), *Trends in Business Organization: Do Participation and Cooperation Increase Competitiviness?*, JCB Möhr.

Williamson, O. (1975), *Markets and Hierarchies*, New York: Free Press.

Williamson, O. (1985), *The Economic Institutions of Capitalism*, New York: Free Press.

Williamson, O. and M. Wachter and J. Harris (1975), "Understanding the employment relation: the analysis of idiosyncratic exchange", *The Bell Journal of Economics*, **6**.

6.   Labor market regulations, social policy and job creation

Colin Crouch

6.1.   INTRODUCTION

Virtually all current policy discussion of labor markets assumes a threefold distinction of a regulated, low-employment continental Europe, a deregulated, high-employment Anglo-America, and a high-employment Japan whose labor markets are difficult to analyse but which do not seem to resemble those of Europe. From this emerges the ostensibly clear political lesson that European labor markets must be deregulated if high levels of employment are to return. This is held to require the elimination of anything that might constitute an impediment to pure market forces in the labor market: protection of employees' working standards, unemployment benefit, and any measures that try to contain the gap between high and low earners. An important moment in the victory of this neo liberal approach was the publication in 1994 of the *Jobs Study* (OECD 1994a and b) by the Organization of Economic Cooperation and Development. The main political message was clear and was repeated in the "editorial" articles in subsequent *Employment Outlooks* (OECD 1994c and 1995).

The detailed presentation of evidence in the *Study* at times provides a measured and less ideological assessment of the situation, and some individual discussions (such as that on training and education (1994b, ch. 7) implicitly contradict much of the core argument.[1] More recently, in the 1996 and 1997 issues of *Employment Outlook*, the OECD has shown greater ambivalence. Doubts are evident about the consequences for the behaviour of workers of the low wages, insecurity, poor working conditions and frequent job changes that the Organization had been recommending as the best means of getting the unemployed back to work (OECD 1996, p. vii); and about the threats to social cohesion which might be posed by the rise in inequality that seems to be associated with the reforms (OECD 1996 and 1997). There has also been some acknowledgement that the decisive conclusions of the 1994 documents may not have been justified. Thus, it is suspected that low wages

130

do not seem to increase employment chances (OECD 1996, p. 76); that the relationship between labor turnover and unemployment is not that clear (ibid., p. 168); and that there is little evidence that employment protection really has an effect on employment (ibid., pp. 171–2). It has also been suggested that while structural job protection might lead to higher long-term employment, it might actually reduce the number of people who experience some unemployment; and that labor flexibility might reduce employers' willingness to invest in human capital (ibid., p. 176).

However, it has been the simple neo-liberal argument of 1994 that has continued to inform political rhetoric and public discussion: if labor markets could be deregulated, especially through reducing the level of employees' job rights and the generosity of unemployment benefits, full employment might be restored. Because this thesis has been so widely accepted, and the original *Jobs Study* played an important part in disseminating it, it is worth while considering in some detail the strength of the case that was made.

A large amount of sophisticated empirical evidence was deployed to support the case, although in many instances the results were inconclusive. The OECD then surprisingly fell back on *a priori* reasoning. For example, attempts by the *Jobs Study* to demonstrate that unemployment compensation affects the job-seeking behaviour of the unemployed (OECD 1994b, p. 44), or that minimum wages raise the level of unemployment (ibid., pp. 46ff.) found very little tangible empirical support. The Organization therefore had recourse to a first-principles argument that there must be some effect of the kind predicted (ibid., pp. 51ff.). A summary of the cases for and against employment protection displays inconclusive empirical evidence but falls back for a conclusion on the *a priori* argument that protection of employees' job rights is likely to reduce employment because anticipated dismissals costs are an aspect of labor costs and are therefore likely to discourage hiring (ibid., pp. 73–6).

The argument that the superior employment performance of the Scandinavian economies in the past had been achieved through centralized or coordinated bargaining is inconvenient to neo-liberal theory. The OECD therefore argues that this relationship is suspect, because in theory it must primarily be private employment which will react to the cost of labor, whereas in fact it was public employment that expanded most in Scandinavia (ibid., 1994b, p. 20). The neo-liberal prejudice against public employment as rent-seeking and incapable of being managed efficiently is here used to undermine evidence that might disconfirm the prejudice. In the same passage, employment growth in the decentralized countries (primarily the UK and the US) is contrasted favourably with job creation in Scandinavia, because in the former cases it was "solidly based" on private-sector job expansion. It is again an *a priori* assumption that there is some quality of "solidity" possessed by jobs, any jobs, in the private sector that cannot be shared by those in the public domain.

Perhaps the most important point where this occurs in the *Jobs Study* is when dealing with the case of Japan. The fact that that country, which has continued to experience rapid job growth, also has very long job tenures and has been ranked by some observers as intermediate (rather than low) in its degree of job regulation (for example, Bertola 1990), potentially causes major difficulties for the deregulation thesis. The OECD therefore argues that the Japanese employment system does not really provide job protection (OECD 1994b, p. 79). The reasoning for this is as follows: because there is little state social security in Japan, it is important to employees that employers offer them job security; therefore, in order to attract labor, employers make such an offer. Because this is seen as a labor market decision by employers and not regulation by the state, it is not regarded as a form of regulation – even though it has the same effect on security for those workers concerned as would a legislated system.

It might be objected that, unlike statutory protection which is likely to be universal, the Japanese system, which necessarily limits guaranteed long-term employment to certain categories of workers in large corporations only and maintains other categories of less-well-protected employees, including those on special temporary contracts, contains its own flexibility via a segmentation of the labor force. Only a third of the Japanese workforce is covered by long-term employment guarantees. This is a valid and important point, but it is not an argument which should be deployed by the OECD researchers, who are in general very critical of segmentation as a source of rigidity. They justly regard devices which accord different levels of statutory protection to different categories of workers as creating barriers between insiders and outsiders and as generally impeding the free flow of labor. In particular, they criticize the policies of various European governments (for example, France and Spain), which have tried to reconcile continued protection for much of the workforce with the need to reduce high youth unemployment by developing special legal categories of temporary employment (ibid., p. 78). The OECD unequivocally prefers policies which remove protection from all workers, as this is more consistent with the pure market model of labor being available as an uninterrupted flow rather than coming in certain defined "lumps".

However, the Japanese employment system, which embodies one of the world's most segmented labor markets, is not subjected to the same criticism. Neither does the *Jobs Study* regard the ethnic structure of the US economy as providing the basis of any segmentation in the labor market, despite the existence of a number of studies arguing this very point; nor does it see segmentation in the particular labor market role played by students and elderly people in the US and elsewhere (*vide infra*); or in the practice of many large firms in many countries of offering very diverse packages of job security to different types and levels of staff. In each case the explanation is the same: from a rigid neo-liberal perspective such distortions as segmentation cannot by definition be produced by the actions of firms acting in free markets, but only by governments (ibid., p. 79). If a distortion cannot be traced back to some piece of legislation, then, by definition, it is not a distortion.

Similarly, the Organization deplores the existence of imperfect competition in product markets (ibid., pp. 23ff.), but attributes this entirely to government policy. This shows no recognition of the fact that some markets, mainly those requiring heavy investment and bringing large economies of scale, will almost always feature imperfect competition. Oligopolistic firms may be fiercely competitive, but they do not adhere to the theoretical model of *perfect* competition, in which no individual actor can take strategic action but all are price-takers responding to market signals which remain sovereign. Large corporations have the capacity to establish internal labor markets, company cultures, human resource management programmes to encourage long service – all of which create "insiders", act as sources of rigidity in the labor market, and produce segmentation effects.

Another feature of the *Jobs Study* is the use of anecdotal and *ad hoc* adjustments in order to deal with inconvenient evidence, in particular making use of the formula that situations had recently changed where the available evidence points in the wrong direction. For example, there is some perplexity at the fact that a survey by the International Organization of Employers (IOE) had ranked the level of job protection in Finland, Norway and Sweden only moderately high. The *Jobs Study* therefore comments that this protection had increased in recent years (ibid., p. 77) – although in fact all the increases listed took place several years before the IOE study referred to and had presumably been discounted by it. On the other hand the fact that French employment policy has been deregulating labor markets consistently for several very recent years – with no improvement in unemployment levels – does not merit any suggestion that employment in that country is perhaps not now as protected as it once was.

When discussing labor market immobility caused by non-transferable occupational pensions schemes one might have expected the OECD to confront the fact that universal state pension schemes constitute a solution to this problem, and that this might be one way in which some northern European economies embody some compensatory flexibility at a point where the US (where 70 per cent of pensions, the highest level in any country, are not portable) evinces unusual labor market rigidities. This might then have provoked a fascinating and useful discussion of ways in which different kinds of labor market regime might show different patterns of flexibility and rigidity. However, the *Study* simply dismisses the awkward US evidence with the comment that the percentage of non-portable pensions in the US is "falling" (ibid., p. 68) – with the unspoken and unjustified implication that its past effects therefore do not have to be considered.

At another point, where the Organization is pressing its case for considerably increased income inequality as a means of reducing unemployment, it presents a chart, and an impressive correlation coefficient, demonstrating that the more that incomes widened during the 1980–89 period, the more employment grew (ibid., p. 2). There are three curious things about this evidence. First, the UK appears as a total outlier, being the only other country apart from the US to have experienced a major increase in inequality but having one of the most negative job growths. This is explained away by the OECD by the fact that during the latter 1980s UK employment experience improved; but by taking various subperiods of time defined in an *ad hoc* manner to suit the evidence, one could demonstrate that any other country's situation was different from that displayed. This is an instance of special pleading for a case rather than neutral examination of evidence.

Second, the income development data used are for the whole economy, while the job growth data are for private-sector jobs only. It is entirely possible that one reason for private-sector jobs growing during the 1980s was a tendency for economic activities to move from the public to the private sectors, either directly through privatization or indirectly through reductions in public services, some of which will have been compensated by a growth of private equivalents. Private-sector job growth may therefore not have been *net* job growth; this will be very relevant to an appraisal of British private-sector growth during the 1980s, a period of considerable privatization. Further, given that incomes are more unequally distributed in the private sector than in the public, it is not at all surprising that countries which saw high private-sector job growth (partly at the expense of public-sector job growth) also saw an increase in inequalities.

Finally, there is an additional oddity that the incomes data used relate to male earnings only, while most job expansion during the period was of female employment. The link between male earnings development and female job growth needs to be specified before we can accept the plausibility of the case that increases in inequality among the former produced job growth among the latter.

Neo-liberal arguments incorporate in their assumptions certain generalizations about countries in general which are in fact based on the specific circumstances of the United States; the fault here lies not so much with neo-liberal politics as with the academic economic theory on which it draws, and which has for many years now been one-sidedly based on US models. Some instances of this can also be found in the *Jobs Study*. For example, it complains about the cartelization of product markets produced by industry-level collective bargaining in European countries (ibid., p. 52). This is however true only if one assumes a more or less closed economy in which foreign trade constitutes only a small proportion of economic activity – as in the US case. The small European economies have been highly open, while the German one (the only enduring case of coordinated industry-level bargaining in a large country) is unusually dependent on exports and has a collective bargaining system heavily dominated by particularly export-sensitive industries – mainly metal, also chemicals (see Crouch 1990). In an internationally open economy centrally organized actors in collective bargaining have to confront the price implications of their actions in relation to competitors in other countries over whose behaviour their organizations have no control. Within internationally traded sectors therefore the organization of the labor market does not have the same automatically cartelistic implications in some European countries as it would have in the US.[2]

The *Study* similarly attacks industry-wide collective bargaining as likely to protect uncompetitive privileges for insiders (OECD 1994b, p. 52) without taking account of the implications of international trade for collective bargaining in open economies. It is therefore puzzled to find (ibid., p. 30) more evidence in the US or Canada of inter-industry wage premia – implying a higher level of imperfect competition – than in Europe.

6.2.   THE NEO-INSTITUTIONALIST CRITIQUE

The central arguments against the neo-liberal or deregulationist thesis are of two kinds – both also based primarily on *a priori* reasoning and difficult to test. There is first a "moral" or "social" argument that worries about the effect on people of the poverty and insecurity that seem to be consequences of unregulated labor markets. In this chapter I shall not be concerned principally with these issues, but with the second set of objections, those presented by the set of approaches broadly called "neo-institutionalist". The central thrust of these arguments is to point to the limited nature of the model of action embodied in neoclassical economic theory, which is concerned almost exclusively with decisions based on prices determined by a perfectly competitive process. The efficiency of action is regarded as being reduced whenever there is a departure from the purity of this process. Such departures might come from impositions of a need to take account of factors not embodied in the price, or to take account of the actions of others through mechanisms other than that of price, or to slow down speed of response. Institutionalist analyses, in direct contrast, concentrate on potential losses to human efficiency that might result from sole reliance on pure market signals: an incapacity to communicate through channels other than those of price signals; an incapacity to respond to externalities; the waste that might flow from the short-term nature of horizons imposed by the emphasis on speed of decisions and their implementation.

Where the labor market is concerned, this has the following implications.

First, once the legal right of employees to form unions is conceded, the potentially inflationary consequences of this organization will be most effectively contained if these organizations and their counterparts among employers are capable of acting with strategic capacity and are unable to externalize any negative consequences of their actions.

Second, where it is difficult for employers to fire workers, the former have an incentive to improve the quality of the workforce which will be lacking in unregulated labor markets; therefore while, in the latter case, it will be possible for individual employers to use rapid changes in hiring and firing to recruit a high-quality workforce, this will be simply an exchange process and will not lead to any overall improvement in workforce quality.

Third, where employers are organized in associations capable of exercising sanctions against member firms, they will have incentives to collaborate in positive-sum exchanges, including those likely to improve the quality of labor, while those who are not organized will be limited to zero-sum exchanges.

Fourth, employees who have both expectations of security of employment and the ability to organize themselves to make "voice" contributions to working arrangements will be more likely to contribute to the model of the "committed company" commended by the human resource management literature.

According to neo-institutionalists, therefore, pure short-term, free market exchanges might lead to suboptimal performance in a number of respects. They therefore do not necessarily agree that all measures to make the labor market resemble more closely a pure market will improve economic performance and therefore, in the longer run, employment levels. If such measures destroy institutions working in the ways outlined above, the net effect of a strengthening of market forces could be negative. Institutionalists are on weak ground if they try to use these arguments to defend every example of a labor market institution. Many impediments to markets are simply impediments to efficiency with few countervailing gains: for example, collective bargaining arrangements that fail the strict conditions for strategic capacity capable of excluding externalities; or inter-firm arrangements that are merely protectionist.

These arguments are not necessarily connected to a "moral" or "social" case for protecting existing labor interests which has preoccupied social democratic political movements.[3] There are distinct affinities between neo-institutionalism and social democracy in that the former stresses the potential positive contribution of employee security and the organization of their interests, although institutionalists should not be indiscriminate in their support of whatever associational arrangements and security policies happen to have been developed by any particular political movement. Similarly, neoclassical economists are not necessarily associated with neo-liberal political positions, although again the empirical association is strong.

Neo-liberals are not without a capacity to respond to the new institutionalists' contentions. They can propose that individuals need to be given adequate incentives to invest in improving their own labor capacity, and they can find many empirical examples where this occurs. They can also demonstrate that, if it is required by the product markets, employers will often have adequate incentives to invest in improving the quality of labor.

However, these remain the weak points in the neo-liberal position. At the level of general labor market policy it is today virtually unchallenged: if governments and policy experts hold back from a thoroughgoing labor market deregulation it is usually only because they recognize certain political difficulties in implementation, not because they doubt its economic efficacy. However, on questions of improving the skill level and the general commitment of the labor force there are more substantive doubts. These were evident in the *Jobs Study* itself, in that (as noted in note 1) its chapters on education and training are far less deregulationist and neo-liberal than those on general labor market policy, and in fact contradict these schools on a number of points.

6.3.   RE-EXAMINING EMPLOYMENT AND EMPLOYMENT REGULATION

If some governments and the OECD are now having second thoughts about deregulation, it is because they fear that there might be negative consequences from some of the otherwise beneficial results of deregulating the labor market. However, I want also to question the confidence with which the *Jobs Study* insisted on these allegedly beneficial results.

In particular its argument relies on generalization at a very high level: an only occasionally differentiated "Europe" is seen as having a high level of regulation, which is itself seen as being of a monotonic quality. "Employment" is treated similarly: a job is a job is a job – the only qualitative differences in employment that are recognized being segmentation produced by government policy aimed at establishing special statuses of short-term contracts (ibid., p. 78) and the allegedly non-solid quality of public-service employment. The detailed analyses of the *Jobs Study* differentiate individual countries, and demonstrate considerable diversity in European experience. In drawing its conclusions, however, the study usually lumps together a large unit called "Europe" and sets it against North America (or usually just the US), doing so in the graphical presentations on its cover and in its headline and summary pronouncements (for example, OECD 1994b).

The failures to make qualitative distinctions are partly the consequence of economists' preference for regression analysis, which requires the reduction of diverse aspects of a complex phenomenon to an apparently simple, monotonic, measured scale. Although much of the use of evidence in the *Jobs Study* is more sophisticated, this is never taken to the point of identifying different *types* of regulation and their possibly differing consequences. The search for a simple undifferentiated concept, in this case "employment protection", as the key explanatory variable, is justified by the OECD with the good argument that one should prefer a theory that works at a level of overall generalization over one that draws attention to a series of empirical amendments and caveats. However, hypotheses derived at the generalizing level must also be consistent with variation and differences found at more detailed levels. It is on this score that I find much of the current orthodoxy unconvincing and argue that the policy conclusions which can be derived from an analysis of recent labor market changes need to be far more careful and discriminating.

6.3.1. Job Growth

At first glance it is true that employment expansion in the US and Japan has been considerably superior to that in western Europe. The *Jobs Study* (OECD 1994a, Table 1.1) showed that, during the period 1979–90, there was 1.6 per cent and 1.1 per cent job growth in the US and Japan, respectively, whereas the only western European countries to experience positive employment growth were Norway (0.7 per cent), Germany and Finland (both 0.6 per cent). However, as the *Study* then acknowledges, this leaves out of account the fact that European populations of working age were growing more slowly than those in Japan and the US. A more relevant figure is the growth in the number of jobs per capita of the population of working age (conventionally defined as ages 15 to 64). This reveals a less dramatic contrast (ibid., Table 1.2). The US still had the fastest rate of job growth, but down to 0.6 per cent; second were Finland and Sweden (0.3 per cent), fourth Japan (0.2 per cent), fifth the UK (0.1 per cent); Denmark, Greece and Norway had zero growth and all other European countries had negative levels. It is notable that, apart from Greece and the UK, the European countries with the most positive job creation levels were Scandinavian, those most outstanding for their advanced levels of welfare state provision, redistributive taxation, employee rights and strong trade unions.

The OECD data relate to the major period of economic transformation that took place in the wake of the oil shocks and other inflationary crises of the 1970s. In Table 6.1 I have tried to bring the account up to date by considering what has happened during the first half of the 1990s, when there had been a new worldwide recession and a further advance of neo-liberal policy influence. Here I have used a slightly different indicator from the original OECD *Study*. This had measured *all* job growth but as a proportion of the population aged 15–64 only. This would give a statistically exaggerated view of per capita job growth in any countries where there was also a rise in employment among the over 65s; as we shall see in due course, this is a relevant point for the issue of job creation. I have therefore taken the growth in employment only among those aged 15 to 64 as a proportion of the total population in that age range.

Table 6.1
Annualized changes in employment/population ratio, 1990–95,
population aged 15–64

Country	1995	1990	Annual change	Rank order
Austria	68.7	65.5	0.64	1
Belgium	55.7	57.1	−0.28	11
Denmark	73.4	77.1	−0.74	13
Finland	61.3	74.1	−2.56	18
France	59.5	60.6	−0.22	10
Germany*	65.1	64.8	0.06	7
Greece	54.2	55.0	−0.16	9
Ireland	55.0	52.4	0.52	2
Italy	52.1	55.7	−0.72	12
Netherlands	64.3	61.7	0.52	2
Norway	74.0	73.9	0.02	8
Portugal	65.7	72.0	−1.26	16
Spain	45.9	49.9	−0.8	14
Sweden	71.1	80.9	−1.96	17
Switzerland	79.2	77.6	0.32	4
UK	67.8	71.8	−0.8	14
Japan	74.1	72.6	0.3	5
US	73.5	73.0	0.1	6

Note: * The 1990 figure is for the former western Federal Republic; that for 1995 is for united Germany.
Source: OECD *Employment Outlook*, July 1996 (Paris: OECD 1996).

Japan and the US still have strong positive performances, but they are not the strongest; that position is in fact occupied by European countries, while the leading European neo-liberal case, the UK, had one of the worst negative records.[4] In appraising German performance one must bear in mind that the 1990 figure relates to the old West Germany, while that for 1995 relates to the whole of the new Germany. The small positive per capita job growth in that country – almost as high as that in the US – was therefore achieved amidst the reconstruction crisis in the east. It is also notable that, alongside the UK, the most negative experiences have been concentrated among two groups: the southern European countries and the Scandinavians (except for the special case of the Norwegian oil economy).

6.2.2 Employment Regulation

The main concern of the *Jobs Study* was to demonstrate that job growth would correlate inversely with the degree of job regulation or employment protection. The OECD report therefore proposed an interesting variety of measures of the strength of labor market regulation, and found strong correlations between some of them and measures of employment growth (OECD 1994b, Table 6.9). However, when the data were recalculated after removing the four southern European countries, Greece, Italy, Portugal, Spain (among which, with the exception of Portugal, western European unemployment is heavily concentrated), a different picture emerged. The *Jobs Study* claimed that the correlations were largely unaffected by this, but in fact there was now a considerable lack of explanatory power in nearly all the tests, the only measure performing well being the index of job strictness produced originally by the IOE and subsequently extended by the OECD to include all countries in its coverage. As already noted in the above discussion of the OECD's use of evidence and as pointed out by the *Jobs Study* itself (ibid., p. 76), the principal differentiating characteristic of this index is that it rated the degree of regulation in the Scandinavian labor markets less stringently than did other measures.

We therefore already have indications of two important subregional effects within Europe: exclusion of the southern European countries makes a considerable difference to the strength of the findings; and there is disagreement over how to interpret the impact of Scandinavian job regulation, the more moderate assessment of the strength of regulation in those countries producing the better results.

There is another questionable feature of the OECD's correlations. Although some of the measures used take account of collective bargaining and other aspects of labor market institutions, the main weight is borne by estimates of the strength of government regulation.[5] Also, the strength of government regulation is assessed through an examination of the mere existence of legislation. Not only is non-statutory regulation given little attention, but it is assumed that all legislation is implemented.

There are grounds for questioning both assumptions of this legalistic methodology. On the first, I have already discussed above the major problem that the OECD has with Japan. This country has, within its great firms, possibly the most institutionalized labor markets in the world; but because the factors which reduce the disposability of labor result from corporate strategy rather than government regulation, they are disregarded as not really being job regulation – an ideological rather than a scientific conclusion. Also, Denmark is regarded by the OECD as a low-regulation country because it has little statutory regulation of the terms of hiring and firing. However, as we know from much research, the Danish labor market is very thoroughly organized by employers' associations and trade unions which negotiate regulation of the labor market through powerfully binding agreements (Due et al. 1994). For example, the recently agreed directive on parental leave within the framework of the Protocol on Social Policy of the Treaty of Maastricht was implemented in Denmark, not through legislation, but through a collective agreement of the social partners. Denmark also has a very well-developed welfare state and strongly redistributive taxation; it hardly suits the neo-liberal ideal of a free market society any more than does Japan, although in very different ways.

This raises an important methodological question. Neoclassical economics (from which neo-liberalism here draws its analysis) does not have a concept of society. This is not surprising as it is not its task to do so; however, the absence brings some problems when a stage in analysis requires such a concept. The tendency is to regard all social institutions other than government as being in principle easily assimilated to economic theory. Therefore, Danish collective agreements and Japanese employment practices do not count as forms of regulation because they do not come from the state and therefore can somehow be harmonized with free markets. But from the point of view of sociological theory, whose business it is to produce concepts of society, social institutions are often governed by a different logic from the market and can at times resist the market as effectively as (perhaps more effectively than, since deeply embedded and often invisible) the state.[6]

The second issue, the assumption that regulations are implemented in accordance with the strength of their provisions, leads the OECD to regard the high-unemployment countries of southern Europe as having the most highly regulated labor markets. It is widely known that in at least some economic sectors and geographical areas within southern Europe legislated labor regulation is very widely ignored. This will not be true for the public sector or for the large corporations whose opinions become represented in forums like the IOE; and indeed no employer is likely to lobby an international agency in order to say: "don't worry about our employment regulation; much of the time we ignore it". It does, however, apply to many small firms; and it is small firms which have been significant producers of employment growth in many countries in recent years. It must also be remembered that self-employment is particularly high in most of southern Europe. This form of work is by definition not governed by employment legislation, and must provide a major element of flexibility.

It is also likely that, where job regulation is poorly implemented, implying the existence of considerable "black" employment, the existence of many jobs will go unrecorded and some people who are in fact in work will falsely declare themselves to be unemployed; this might well include some of the self-employed. Taken together these data will give the impression of a combination of extremely low levels of employment, high levels of unemployment and very strict job regulation where in fact the reality is very complex. It would be very dubious to permit the testing of any thesis about the relationship between employment and labor regulation to be heavily affected by recorded data from this part of Europe. However, as we have seen, whether or not southern Europe is included has a considerable effect on the strength of correlations found for the OECD's hypotheses, because these countries occupy extreme positions on the measurement scales of both low employment and high regulation.

Some southern countries also have very weak trade unions, and most of them have poorly developed welfare states.[7] The proposition, necessary to the OECD's overall evidence on the rigidity of European labor markets, that labor is more easily hired and fired in Denmark and Japan than in Greece, Italy and Spain, is not convincing.

An alternative approach, which is also used by the OECD *Study*, is to assess *de facto* labor rigidity by considering the length of employees' tenure with a particular firm. It is argued that employers need the freedom to dispose of employees easily if they are to be willing to hire them. We should therefore find job growth higher in those countries where average job tenure is lower. Unfortunately standardized data on this latter variable are available for only a few countries (Table 6.2). There is a slight tendency for job growth over both the 1979–90 and 1990–95 periods to be negatively correlated with average tenure length, though in neither case does this reach anything like statistical significance.

It can be argued that data on overall job tenure do not really tell us about the margins at which employers seek flexibility in their labor forces, since large numbers of employees are included whom employers have no wish to lose. We might perform a better test on the margins by considering only short-term stays, which we might assess by considering the percentage of employees who left their jobs after less than a year. This is also shown in Table 6.2. Here the sign is wrong for the deregulation thesis for the 1979–90 period but supportive of it in 1990–95, although in neither case is there any statistical significance.

Table 6.2 Employment tenures, c.1992		
Country	**Average stay in a specific job (years)**	**% in specific job for less than one year**
Austria		13.8
Finland	9.0	11.9
France	10.1	15.7
Germany*	10.4	12.8
Netherlands	7.0	24.0
Norway	9.4	14.9
Spain	9.8	23.9
Switzerland	8.8	17.6
UK	7.9	18.6
Japan	10.9	9.8
US	6.7	28.8

Note: *   Unified Germany.
Source: OECD *Employment Outlook*, 1993 (Paris: OECD 1993) .

We must consider in more detail the OECD's strategy of reducing all labor market regimes to a monotonic scale ranging from high to low levels of protection. (Subsequently, as we have seen, it makes an *ad hoc* argument about the character of Japanese labor markets because otherwise that country is inconvenient for the deregulation thesis.) This requires a series of dubious assumptions: that it is possible, say, to assess on a single scale the relative importance of so many months' protection against unfair dismissal and of a certain kind of control over the activities of private employment agencies; and that these different regulatory components add up to a single final end-product – employment rigidity – with no qualitative differences among types of rigidity. Full details of a labor market regime should include, in addition to some indicators of statutory employment protection, an estimate of the strength of labor within collective bargaining (given, for example, by trade union membership density) and an indication of both the general level of state intervention in the market (given by the total size of public spending) and the specific level of the taxation costs imposed on firms when employing labor (given by employers' contributions to social security funds).

Even then we should still be following the OECD in generalizing across whole countries, whereas in reality it is likely that different economic sectors and also different sizes of firm encounter different levels of job protection. Employment in public services is likely always to be relatively protected, because, whatever the character of the political regime, public employers have difficulty in not abiding by codes of reasonable treatment of employees and are particularly constrained to obey legal regulations. *Ceteris paribus*, employment in the manufacturing sector is more likely to be protected than that in most private services, because it is nearly always more strongly and effectively unionized. The core employees of large firms are usually likely to be better protected than workers in small companies, even where the full rigours of an employment system such as that in Japan are not operative.

Looking at the data in these terms, there was most job growth (or least job loss) in the 1979–90 period in Japan, the US and in the Scandinavian countries. The worst performers were the southern Europeans and the core continental European countries. The good performance of the unregulated US and the poor performance of the core continentals is consistent with the deregulationist hypothesis, but the good performance of Scandinavia and the poor performance of the largely ineffectively regulated southern Europe is not. In contrast, an institutionalist theory would have predicted the Scandinavian and southern European positions but will have been surprised by the American case. In the more recent, 1990–95, period the evidence is again mixed. Scandinavia has now started to perform as anticipated by neo-liberal theory, but the UK should have performed much better. Also, the performance of the core continentals (even when one has removed the southern Europeans from the category) is far more diverse than is justified by the common generalizations of the OECD and others about "Europe". More important, certain countries in the group, including some which appear to be highly regulated on any measurement, such as Austria and Germany, have performed as well as Japan and the US and considerably better than the UK (or indeed than France, which had implemented many deregulatory policies in previous years).

6.2.3.   Who Works?

In addition to considering job growth we should examine the overall contours of employment. I prefer to do this in terms of who works rather than of unemployment rates. Unemployment data have become an unsatisfactory basis for labor market analysis. Counts of unemployment are heavily affected by different national rules for defining the unemployed. Unemployment levels are politically sensitive, and definition as being unemployed usually entitles persons to benefits; both factors give people various incentives to present themselves as unemployed while giving governments incentives both to change definitions of unemployment in a way that reduces the estimate, and to take measures to make registration as unemployed difficult.[8] The OECD itself, commending British policies during the 1980s of "frequent monitoring" of unemployed people, points out that "even quite low levels of contact with unemployed people reduce the number of benefit claims" (OECD 1994b, p. 104). And the UK's Youth Training scheme was praised because it provided an opportunity to remove large numbers of young people from eligibility for benefit (ibid., p. 105). The role of unemployment registration as a measure of excess supply within the labor market is here completely lost in the policy-maker's concern, for political and cost reasons, to be able to present a lower number of claimants. If governments do this differentially, comparisons between unemployment levels might simply reflect different regimes of counting and of severity of treatment of potential claimants.

Similarly, a person's decision to declare himself or herself to be unemployed might be a claim for benefit rather than a declaration of entry into the labor market, and the varying severity of different benefit regimes will affect claimants' capacity to fudge this distinction.

Further, today's labor markets differ from those of previous decades in that far more married women now perceive themselves as members of the workforce; like men, they are either in paid employment or registered as unemployed. But a third option remains for women: to be regarded as housewives and mothers and not to register as unemployed if they do not have paid jobs. Women's decisions as to how to define themselves will have a major effect on the unemployment rate. Further still, both men and women leaving the labor force in the latter part of their working lives might perceive themselves as retired rather than unemployed, although they might take employment of various kinds if it appears. It is difficult to determine whether or not housewives and retired people are "in the labor market". They are unlikely either to describe themselves as unemployed when approached by a labor market survey researcher or to try to register at their local benefit office. They may well, however, respond to a sudden job opportunity or even start looking for work.

Finally, a similar question can arise among younger age groups, where people might "park" themselves in education courses rather than either become unemployed or take unattractive work; or if pursuing educational courses might take part-time work to help pay their way through it. Whether they will register as unemployed will depend partly on their self-perception, partly on rules for benefit entitlement which often make it illegal for students to register as unemployed.

The economic concepts that inform standard labor market analysis assume that two types of person are "active" in the labor market: those actually in jobs and those who have registered as unemployed and are hence in principle offering themselves on the market for work. These two groups together comprise the "supply" of labor. A high rate of unemployment therefore indicates excess supply, carrying with it the strong presumption that a reduction in labor's price would reconcile the imbalance. It is on that basis that most current analysis depends for its recommendations that the cost of labor must be reduced, whether through cutting wages, reducing security levels and other rights, or reducing the non-wage costs of labor. However, registration as unemployed is less a signal of a desire to enter the labor market than a request for social security benefit; the two decisions are related but far from the same. It is possible that government rules do not permit someone to claim benefit, though he might well remain actively searching for work.

I shall therefore concentrate on a comparison of numbers *in work* rather than on unemployment. We look first at the simplest feature of the labor market: the proportion of the relevant population which is in employment. This relevant population is conventionally defined as those between the ages of 15 and 64. I wish to make two changes to this. First, increasingly large numbers of young people between the ages of 15 and their twenties remain in education. I therefore remove from the population all people in full-time education. (This will lead to the opposite and unavoidable inaccuracy, as increasing numbers of young people in some countries are working part-time during their studies, but we shall discuss this in due course.)

I also remove the artificial constraint of the age 65 cut-off. Retirement ages vary across countries, and various numbers of people work after formal retirement. Especially if we consider (as did the *Jobs Study*) all jobs that have been created, irrespective of the age of those performing them and of the number of hours per week involved, we need to remove any artificial cut-off age that might exclude some members of the potential working population. I do exclude from consideration the population aged over 80, since work is very unlikely to be continued by people of this age. The population universe is therefore everyone between the age of 15 and 80 who is not in full-time education. Table 6.3 shows the proportion of this population actually in work in a number of countries, by gender, in the years around 1990. In addition to simple rank order we can group the countries into those with a moderate level of employment (those having levels within one standard deviation of the mean), a high level (above this range) and a low level (below this range).

Japan tops the list among overall providers of employment, although it is followed by three of the Nordic countries, Portugal and Switzerland, within the high-employment group. The UK and US occupy moderately high positions, ahead of the "core continental" group which is in turn (except for Belgium and Ireland) clearly ahead of the southern Europeans. There is support here for the deregulationist thesis, *but* also for those arguments that draw attention to the heterogeneity of "Europe" and of the difficulty of accommodating a simple deregulationist thesis to a situation that has high employment in Scandinavia and low employment in southern Europe.

If we now consider the genders separately, among men Japan is joined by the two anomalous cases of Portugal and Switzerland as the three high employers, although the US (but not the UK) also ranks high. Below this there is no discernible pattern of country types within Europe. In fact, all countries are heavily bunched here (with a standard deviation of only 7.92 per cent of the mean). It is female employment which accounts for the greatest absolute differences among countries as well as the most recent rates of growth (standard deviation of 19.19 per cent of the mean). Here all four Nordic countries predominate, followed by Japan, Portugal, the UK, the US and then the other western European cases. It can certainly be concluded that the core countries of western Europe – including all the original European Community members – have lower female employment levels than either the non-European cases or those (Portugal, Scandinavia, the UK) which are for various reasons outside the core. Southern Europe is, with the exception of Portugal, towards the foot of the table.

With the exception of Greece, all countries with low reported female employment have had prolonged periods of government by political parties or dictatorships close to the Catholic Church.[9] With the exception of Portugal, all countries with high female workforce participation lack this experience, diverse though their political and religious composition might be. The Portuguese exception can be explained. During the prolonged period of pro-Catholic dictatorship, Portugal did have a low female participation rate similar to that of other Catholic countries. This changed rapidly and suddenly following the Marxist military coup that overthrew the dictatorship in 1975. Laws regulating female employment were then changed drastically in a manner that was never imitated in Spain.

Table 6.3
Proportions of population aged 15–80 in employment, c.1990

Country	All employment (%)						All in part-time work (%)			All full-time employment (%)					
	Men		Women		All		Men	Women	All	Men		Women		All	
	%	rank	%	rank	%	rank				%	rank	%	rank	%	rank
Austria	74.18	9	47	12	60.11	11	4	26.9	13.9	71.21	6	34.32	9	51.75	7
Belgium	65.67	18	46.3	13	55.81	15	2.8	29.8	13.6	63.83	16	32.5	11	48.22	14
Denmark	74.89	7	60.4	2	67.62	3	10.4	35.5	21.6	67.1	11	38.97	4	53.01	4
Finland	66.04	17	58.4	3	62.14	9	5.7	11.3	8.4	62.28	17	51.82	1	56.92	3
France	69.26	15	48.7	10	58.85	12	5	28.9	15.6	65.8	12	34.65	8	49.67	11
Germany *	74.63	8	48.7	11	61.35	10	3.6	33.8	16.3	71.94	5	32.24	12	51.35	10
Greece	70.99	13	38.2	16	54.26	16	2.8	8.4	4.8	69	7	34.95	7	51.66	8
Ireland	69.28	14	35.1	17	52.25	17	5.1	21.7	11.3	65.75	13	27.5	15	46.35	16
Italy	75.07	6	38.5	15	56.49	14	2.9	12.7	6.4	72.89	4	33.65	10	52.87	5
Netherlands	72.62	11	44.7	14	58.5	13	16.8	67.2	37.4	60.42	18	14.66	18	36.62	18
Norway	76.12	5	57.4	4	66.61	5	9.4	46.6	26.5	68.96	8	30.66	14	48.96	12
Portugal	77.69	3	56.4	6	66.65	4	4.2	11.6	7.5	74.43	3	49.87	2	61.65	1
Spain	66.23	16	31.5	18	48.54	18	2.8	16.4	7.5	64.38	15	26.33	16	44.9	17
Sweden	71.68	12	66.9	1	69.26	2	9.4	40.3	24.3	64.94	14	39.92	3	52.43	6
Switzerland	83.03	2	49.7	9	66.19	6	8.6	54.7	28.3	75.89	2	22.53	17	47.46	15
UK	73.09	10	56	7	64.49	7	7.7	44.3	24.1	67.46	10	31.18	13	48.95	13
Japan	88.73	1	57.4	5	72.59	1	10.1	34.9	20.1	79.77	1	37.35	5	58	2
US	76.48	4	51.1	8	63.1	8	11	27.4	18.6	68.07	9	37.13	6	51.36	9

Note: *   Former western Federal Republic.
Source: Various ILO and OECD publications.

The different genders therefore tell different stories. The pattern of male employment lends some support to the deregulation thesis and also suggests little diversity among European nations, though male employment does not explain much of the overall picture: less than 2 per cent more employment in the US than in Italy or Germany. The female pattern supports a totally different explanation based on disincentives to female employment embodied in Catholic social policies of various kinds. These range from a tendency for the provision of child care for working mothers to be very low in Catholic countries; for social insurance benefits to be orientated towards male "breadwinner" incomes; and for state welfare policies often to make assumptions that the sick or elderly will be cared for by a relative if one exists in the household – and given the stress on males as breadwinners, these obligations fall mainly on women.

Much writing on female employment has argued that it is the positive policies associated with the Scandinavian countries that explain high female participation rates (Esping-Andersen 1996). The evidence reported here suggests rather the negative thesis that in various ways Catholic social policy might discourage what might otherwise be assumed to be a desire by women to work. This evidence is therefore supportive of a deregulationist thesis, but concerning a very particular kind of regulation only.

6.2.4. Part-time and full-time; Young and Old

So far we have regarded a job to be a job, as does the OECD. There is however a difference between full- and part-time employment. The creation of a full-time job clearly indicates a greater job creation capacity than a part-time one. In arguing this I do not intend to join the debate over whether the creation of part-time jobs is worthless or somehow exploitative, or whether part-time workers would prefer full-time jobs if they were available (Blossfeld and Hakim 1997), but merely to make the neutral quantitative point that the difference between the two forms of work must be taken into account. To take an extreme case: let us assume two economies; in one there is a 1 per cent growth in jobs, all these jobs being of 40 hours a week duration; in the second there is a 2 per cent growth in jobs, but they are all for 20 hours a week. An equal amount of work has been created in the two economies, but the OECD would regard the second as having been twice as effective in job creation.

Do factors of this kind help explain some of the differences in job creation? Unfortunately we cannot tell which of the jobs being claimed in the OECD's jobs *growth* figures have been part-time, but with one important caveat we can examine what proportions of persons working are in full- and part-time jobs. The caveat concerns the definition of part-time. These vary widely and are completely non-standardized; we certainly cannot assume that part-time jobs are 50 per cent of full-time ones. In some countries (Denmark, Sweden, to some extent the US, jobs might be considered part-time if they are between 30 and 35 hours a week, whereas in Belgium, France, Germany and the UK they are rarely above 29 hours. It is impossible to take proper account of this, other than to modify the strength of any conclusions which we might draw. However, the later columns of Table 6.3 show the effect on the data given in the earlier columns of removing from account all part-time work; in other words they provide a measure of full-time employment.

The effect of removing part-time work is, not surprisingly, greater on levels of female employment. In particular the strong "Catholic effect" disappears; the relationship between level of full-time employment and political domination by Catholic parties that obtained for the overall female employment figure no longer obtains. Catholic social policy would therefore seem to have inhibited, not the participation of women *per se* in the labor force, but the possibility of combining work and family roles. It may therefore operate as much at the wider level of child-care provision, and so on, as through job regulation in particular. Why this happens would require more detailed research into the family position of full-time and part-time working women – and also an attempt at taking account of possible non-reporting of employment in southern Europe. It is at least possible that low levels of employment in some countries can be partly explained by a highly specific set of arguments about Catholic social policy and female part-time working rather than anything general about employment protection.

I want here however to concentrate on the effect on *male* employment of removing part-timers. When we concentrate solely on men in full-time work, there is no effect on Japan's relative ranking (even although its male part-time ratio is high), but the relative rank of the US sinks to a very median position, behind several core continental cases, although above most Nordic ones.

Therefore, if the US has a distinctively high capacity to provide work because of its low level of employment regulation, this is very largely through part-time work, especially among men. This places the concept of the US "job machine" in an important perspective. The same conclusion cannot be drawn about Japan.

Under what circumstances do men work part-time? The number who do so because they have become "househusbands" is probably very small, certainly outside the Nordic countries. There will be some who are disabled, but most significant must be those who can find only part-time jobs, or who are working while they are studying, or who are elderly and do not want to manage a full working day. (Of course, female part-timers will include all these groups too, in addition to the more familiar "dual-burden" working housewives.)

I have above raised the question of the age range over which proportions of the population in employment should be considered. At what ages do people in various countries tend to stop working? Ages of statutory retirement vary, while an aspect of US labor non-regulation is the absence of any statutory retirement age at all. Even where retirement is normal, people sometimes continue working until later years or take on new kinds of work. At the other end of the age scale we have assumed that we should remove from consideration among the potentially employed all those persons in full-time education. However, it is possible for someone to be in full-time education and yet also to be in some kind of employment. This, too, varies by country. The OECD's assessments of job growth, and our own assessments above of the total workforce, include as "in work" all elderly persons and students in some kind of employment.

Let us first consider the young. Table 6.4 shows the proportions of 18-year-olds in employment who were also in education in 1984 and 1994. (Smaller numbers continued in that situation at least until age 26.) It is notable that in some countries – Denmark, the Netherlands, the US, to some extent the UK and, among women only, Ireland – there were particularly high levels of employment among young persons in education. This suggests strongly that part of this employment growth was among students paying their way through college; and the above statistics for the total population in work as a proportion of the 15–80-year-old population not in full-time education was excluding from the denominator many young people who were in fact in jobs – presumably largely part-time ones; one assumes that most people both in employment and in education are working part-time.

A further useful statistic is that for young people who were neither at school nor in work, which may be a more reliable indicator than the unemployment rate, also shown in Table 6.4. It is interesting to note that the worst performing country here was the UK, which has initiated deregulationist policies more extensively than any other European country, while the US itself was not among the best performers, which were in fact found in continental Europe.

To further test the hypothesis that institutional labor markets protect insiders and therefore exclude the young, we can compare unemployment rates for different age groups. An important aspect of the deregulationist argument is that employment regulation protects insiders and is therefore likely to result in particularly high unemployment rates among the young. The OECD therefore duly draws attention to the fact that youth unemployment is proportionately much higher than adult in its so-called high-protection countries (OECD 1996, p. 79), but fails to note that among 15–19-year-olds it is also particularly high in the US and only average among 20–24-year-olds (see Table 6.5). It must also be pointed out that these figures are for registered unemployment and may therefore to some extent merely reflect different government policies towards registration by different age groups; in appraising the UK's favourable rankings in the table one must bear in mind the point cited above, that that country was singled out for praise by the OECD for finding means of preventing young

Table 6.4

Educational and employment position of 18-year-olds

Country	Males				Females			
	% of those employed also in education		% in neither work nor education	% registered unemployed (15–19)	% of those employed also in education		% in neither work nor education	% registered unemployed (15–19)
	1984	1994	1994	1994	1984	1994	1994	1994
Belgium	7.1	11.5	13.0	32.5	3.2	6.7	13.5	37.5
Denmark	23.9	50.8	4.4	8.5	32.5	63.5	10.6	5.1
France	1.9	15.6	10.7	21.9	5.7	27.6	10.1	34.5
Germany*	5.8	12.0	7.8	5.8	7.3	15.4	8.2	6.8
Greece	5.8	5.1	10.8	20.6	2.1	8.5	20.8	47.6
Ireland	5.9	10.8	16.8	32.8	6.9	23.3	11.9	34
Italy	2.1	2.6	15.2	33.0	2.5	2.6	19.7	42.4
Netherlands	23.7	55.1	5.3	16.0	18.8	65.7	4.7	12.0
Portugal	10.2	16.0	7.2	11.3	4	15.8	10.2	19.9
Spain	2.0	11.3	17.2	39.8	0.5	17.8	18.1	58.1
UK	14.6	21.9	23.5	20.8	18.1	33.0	25.4	16.1
USA	43.8	46.3	12.0	19.0	42.9	45.6	16.8	16.2

Note: *   1984, former western Federal Republic; 1994 unified Germany.

Source: OECD 1996.

Table 6.5
Ratios of youth to adult unemployment, 1994

Country		Unemployment rates			Ratios and rank orders			
		(a) 15–19 years	(b) 20–24 years	(c) 25–54 years	a : c	ranks	b : c	ranks
Belgium	M	32.5	18.9	6.4	5.08	15	2.95	14
	F	37.5	22.0	11.2	3.35	14	1.96	10
Denmark	M	8.5	11.5	6.7	1.27	2	1.72	2
	F	5.1	13.8	9	0.57	1	1.53	4
Finland	M	29.8	32.1	17.4	1.71	3	1.84	4
	F	35.1	27.9	14.5	2.42	6	1.92	9
France	M	21.9	24.5	9.7	2.26	6	2.53	12
	F	34.5	31.4	13.1	2.63	8	2.4	12
Germany*	M	5.8	9.0	6.9	0.84	1	1.3	1
(1993)	F	6.8	8.7	10.3	0.66	2	0.84	1
Greece	M	20.6	19.5	4.8	4.29	14	4.06	15
	F	47.6	33.6	10.7	4.45	16	3.14	16
Ireland	M	32.8	24.7	14.4	2.28	7	1.72	2
(1993)	F	34.0	19.6	14.1	2.41	5	1.39	3
Italy	M	33.0	27.8	6.0	5.5	16	4.63	16
	F	42.4	34.6	11.7	3.62	15	2.96	15
Japan	M	8.3	5.0	2.0	4.15	13	2.5	11
	F	6.8	5.0	2.8	2.43	7	1.79	7
Netherlands	M	16.0	12.4	5.6	2.86	11	2.21	7
	F	12.0	7.8	8.0	1.5	3	0.98	2
Norway	M	12.7	10.7	4.7	2.7	10	2.28	9
	F	11.0	8.7	3.5	3.14	12	2.49	16
Portugal	M	11.3	12.4	4.8	2.35	8	2.58	12
	F	19.9	15.1	7.0	2.84	11	2.16	11
Spain	M	39.8	36.4	16.4	2.43	9	2.22	8
	F	58.1	47.4	28.4	2.05	4	1.67	5
Sweden	M	17.7	19.3	7.9	2.24	5	2.44	10
	F	15.4	13.9	5.8	2.66	10	2.4	12
UK	M	20.8	18.3	9.8	2.12	4	1.87	5
	F	16.1	10.7	6.4	2.52	8	1.67	5
US	M	19.0	10.2	4.9	3.88	12	2.08	6
	F	16.2	9.2	5.0	3.24	13	1.84	8

Note: *   Unified Germany.
Source: OECD 1996.

people from registering as unemployed. Germany's position is particularly interesting here, in that for both genders in the teenage group and among women in their early twenties the youth unemployment rate was actually lower than that for older workers. The only other ratio below unity was that for Dutch women in their early twenties.

In the German case (and the same would probably be shown for Austria and Switzerland if we had their statistics) the answer lies in the capacity of the apprenticeship system to absorb young workers. The German model of apprenticeship itself depends for its success on cooperative networks among firms of precisely the kind that the OECD finds most offensive to its neo-liberal ideal; it also constitutes a leading example of how institutions that might be thought to be cartels protecting insiders can in fact embody mechanisms that offset this tendency if only they are subjected to empirical research and not written off through *a priori* ideological neo-liberal reasoning. Turning to elderly workers, in both Japan and the US people remain in the labor force longer than elsewhere, and this explains part of the high participation rates in these two countries. To what extent this results from a desire by elderly people to remain participating actively and to what extent it is a reflection of low pensions for large proportions of the population it is impossible to say. It is, however, relevant to note that jobs specifically available for the elderly do not necessarily make a general contribution to employment opportunities. One also assumes that most elderly people in the workforce are in part-time employment, and these cross-national differences in elderly working may also help further explain the differences in part-time working, particularly among men.

Different national age structures of employment suggest an interaction with social policy. The German apprenticeship system makes possible early labor force entry through the acquisition of skills; Japanese labor market entry is delayed while young people acquire skills; in the US and possibly British case youth participation is partly inflated by students' part-time working or, in the British case, by a large amount of early school-leaving. At the other end of the age range the generosity of pension arrangements seems to explain labor force behaviour.

The age spread of employment might be considered relevant to issues of the underlying flexibility and adaptability of labor markets. The more rigid the labor market, the more likely it is that existing employees will have established their place and will prevent access to jobs by newcomers. There will then be a further difference determined by whether a high rate of employment is sustainable across the life course or whether, as it were, high youth employment has to be purchased at the "cost" of low employment among older workers. I put "cost" within inverted commas because a low level of employment among older workers may be variously interpreted. To the extent that the economy gains from having younger, more recently educated people doing its work while people in their declining years enjoy more leisure time on comfortable pensions, there may well be a positive sum in a pattern of high employment among the young and low employment among older age groups. To the extent that the economy loses the experience of older workers who in turn are reduced to lives of poverty, there is a negative sum. It is difficult to evaluate this complex question. Presumably, if economies are flexible and adaptable, there should be a premium on youth and recency of educational experience, leading one to reason that there will, in many fields, be gains from a more youthful workforce. It is extremely difficult to evaluate the quality of life of the early retired. Evaluating differences in women's participation requires even more complex judgements, as it involves evaluations of the relative values of different kinds of social order.

Overall we can conclude at this point that among the explanations of the apparently dramatic differences between US and Japanese employment rates on the one hand and European on the other are a greater proportion of part-time male work in the US (and certain European countries), probably concentrated mainly among the elderly and students, and therefore offering little guidance to employment opportunities for the core 15–64-year-old workforce. Among women these factors are also at work, but supplemented by the further differentiation which separates countries which have been strongly influenced by Catholic social policy from others.

These age questions raise a further issue. I commented above on the way in which the OECD perceives labor market segmentation only where it is introduced by state policy and not where it results from imperfect competition and monopsony or other factors not deriving from government action. This is a further example of the argument made above in connection with Danish and Japanese non-statutory regulation: the structures of social relationships can produce their own "rigidities", which are not produced by the state but which are not easily assimilated to the market either. In the student and elderly components of the labor market we have major examples of segmentation: neither of these forms of labor is generally available in the market, but eligible for and offering itself for very specific kinds of work.[10]

6.2.5. The Sectoral Distribution of Jobs and Job Growth

It is possible that both deregulationist and institutionalist theses have explanatory power in accounting for labor market developments, but are concerned with different kinds of employment. One basic way of assessing this possibility is to consider different patterns of employment and its growth in different sectors of the economy. The *Jobs Study* enables us to break down employment growth in different countries over the 1979–90 period according to a useful analysis of sectors.

From this it is clear that manufacturing has been in decline as a sector of employment, but it retains its central importance as the most heavily internationally traded sector and therefore one in which competitive pressures should be particularly strong. It is also one in which trade unions have had their main strength and where labor regulation originated and has been most important. The deregulationist hypothesis should therefore lead us to expect the superiority of the UK and the US, and possibly Japan, to show particularly effectively here, with the Nordic countries having the worst records. In fact, only Greece and Japan saw a net increase in manufacturing employment; the US was in mid-table among several European countries; and the UK had the worst record of all. With the exception of Norway, the Scandinavian countries were highly placed. Neither the deregulationist thesis *stricto sensu* nor the vulgarized form of it as "Japan and the US versus Europe" explains employment growth in this key sector. The relatively strong performance of some Scandinavians and the German economy is as anticipated by several forms of neo-institutionalist theory, which argue for the importance of organized industrial relations, strong mutual commitments between workforce and management and strong social infrastructure in sustaining high performance by the advanced countries in manufacturing. Institutionalists would also claim Japan to be an institutional economy in this sector.

Important for recent employment growth has been the commercial or trade sector (retail and wholesale sales). Here there is clear evidence of superior employment growth among the southern Europeans and the Anglo-Saxons. My characterization of the former as those in which regulation is often evaded in small enterprises and hence as low-regulation countries should be particularly important here, where much employment is in small firms. According to my grouping of countries, therefore, this pattern of growth is fully consistent with the deregulationist hypothesis. According to the OECD's ranking of the southern European countries as strictly regulated, however, the evidence is contradictory.

Overall, four sectors saw important job growth during the period covered by the OECD study: trade, finance and business services, private community and social services, and public services. Of these the one that best suits the deregulationist thesis is retail and wholesale trade. Finance and business services is the most strongly growing sector of all but very small. Private and public community and social services have both grown, but with opposite implications for deregulationist and neo-institutionalist theses. Manufacturing has not in general been a growing sector, but maintenance of it has been more compatible with the expectations of institutionalist hypotheses. On the other hand, another overall declining sector, personal services, has shown growth in some places in a manner strongly supportive of the deregulationist thesis.

The problem with considering growth patterns within a range of countries that includes, on the one hand, such old industrial nations as Germany, the UK and the US, and on the other, recent industrializers such as Greece and Portugal, is that historical modernization processes become caught up with changes taking place within already advanced economies.

To some extent, of course, this is not merely a methodological problem but a substantive issue: the fact that Greece is undergoing industrialization at a time when many countries have already been through that process means that Greek industrialization will never resemble that of, say, France or Sweden. We cannot here develop a model that addresses these complex processes, but we should, besides considering change flows, also consider the existing stock, that is consider the absolute sizes of the different sectors in different countries. By the early 1990s, how did national economies differ in their capacity to provide employment for their populations in different sectors of the economy, and to what extent are the patterns found compatible with the expectations of the deregulationist thesis?[11]

According to the deregulationist thesis and the regulatory ranking of countries by the OECD, we should find the US, Japan and the UK in the upper parts of most lists, although neo-institutionalists would claim that labor markets in the Japanese manufacturing sector are more accurately defined as institutional than as pure; and I would argue that southern European countries should not be regarded as highly regulated in all sectors where evasion of labor regulation should be possible (parts of all sectors except public services).

The US and Japan – although not the UK – occupy high positions in a number of sectors, but with contrasting distributions. Japan has the very highest level of manufacturing employment, among both genders, while the US has only moderate levels overall and among males one of the lowest. Japan is accompanied by the institutional economies of Austria, Germany and the Nordic countries (less Norway), although also by the UK, as a high-manufacturing employer. If a neo-institutionalist interpretation of Japanese employment in manufacturing is accepted, the institutional thesis rather than the free market one is sustained for this sector.

It is in distribution that Japan and the US share dominance, ahead of virtually all European countries; this is a sector within which Japan should be regarded as unregulated. The US also has a dominant position in financial and business services while Japan has a moderate one. Perhaps surprisingly, the US is a large employer of people in community and social services (public and private combined), although Japan scores low; Japan is moderate but the US low in personal services. The case for a joint Japan/US distinctiveness therefore lies essentially in the distributive sector. Japan's overall performance relies mainly on a combination of strengths in this and in manufacturing – a sector where the US is weak; US performance relies on distribution, financial services and, to some extent, community and social services – sectors where Japan is relatively weak. The UK shares profiles with the US only in financial and business services. It does share manufacturing dominance with Japan, but alongside two core continental cases; it is only a moderate employer in distribution and in community and social services, the other areas of US strength.

If we disaggregate by gender, by far the biggest source of diversity is in the proportion of women employed in community and social services, the extreme contrasts being between Scandinavia and the US on the one side and southern Europe and Japan on the other. The second and third biggest sources are males in the primary sector and manufacturing, but then follow both genders in distribution, with Japan and the US being major employers in both cases.

The relatively low level of female employment in community and social services in southern Europe deserves special comment. Given that this is primarily in the public sector it is likely that the low level is real and not the result of concealment of employment in the black economy. If this is a matter of job regulation, it is of a very particular kind, and could most easily be addressed by the development (whether public, charitable or market) of these services in those countries. Given that they can only be developed *en masse* in relatively poor countries where they are publicly provided, one might conclude that an expansion of the welfare state is needed to promote job growth rather than a reduction of employment protection.

6.4.   CONCLUSIONS: EMPLOYMENT AND GLOBALIZATION

We are left with the distributive sector as the most plausible embodiment of the deregulationist thesis. Japan and the US share a strong presence here (although so do some Scandinavians), and almost the entire case for a distinctive and shared US and Japanese employment performance rests on their overall employment levels (although not relative growth) in this sector. It is also a sector where the designation of Japan as unregulated is more convincing than in, say, manufacturing. Apart from some aspects of transport and communications,[12] this is not in general an internationally traded sector, which warns us of an important point: a separation between international competitive success and labor regulation, although these are often coupled in political rhetoric.

It is frequently argued that, unless the advanced countries deregulate their labor markets, they will lose out in competition with new producers in the newly industrializing countries. However, as we have seen above, it is in the main sector of international trade, manufacturing, that many countries with institutional labor markets have retained their prominence, more so than in low-regulation cases. The following logic seems to be in operation. In most advanced countries there have been strenuous attempts to raise productivity in the export and import substitution sectors; labor has been replaced by technology; low-skilled labor has been replaced by high-skilled; and inefficient producers have closed down. Niches have been found in globally competitive markets, not by reducing labor standards, but by improving productivity. This has often led to improved standards for those remaining in employment, but a large decline in their numbers. The competitive pressure from global competition has therefore fallen indirectly on those *forced out* of employment in the sectors directly engaged in the competition. Many of these have become unemployed; although the evidence is mixed, there are clear indications that *part* of the rise in unemployment in Europe and elsewhere has been the result of the new competition (Wood 1994, ch. 8). Many others, however, have found employment in services sectors not directly touched by global competition. The process has often been even more roundabout than this implies. Workers do not necessarily move from one sector to another; rather, one generation stays in the old sector while its sons and daughters find employment in the new; or the wives of men made redundant or taking early retirement find the new employment and thereby sustain the family's income.

The growth of non-traded services has not been *caused* by globalization. In many cases it has been fortuitous that employment opportunities have opened in these services at a time when employment was contracting in manufacturing; and many of the jobs created have been at high skill levels. In particular, what we have seen to be the biggest single component of the services sector – community and social services – employs proportionally more highly educated personnel than either manufacturing or the distributive and communications services which are closely allied to manufacturing (Crouch 1998, ch. 4). At least in most European countries, a majority of community and social services are either publicly or charitably provided, and employment of this type typically enjoys high levels of security. Nevertheless, public employment has not been free from the pressure of globalization. Since an important part of the cost advantage of third world producers and relatively low-cost advanced countries comprises the low taxes and social costs borne by businesses, many advanced countries have tried to improve their competitiveness by reducing their own social expenditure, which eventually has an impact on the employment conditions of public employees in social and community services. Governments have also used reductions in taxation (and therefore in expenditure) as indirect inducements to workers not to press for increased wages and thereby to constrain labor costs. Finally, the ability afforded by globalization to some firms to "regime shop" may involve governments in competitive reductions in taxation on business and managerial incomes, again with negative consequences for public employment. This can be seen in the evidence reviewed above of the recent collapse of employment in the Nordic countries following the introduction there of neo-liberal orthodoxy.

Increased productivity and intensified competition in manufacturing alongside this forced decline in public services are now leading to greater reliance being placed on other services sectors – distribution and communications, business services, and personal and domestic services – to provide employment opportunities. They have been doing so through a process of growth that initially had nothing to do with globalization but with changes in patterns of consumer demand, the implications of differential productivity rates in different sectors of the economy, and the tendency for manufacturing firms to contract out a range of service activities to firms in the business services sector. This process of job creation has been at varied skills levels: business services, like public services, have provided a large number of professional and managerial positions; the distributive sector has mainly contributed routine non-manual jobs; private services have provided some professional and routine non-manual, but also some unskilled manual employment (Crouch 1998). In all cases, again including the community and social services sector, most of the employment creation, especially at the lower levels of skill and earnings, has been taken up by women.

Globalization has been only indirectly involved in these main processes: it is only in so far as pressures to improve productivity (and therefore probably to reduce employment levels) are higher in internationally traded sectors which have become more competitive as a result of globalization than in protected sectors that it has been one among many general causes of the rise of the service sectors. There is, however, a more specific indirect contribution of globalization to certain kinds of employment growth which is more clearly an aspect of a decline in labor rights. This takes the following form. The decline in the demand for labor in manufacturing, created *partly* by globalization, leads to a rise in unemployment among low-skilled people. Employment can be created for them in labor-demanding, and therefore low-productivity, sectors only if they are inexpensive to employ. This requires not only low wages but also low indirect labor costs and low levels of security. It is this line of reasoning that has led the OECD and the consensus of economic experts to advocate a *general* deterioration in the regulation of labor markets.

No one expects the actual levels of security and employment terms of higher-paid employees to be adversely affected by the removal of legislated or bargained security arrangements; such employees would continue to benefit through labor market forces – one outcome of which is a segmentation of labor markets because, however much a nuisance OECD experts might find the fact, the labor market is an inherently "lumpy" one. The aim of the deregulation strategy is to produce more employment at the low end of the skill and income chain, simultaneously engineering a general shift in the character of security away from public policy and towards employer discretion as well as a major increase in social inequality.

In the course of this discussion we have found some evidence to confirm the OECD's account that the Japanese and US populations are more heavily engaged in economic activities than many of their European counterparts. We have, however, also found good reason for querying the simple argument that deregulation of the labor market is the main *explanandum* of a gap between Japan/US and Europe. First, we have disputed the bracketing of Japan and the US as two "deregulationist" cases set against a monolithic Europe. Instead we would identify a number of different labor market regimes, among which it is particularly important to distinguish between sectors and to separate Scandinavian and southern European patterns within Europe. Regarding the countries of southern Europe as the main exemplars of labor protection – an attribution necessary to the deregulation thesis – is also problematic on two grounds. First, there are legitimate doubts concerning the implementation of legislation there; and second, the forms of labor regulation and other social policy are more influenced by Social Catholic thought rather than the social democracy which is neo-liberals' prime political target.

The superior employment performance of the US, and of some European countries, can be explained largely by their particularly high incidences of part-time working, most interestingly *male* part-time working. There is also evidence that much of this is accounted for by work by students and elderly people. It is far less clear that there is any superiority in US employment among the core job-seeking 15–64-year-old population, at least the male proportion of which should be presumed to be seeking full-time work. There may or may not be reasons for seeking to encourage greater numbers of students and elderly people to be in paid employment. However, two points must be borne in mind. First, highly specific changes can be made to social policy and labor regulation provisions to encourage employment among these groups should such employment be deemed desirable. The OECD's arguments in favour of general rather than specific regulatory relaxation (or change) on the grounds that it is bad to encourage segmented labor forces fails when it is realized that the principal categories of employment likely to be encouraged by deregulation are themselves highly segmented categories.

Second, the sector which seems to be making by far the biggest contribution to US (and Japanese) employment superiority is the retail and wholesale trade sector, which in general provides low-productivity, relatively low-skilled and non-internationally traded services. The principal rivals to this for employment creation are publicly provided community and social services – which in fact have to be reduced if the deregulatory economy is to thrive. It needs to be demonstrated that there are overwhelming advantages in basing an economy on the former at the expense of the latter. By all means let countries try to increase financial and business services, and identify specific rigidities (such as employment-based taxes) which could be abolished. But we must avoid two other corollaries of the present ideological state: rejection of the public-service option, and an insistence on an over-generalized definition of (and consequently over-generalized attack on) labor market protection.

In its discussions of wage determination, the OECD takes seriously the evidence of Calmfors and Driffill (1988) and other observers that counter-inflationary wage behaviour is likely to be found at two extreme ends of a continuum: completely centralized or coordinated bargaining, or complete market determination (OECD 1994b; pp. 20–22). It argues, with good grounds, that the ideal of *complete* centralization is unlikely to be achieved in future, even if it possibly had been in some countries in the past. Continuing the logic of the U-curve argument it points out: "a near-complete centralisation arguably aggravates any tendencies for wage-wage spirals as rival union blocks attempt to show their relative merit in achieving wage increases" (ibid., p. 22). Since near complete systems are more likely than complete ones, it concludes that it would be best to move entirely away from that kind of model, and therefore advocates complete decentralization – ideally movement to the extreme pure market pole.

However, the Organization does not face up to the fact that complete pure markets in labor will also be impossible to achieve, and that decentralized systems will be near decentralized just as centralized systems turn out to be near centralized, which former the logic of the U-curve would suggest will be as deficient as the latter. While the OECD does not recognize this problem explicitly, it seems to do so tacitly by stressing the need to bolster decentralized systems with "credible non-accommodating macroeconomic policy ... [and] enterprises ... subject to the full rigor of market discipline". Near-centralized systems are not seen as being eligible to remedy their weaknesses with this kind of additional support, even though a combination of this kind characterized German and Scandinavian industrial relations systems at various points of the postwar period (Crouch 1994; Streeck 1994). The OECD, as ever, forgets the market discipline wrought by constant exposure to foreign competition experienced by certain European as opposed to US industries.

The search for the total automaticity of the perfect market in place of the difficulty of managing modern economic systems accounts for much of the attraction of neo-liberal remedies for political parties of all colours at the present time. If awkward issues such as wage determination and working conditions could be put on the automatic pilot of the market, policy-making would be so much simpler. If, however, the perfect market is as unattainable as perfect centralization, and we are forced permanently to exist in the uncomfortable bend of the U-curve, then the policy remedy simply to get as close to the perfect market extreme as possible may be taking us in a hopeless direction; and indeed, if the *Job Study*'s own discussions of training are to be credited, considerable damage may well be done to important institutions in the process. Rather, policy should be concerned with ways of managing the problems of being trapped in the U-curve – just as the OECD itself acknowledges when it commends the support of non-accommodating monetary policy. If governments are considered to have the capacity to run policies of that kind, they can also manage policies that can impose tough constraints on the behaviour of institutional market actors rather than seeking to abolish the capacity of those actors.

NOTES

1   For example, the Japanese case is cited as suggesting that investment in training and stability of employment, including low job turnover, may be mutually reinforcing (OECD 1994b, pp.122, 123), while the rest of the *Study* encourages instability of employment. The training discussion also points out that the countries which secure the highest education enrolment rates among young people after the compulsory school-leaving age are those where vocational education is highly organized, with clearly defined and collectively organized and accepted responsibilities (p.130); but the rest of the *Study* seeks to undermine all forms of supportive organization in the labor market above the level of the enterprise. The training discussion is also aware of high youth unemployment in North America, caused partly by the need for so much trial and error in finding suitable work (p. 140), and attributes this in part to the absence of certification of skills in the US (p. 144). But this is itself a consequence of the autonomy of enterprises and absence of either public regulation or strong employers' organizations – essential characteristics of what the *Jobs Study* otherwise finds so praiseworthy about the US economy. The training discussion might also have noted that this frequent trial and error of young people's labor market experience, which it sees as unfortunate, accounts for at least part of the high number of people leaving jobs within a year in the US – a phenomenon which in general, as will be seen below, the *Study* praises as evidence of labor market flexibility.

2   Even when a US industry is heavily engaged in international trade, the sheer size of the US economy is likely to make that industry a global price leader in a way rarely open to European producers. Of course, the argument here assumes that the economies concerned are not protectionist. For nearly all the postwar period this condition has more or less obtained for the German and Scandinavian economies at the heart of the argument.

3   Indeed, the world's primary case of an institutional economy (including labor markets), that of Japan, is one in which social democracy has been weak.

4   This did change in the mid-1990s, as did the position in some other countries.

5   Particular use is made of a ranking devised by Bertola (1990). This author had developed a single scale of level of restrictiveness based on a purely qualitative discussion of different components of labor market regulation by Emerson (1988). Emerson had in fact stressed the complex diversity of labor market regimes, drawing attention for example to the role of private litigation in establishing employment rights in the US where statute was perhaps more likely to be used in many European countries. Most of his data used sources from the mid 1980s and therefore, like the IOE study of 1987, cannot take account of the differential

progress of deregulatory policy in various European countries during the late 1980s.

6   An interesting example of this phenomenon from a different field from the labor market is the frequent perplexity of western economists and governments at the difficulty of selling goods to Japan. It is assumed that somehow this must be the result of something that the Japanese government does; the idea that Japanese consumers might have an extensive and collective aversion for imported goods is regarded as inconceivable.

7   It is true that in some countries, including France and Spain, there are legal measures for extending the scope of contracts to non-union firms. However, that cannot compensate for weakness of bargaining power produced by unions' poor membership levels (and therefore such resources as strike pay) in the first place.

8   See King (1995) for a detailed study of the changes over time and the highly political character of policy on benefit entitlement in the UK and the US.

9   It may well be that the Greek Orthodox Church has had similar implications for Greece, but in the absence of other Greek Orthodox cases we shall have to set that country aside.

10   It could in fact be argued that youth and old age are, in part, segmentations produced by government. In all advanced countries various stages of youth are statutorily defined through requirements to attend school and protection of people under certain ages from various activities. In many countries old age is also defined by eligibility rules for state pensions.

11   The figures on which this discussion is based are available from the author.

12   It must be remembered that we are here interested in labor markets rather than capital ownership. If, say, a US firm owns a telecommunications network in the UK, this counts for our purposes as UK employment, not a US export.

REFERENCES

Bertola, G. (1990), "Job security, employment and wages", *European Economic Review*, **34**, 851–86.

Blossfeld, H., and Hakim, C. (1997), "Between Equalization and Marginalization: Women Working Part-time in Europe and the United States of America", Oxford: Oxford University Press

Calmfors, L. and J, Driffill (1988), "Bargaining structure, corporatism and macro-economic performance", *Economic Policy*, **6**.

Crouch, C. (1990), "Trade unions in the exposed sector: their influence on neo-corporatist behaviour", in R. Brunetta and C. Dell'Aringa (eds), *Labor Relations and Economic Performance*, London: Macmillan and International Economics Association.

Crouch, C. (1994), "Incomes policies, institutions and markets: an overview of recent developments", in R. Dore, R. Boyer and Z. Mars (eds), *The Return to Incomes Policy*, London: Pinter.

Crouch, C. (1998), *Western European Societies: Social Change in Contemporary Europe in a Global Context*, Oxford: Oxford University Press.

Due, J., J.S. Madsen and J.C. Strøby (1994), *The Survival of the Danish Model*, Copenhagen: DJØF.

Emerson, M. (1988), "Regulation or deregulation of the labor market?", *European Economic Review*, **32**, 775–817.

Esping-Andersen, G. (1996), "After the Golden Age? Welfare state dilemmas in a global economy", in G. Esping-Andersen (ed.), *Welfare States in Transition: National Adaptations in Global Economies,* London: Sage.

King, D. (1995), *Actively Seeking Work*, Chicago: University of Chicago Press.

Organization for Economic Cooperation and Development (1993), *Employment Outlook, July 1993*, Paris: OECD.

Organization for Economic Cooperation and Development (1994a), *The OECD Jobs Study: Evidence and Explanations. Part I – Labor Market Trends and Underlying Forces of Change*, Paris: OECD.

Organization for Economic Cooperation and Development (1994b), *The OECD Jobs Study: Evidence and Explanations. Part II – The Adjustment Potential of the Labor Market*, Paris: OECD.

Organization for Economic Cooperation and Development (1994c), *Employment Outlook, July 1994*, Paris: OECD.

Organization for Economic Cooperation and Development (1995), *Employment Outlook, July 1995*, Paris: OECD.

Organization for Economic Cooperation and Development (1996), *Employment Outlook, July 1996*, Paris: OECD.

Organization for Economic Cooperation and Development (19967), *Employment Outlook, July 1997*, Paris: OECD.Singelmann, J. (1978), *From Agriculture to Services: The Transformation of Industrial Employment*, Beverly Hills: Sage.

Streeck, W. (1994), "Pay restraint without incomes policy: institutionalized monetarism and industrial unionism in Germany", in R. Dore, R. Boyer and Z. Mars (eds), *The Return to Incomes Policy*, London: Pinter.

Wood, A. 1994, *North–South Trade, Employment and Inequality: Changing Fortunes in a Skill-Driven World*, Oxford: Clarendon Press

7.   Multinationals, "relocation", and employment in Europe

Anthony Ferner*

7.1.   SUMMARY

Multinational corporations employ millions of people in Europe, and over 70 million worldwide. Through their role in foreign direct investment (FDI) and international trade, they are the motors of the "globalization" of the international economy. This chapter considers their impact on employment in Europe.

In recent years, an old debate, on the "relocation" of production to low-cost economies, has resurfaced with renewed vigour in France, Germany, and elsewhere. The reasons for this re-emergence are explored, in particular two interlinked factors: the growing international coordination and integration of productive activities within multinationals, and the rapid integration into the world economy of huge new markets in central and eastern Europe and in Asia.

The chapter uses both quantitative data and recent prominent cases of relocation to analyse the forms and extent of relocation, both between Europe and the developing world, and within Europe itself. It argues that in some respects, the scale of the problem has been exaggerated. Many activities are not susceptible to relocation, FDI to lower cost countries is often driven by a "market-seeking" rather than "efficiency-seeking" rationale, and outward investment often appears to have a net employment-generating effect in home economies through the export of capital goods, knowledge-intensive components, and professional and managerial skills.

None the less, there are a number of worrying aspects: the rise of low-labor-cost areas on the European Union's eastern borders; the expanding range of economic activities which may be "spun off" from other productive processes and moved to remote locations; the increasing competition from countries such as India in high-skill, even "leading edge", sectors such as computer software. More generally, while economists may argue that in the long run "efficiency seeking" by multinationals helps raise efficiency and competitiveness, and hence employment, in home countries, relocation generates massive social consequences in the short run.

Relocation is not just a threat between Europe and the developing world, but within Europe itself, where the single market has prompted concerns about "regime competition" and "social dumping". The redistribution of employment by multinationals between countries may not affect aggregate employment levels in Europe; but it certainly matters if it leads to the same number of people being employed on worse pay and lower security.

The chapter concludes by briefly examining some European employment policy questions posed by international relocation. Can government attempts to reduce the cost of labor be a viable strategy for stemming the loss of jobs to South-East Asia and elsewhere? What role can be played by international clauses on labor standards? How can the European Union avoid a competitive bidding down of pay and conditions of employment, and the deleterious employment effects of "grant-chasing" by multinationals? Finally, can collective action by unions and workforces at national and international level help regulate the impact of multinationals on employment levels and stability?

7.2.   INTRODUCTION

At a time of chronic and worsening unemployment in much of Europe, the ability of multinational companies (MNCs) to generate – or destroy – jobs in both host and home countries has been the subject of sometimes heated debate. The problem was highlighted by the dramatic announcement in February 1997 of the closure of the Renault plant at Vilvoorde near Brussels, with the loss of more than 3,000 jobs, and by ABB's plan published in June 1997 to relocate 20–30,000 jobs in western Europe to eastern Europe and Asia. In France, argument has raged over *délocalisation* – the replacement of domestic production by operations in low-labor-cost regions; in Germany, the *Standort* debate has asked whether high wages and high levels of labor market regulation are deterring inward investment and speeding the flight of German capital to more "favourable" destinations.

This chapter is an attempt to clarify some of the issues concerning MNCs and employment. It considers the relocation debate in some detail. One of the key threads running through the chapter is the competitiveness of national "labor regimes", since this has been at the centre of debates on the relocation of investment. Is the fate of high-wage societies with high levels of labor protection inevitably to lose employment to low-wage economies? Can they only avoid such a fate by adopting the unpalatable alternative of drastically lowering their own labor standards?

The argument begins with a brief overview of the scale of employment in MNCs. Second, it suggests that the current concern with MNC relocation and employment reflects three interrelated developments in the world economy: the emergence of large new economic areas that are being progressively incorporated into the world economy; structural changes in transnational corporate organization as MNCs' operations are increasingly integrated across national borders; and technological innovation and the associated changes in productive structures. Third, it examines the *délocalisation* debate, and assesses the evidence for the claims being made. While questioning whether the export of jobs to countries with low wages and low labor standards is as much of a threat as has been presented, it pinpoints particular areas of concern in relation to "social dumping", and in relation to the growth of high-skill sectors in low-wage economies. Finally, the chapter looks at some of the policy implications for European countries and for the European Union (EU) itself.

7.3.   MNCS AND EMPLOYMENT: AN OVERVIEW

MNCs are key actors in the world economy, the driving forces behind the processes of "globalization" of production. The sheer size of their operations is striking. In 1995 the stock of outward and inward investment both amounted to roughly $2,700 billion;[1] the EU countries accounted for 44 per cent of outward and 39 per cent of inward stocks. Annual flows of foreign direct investment (FDI), both inward and outward, were running at more than $300 billion in 1995 (UNCTAD 1996, pp. 4–5). MNCs generate a high proportion of world production and international trade. The global sales of foreign affiliates reached $6,000 billion in 1993 (pp.16–17), and about a quarter of exports of goods and services worldwide were intra-firm.

MNCs are also major employers of labor on a global scale: UNCTAD estimates that some 73 million were employed by all MNCs in 1993, of which about 29 million worked in foreign affiliates; the top 100 MNCs (ranked by foreign assets) employed about 12 million, of whom 5 million (42 per cent) worked outside the home country (1994, p. 29).[2] Table 7.1 ranks these top 100 MNCs according to the size of their foreign workforce, and to the percentage of their workforce abroad. The top eleven companies all employ more than 100,000 in their foreign operations. (Table 7.2 gives examples of further important European MNCs not included in the UNCTAD list.)

The share of MNCs in employment varies significantly from country to country within the EU, both in terms of outgoing and inward investment. Thus in Ireland, Spain and Belgium, foreign MNCs are responsible for an above-average proportion of employment. In Ireland, the share of foreign

Table 7.1
UNCTAD Top 100 MNCs by assets
ranked by foreign employment, 1994

Company	Country/ Sector	Total employment	Foreign employment	Foreign emp as % of total
Unilever	UK-NL/food	307,000	276,000	90.0
Philips Electronics	NL/electronics	253,000	210,000	83.0
Nestlé	CH/food	212,687	206,125	96.9
ABB	CH-S/elec eqpt	207,557	194,557	93.7
GM	US/vehicles	692,800	177,730	25.7
BAT	UK/tobacco	173,475	158,205	91.2
Siemens	D/electronics	376,000	158,000	42.0
Pepsico	US/food	471,000	140,170	29.8
Alcatel Alsthom	F/electronics	197,000	117,000	59.7
IBM	US/comput	219,839	115,555	52.6
Matsushita Elec.	J/electronics	265,397	112,314	42.3
Ford	US/vehicles	337,778	96,726	28.6
VW	D/cars	242,318	96,545	39.8
Fiat	I/vehicles	251,333	95,930	38.2
United Technologies	US/aerospace	171,500	95,600	55.7
Electrolux	S/electronics	114,103	94,469	82.8
Hoechst	D/chem	165,671	92,333	55.7
Sony	J/electronics	156,000	90,000	57.7
Philip Morris	US/food & tob	165,000	85,000	51.5
Sara Lee	US/food	145,874	84,932	58.2
Hitachi	J/electronics	331,852	80,000	24.1
Daimler–Benz	D/trnsprt & commun.	330,551	79,267	24.0
Royal Dutch Shell	NL/oil	106,000	79,000	74.5
Bayer	D/chem/pharm	146,700	78,300	53.4
Ciba–Geigy	CH/chem	83,980	63,095	75.1
Robert Bosch	D/vehicle parts	153,794	62,343	40.5
Motorola Inc	US/electronics	132,500	58,900	44.5
Saint-Gobain	F/building mtl	80,909	58,364	72.1
Hanson	UK/diversified	74,000	58,000	78.4
Procter & Gamble	US/soaps, cosmetics	96,500	57,500	59.6
Thomson	F/electronics	98,714	57,148	57.8
Exxon	US/oil	86,000	55,000	64.0
Bridgestone	J/rubber	89,711	52,000	58.0
Akzo	NL/chem	70,400	51,700	73.4
Sandoz	CH/pharma	60,304	51,258	85.0
Roche	CH/pharma	61,381	50,869	82.9
BMW	D/vehicles	109,362	50,474	46.2
BP	UK/oil	66,550	48,650	73.1
Rhône–Poulenc	F/chem	81,582	46,430	56.9
Carrefour	F/distribution	90,300	44,200	49.0
Elf Aquitaine	F/oil	86,500	43,950	50.8
Digital Equipment	US/computers	82,800	43,598	52.7
RTZ	UK/mining	44,499	43,112	96.9
Thomson Corp	Can/publishing	48,600	43,100	88.7
Johnson & Johnson	US/pharma	81,537	42,374	52.0
Eastman Kodak	US/sci & photo eqpt	96,300	42,000	43.6
VIAG	D/diversified	86,018	41,288	48.0

Company	Country/ Sector	Total employment	Foreign employment	Foreign emp as % of total
Mannesmann	D/industrial eqpt	124,914	40,487	32.4
BASF	D/chem	106,266	40,297	37.9
Renault	F/vehicles	132,879	39,982	30.1
Hewlett–Packard	US/computers	98,400	39,435	40.1
Toshiba	J/electronics	190,000	38,000	20.0
Gen Electric	US/electronics	216,000	36,169	16.8
Solvay	Bel/chem	39,874	35,695	89.5
Glaxo Wellcome	UK/pharma	47,378	35,523	75.0
Canon	J/computers	72,280	35,101	48.6
Du Pont	US/chemicals	107,000	35,000	32.7
Nissan	J/vehicles	143,310	34,464	24.1
RJR Nabisco	US/food & tob	70,600	33,950	48.1
Pechiney	F/metals	58,234	33,800	58.0
AT&T	US/telecomms	304,500	32,820	10.8
Minnesota Mining	US/mining	69,843	32,581	46.7
Xerox	US/sci & photo eqpt	87,600	32,150	36.7
Alcoa	US/metals	61,700	31,400	50.9
Cable & Wireless	UK/telecomms	41,348	31,128	75.3
Volvo	S/vehicles	75,549	30,664	40.6
Total	F/oil	51,803	29,340	56.6
Sharp	J/electronics	42,853	29,000	67.7
Alcan	Can/metal prods	39,000	28,000	71.8
Toyota	J/cars	172,675	27,567	16.0
Mobil	US/oil	58,500	27,400	46.8
GrandMet	UK/food	64,300	27,006	42.0
Dow Chemical	US/chem	53,700	24,165	45.0
Chrysler	US/vehicles	121,000	24,000	19.8
Veba	D/trading	126,875	23,894	18.8
Mitsui	J/diversified	80,000	23,560	29.3
ITT	US/div. services	110,000	23,366	21.2
International Paper	US/paper	70,000	20,500	29.3
Honda	J/vehicles	92,800	19,668	21.2
ENI	I/oil	91,544	19,527	21.3
NEC Corp	J/electronics	151,069	17,569	11.6
Norsk Hydro	N/chem	32,416	16,208	50.0
Nippon Steel	J/steel	50,438	15,000	29.7
GTE	US/telecomms	111,000	14,793	13.3
BHP	Australia/metals	48,000	12,000	25.0
LVMH Moet-Hennessy	F/beverages	18,779	11,737	62.5
Mitsubishi	J/diversified	36,000	11,146	31.0
Texaco	US/oil	29,713	10,640	35.8
Chevron	US/oil	45,758	10,636	23.2
Amoco	US/oil	43,205	7,541	17.5
Kobe Steel	J/steel	32,485	5,522	17.0
Atlantic Richfield	US/oil refining	23,200	4,631	20.0
Total		**12,189,889**	**5,332,173**	

Note: A few companies in UNCTAD's list are omitted because of incomplete data.
Source: Calculated from UNCTAD (1996, Table I.12, pp. 30–32).

Table 7.2
Employment in selected French, British and German MNCs not in UNCTAD list,
1995–1996, ranked by foreign employment

Company	Country/ Sector	Total employment	Foreign employment	Foreign emp as % of total
BTR	UK/ diversified mfg	152,000	111,000	73
Cie Générale des Eaux	F/water utility, diversified services	221,000	71,000	32
Lyonnaise des Eaux	F/water utility	120,000	51,000	42
Schneider	F/diversified	93,000	48,000	52
Danone	F/food	74,000	47,000	64
Smithkline Beecham	UK/pharma	52,000	44,000	84
Coats Viyella	UK/textiles	60,000	40,000	66
GEC	UK/electrical electronics	83,000	37,000	45
Bouygues	F/construction	92,000	35,000	38
Thyssen	D/metals	123,000	30,000	24
Cadbury Schweppes	UK/food	42,000	28,000	66
BET	UK/diversified holding	101,000	27,000	27
Henkel	D/chem	42,000	27,000	64
MAN	D/industrial equipt	58,000	12,000	21
Continental	D/rubber	46,000	12,000	26

Source: Ferner and Quintanilla (1997) (from worldwide web, annual reports and accounts).

companies in total manufacturing employment was more than 45 per cent in 1995 (up from about 34 per cent in 1975); in sectors such as textiles, chemicals, and metals and engineering, it is far higher (Ruane and Görg 1997, pp. 77, 79–80). The UK, Germany and France are the major EU home countries for MNCs. As Table 7.3 shows, home-country MNCs are responsible for significant proportions of domestic employment. The aggregate *foreign* employment of the MNCs of the US, Japan, France, Germany, the UK and the Netherlands in each case exceeds one million.

Finally, the impact of MNCs on employment varies widely from sector to sector (Dunning 1993, p. 356). In chemicals, motor vehicles, electronics and rubber, employment is dominated by MNCs, both domestic and foreign. Moreover, manufacturing is generally more labor-intensive than services, as reflected in the fact that it commonly accounts for a much greater proportion of foreign employment than of FDI stock. For example, in 1991 outward FDI by German MNCs in manufacturing accounted for 52 per cent of FDI stock but 70 per cent of employment in foreign subsidiaries of German firms; the tendency was even more evident for US and Japanese MNCs. For the service sector, the discrepancy was reversed: for German MNCs, services represented 46 per cent of FDI stock but only 30 per cent of total employment (despite the labor intensity of important service industries such as distribution) (UNCTAD 1994, p. 181). The shift in the pattern of FDI from manufacturing (and the primary sector) towards services has therefore been an important factor in the relatively slow growth of employment in MNCs (see Table 7.4). Despite the internationalization of labor-intensive services such as distribution, hotels, contract catering and cleaning services in recent years, in general, FDI has taken place in less-labor-intensive areas such as privatized utilities (water, tele-communications, electricity) and in financial services (banking and insurance) (ibid. 1994, pp.177–81).

Table 7.3
Employment in MNCs by country (000s)

Country	Year	Worldwide employment in home-country MNCs	Employment in affiliates abroad	Employment in foreign affiliates (%)	Employees in foreign MNC affiliates in country
France	1990	3,680[a]	2,100	57	773[b]
Germany	1989/1990	4,459[c]	2,337	52	1,789
Italy	1987	1,110	511	46	506[b]
Japan	1989	4,064	1,550	38	182
Netherlands	1981	1,454	1,071	74	196[b]
Sweden	1991	1,110	590	53	206
Switzerland	1988	1,095	779	71	130
UK	1981	5,484	1,390	25	775[b]
US	1991	24,909	6,833	27	4,809

Notes: a sample of 100 companies
        b manufacturing only
        c sample of 87 companies
Source: UNCTAD (1994, Table IV.4, p. 179).

Table 7.4
Employment in MNCs by home country and foreign affiliates

	1985	1990	1992
Total employment in MNCs	65	70	73
Employment in parent companies at home	43	44	44
Employment in foreign affiliates	22	26	29
developed countries	15	17	17
developing countries	7	9	12
China	–	3	6

Source: UNCTAD (1994, Table IV.3, p. 175).

7.3.   *DÉLOCALISATION* AND EMPLOYMENT IN EUROPE

The problem of "relocation" – the loss of productive activities to countries with lower wages and more accommodating labor regulation – has in recent years become one of the most emotive areas of debate on MNCs and employment in Europe. The issue is not new. In the 1970s, the proponents of the thesis of the "new international division of labor" pointed out that stagnation and unemployment in the economies of the developed world went hand in hand with rising FDI to developing countries. The study by Fröbel et al. (1980) of German direct investment abroad suggested that many companies were being forced to relocate abroad to stay competitive. This reflected massive differences in labor costs between Germany and FDI locations in developing countries, combined with the development of efficient international transport and communications systems. The haemorrhage of German jobs was particularly strong in the textile and clothing industries, which were characterized by relatively high labor costs and a low proportion of skilled workers. The bulk of the relocated production was what Fröbel et al. called "pure relocation", that is, it was intended to serve the German domestic market through imports.

7.3.1.   The Reemergence of the Relocation Debate

Why has relocation once again become such a burning issue, a decade and more after the earlier debate? There appear to be two major – and interconnected – factors. One is a set of structural changes in the way in which MNCs operate in the international economy, and in particular the growth of internationally integrated industries. The second is the changing nature of world markets. Each is considered in turn.

The "internationalization" of MNCs: from "stand alone" to "international integration"

The stereotypical "traditional" MNC was a company that operated through relatively autonomous country subsidiaries. These served differentiated national markets, and there was little need to coordinate operations transnationally. The growing integration of markets, coupled with advances in transport and in the technology of production and of management control (in particular, the use of information technology together with telecommunications), have encouraged the international coordination and integration of production as well as of research and development, product design, investment financing, inventory management, marketing and distribution systems. Most crucially, technology permits the location of a growing range of activities and tasks remote from the point of delivery or consumption (compare Arthuis 1993).

Increasingly, production facilities in one country may form an integral part of an international productive network, supplying parts, for example, for downstream operations in another country. The car industry is probably the classic exemplar of this process. Within Europe, the completion of the single market project and the elimination of non-tariff barriers to trade make it possible to extend the separation of production and consumption, allowing, say, the German market to be supplied from France. Production no longer needs to be replicated in different locations but may be rationalized and consolidated. Many major European MNCs have as a result embarked on a process of international restructuring to gain the benefits of more integrated and coordinated operations. In sectors such as motor vehicle manufacturing, these developments also have a knock-on effect on major suppliers who are themselves relocating in order to be close to the "original equipment manufacturers", particularly as the spread of just-in-time production methods makes physical proximity imperative.

These developments have made for links of increasing complexity between parent companies and their operations abroad. One tendency has been the emergence within MNCs of the international business division: that is, an organizational structure with overall responsibility for the design, manufacture, marketing and sales of defined groups of products internationally – either worldwide or on a regional, for example, pan-European, basis (Marginson and Sisson 1994). In a number of cases, the headquarters of business divisions may be located outside the MNC's country of origin. Other manifestations of increasing international integration are the formation of dense cross-border networks of supplier firms, the upsurge in strategic alliances and joint ventures, and the successive waves of cross-border mergers and acquisitions (M&As) of the past decade, with peaks in the late 1980s and mid-1990s (see UNCTAD 1996, pp. 7–15).

Such international integration, driven by the pursuit of efficiency gains, is likely to lead to rationalization and cuts in employment. When newly acquired companies, for example, are integrated into existing structures, duplications are eliminated and the workforce is likely to be reduced. The extent of such international rationalization is hard to quantify, but UNCTAD notes that it may help explain the much slower rise in total MNC employment in comparison with the increase in total FDI (1994, p. 174). A sample of more than 300 leading manufacturing MNCs followed by UNCTAD (p. 176) showed a level of direct employment that was slightly lower at the end of the 1980s than at the beginning, following sharp reductions in the first half of the decade; the effect was particularly marked for British and US MNCs, which were in the vanguard of the trend to international rationalization.

An important area of research has focused on opening the "black box" of the firm to understand the implications of this internationalization for internal control processes within MNCs. As Marginson and Sisson (1994, pp. 23–4) argue,

> As the information-processing capacities of company and divisional headquarters have been steadily enhanced, mainly by developments in computer technology and communications systems, intensive monitoring of a range of financial and other performance indicators has become increasingly possible. Corporate offices now routinely monitor data on labor performance, such as unit labor costs, productivity, conflict and numbers employed...

These processes (see also Marginson et al. 1993) facilitate the rationalization of operations between countries, allowing firms to shift production and investment, and hence employment, to those locations where they may be carried out most efficiently.

Recent studies show how companies use sophisticated management information to "reward" or "punish" individual sites by granting or withholding new investment. Under what Mueller (1996) calls "corporate investment bargaining", "plants are under continuous threat that some of their production will be transferred to a competing sister plant at home or abroad" (p. 348).

Many companies have used the *threat* of transfer of investment or production as a lever to improve productivity and efficiency by forcing through changes to work organization, working practices and employment levels. In this way, they are able to bring weakly performing plants up to standards of international 'best practice" (for example Coller 1996), based on what happens in the most advanced plants. Companies then introduce further innovations which are propagated in their turn, in a constantly iterated cycle. Such "coercive comparisons" between plants (Mueller and Purcell 1992) are particularly used in industries where similar or identical plants operate in different countries: a typical case is the motor vehicle industry (for example Martínez and Weston 1995). Both the Ford Halewood and the Renault Vilvoorde cases (discussed in more detail below) rested partly on discussions about relative levels of unit labor costs in different plants.

As Mueller (1996, p. 352) argues, once a company has relocated a part of its operations abroad, its bargaining hand with domestic employees is considerably strengthened, since the threat of relocation cannot so easily be dismissed as bluff. He cites the decision of Daimler–Benz to locate a plant in the US, and Siemens' construction of a new semiconductor plant in the north east of England – "a signal to German stakeholders (including employees) not to take future investment for granted" (p. 354).

In summary, therefore, companies can increasingly engage in rolling programmes of concession bargaining with their employees in different countries, using threats of disinvestment to increase efficiency, then propagating the new "best practice" throughout their operations. If, for whatever reason, workforces are unable to make the adjustments demanded of them, then firms' ability to "scan the horizon" of their activities and compare them accurately across countries is one of the key internal mechanisms permitting firms to make decisions on transnational relocation.

The integration of world markets

The second factor behind the re-emergence of the relocation debate is the increasing integration of world markets. A critical aspect of this is the massive integration of low-wage economies into the global capitalist system in a relatively compressed period of time. Schwab and Smadja (1994) observe that the world market has been transformed dramatically by the sudden entry of about 2.5 billion people. The collapse of communism brought the countries of central and eastern Europe into the world market, and hastened the liberalization of the Chinese economy. Elsewhere, with India being a notable example, the vogue for liberalization has fairly recently encouraged much more positive host-country attitudes towards foreign investment. The upshot has been fierce competition for FDI among countries previously hostile to it.

A second aspect of international market integration is the consolidation of regional common markets, of which the EU and the North America Free Trade Agreement (NAFTA) are the most prominent. Within Europe itself, European integration and the completion of the single market has stimulated the relocation debate. The removal of non-tariff barriers (for example restrictive public procurement rules, incompatible technical standards, constraints on capital markets) allows firms to produce in the lowest-cost locations within the EU (Pain 1996).

7.3.2.   The Relocation Debate: *Délocalisation* and *Standort Deutschland*

In the 1990s, the relocation debate has been particularly sharp in Germany and France. In the former country, analysts have agonized over the prospects of *Standort Deutschland* – Germany's position as a location for investment, particularly in manufacturing. In the period 1991–95, FDI inflows into Germany averaged less than $4 billion a year (compared with more than $17 billion into the UK and $19 billion into France); German FDI outflows were about seven times greater than inflows over the same period, and roughly double their level in the previous five-year period (Barrell and Pain 1997, p. 65). For many, this rapidly accelerating outflow of capital (and the low levels of inward investment) reflect a flight from high-wage costs, labor market rigidity, excessive bureaucracy, tight environmental regulation and burdensome corporate tax regimes. In May 1997, for example, the chair of Robert Bosch, one of Germany's leading international companies, warned that union demands for a shorter working week were endangering the competitiveness of German companies and discouraging foreign investors: "components or tools which we can no longer produce in Germany at competitive prices because of high labor costs, we shall increasingly have to manufacture in more favourable cost conditions abroad" (*Financial Times*, 16 May 1997). In 1997, for the first time ever, Bosch employed more workers abroad than in Germany.

A critical factor in the German debate has been the sudden emergence of a large pool of cheap, but relatively well qualified, labor on Germany's eastern borders, particularly in Hungary, the Czech Republic and Poland. German investment in central and eastern Europe rose from a negligible amount in the 1980s to nearly 8 per cent of its total outward FDI in 1991–94 (Agarwal 1997, p. 101).

In France, the debate was triggered by the report of a Senate working group chaired by Jean Arthuis, subsequently economics minister (see Arthuis 1993). In a context of prolonged high unemployment – currently about 12 per cent – Arthuis claimed that more than a million French jobs were threatened by *délocalisation*. Under increasing competitive pressures to reduce costs, firms looked to transfer production to lower-cost countries, a process facilitated by technological developments which increasingly allow individual production processes, or functions such as maintenance or data processing, to be physically separated from other operations. Relocation might take the form of either direct investment by MNCs, or the hiving-off of activities to subcontractors. Potential new sites were becoming available for relocation as large areas – central and eastern Europe, China – opened up to FDI. The industries most affected by relocation, notably electronics, textiles, clothing and footwear, had had their employees in France cut by half over the previous decade. Companies such as Thomson Consumer Electronics now employs three times as many people in Asia as in France (Woodall 1994). Arthuis went on to advocate a series of protective measures at both French national and European levels, and proposed more stringent rules governing international trade in order to deter relocations to low-cost countries, including a selective increase in customs duties in the sectors most affected.

7.3.3. Relocation, Labor Costs, and Labor Market Flexibility

The debates on relocation vary in their analyses, but a common factor is the key role ascribed to labor costs and to labor market rigidities in driving companies to move their operations abroad.

Labor costs

US Department of Labor figures show huge disparities in hourly compensation costs between the developed and developing worlds (see Table 7.5a). In the textile industry, hourly labor costs in 1995 were about $24 in Germany, $12 in the US and the UK, $2–3 in Hungary and Poland, and $0.5 in China (*Financial Times*, 21 September 1996). Even within

Europe, relatively wide differences remain (Table 7.5b). Significantly, Renault management cited high Belgian labor costs – 25–30 per cent above those in France – as a major factor in the controversial decision to move production from Vilvoorde (*Financial Times*, 7 March 1997).

Table 7.5a Wage costs per hour in developed and developing countries, 1985 and 1994 (US$)		
Country	**1985**	**1994**
West Germany	9.6	27.3
Switzerland	9.7	24.8
Japan	6.3	21.4
Netherlands	8.8	20.9
EU	8.1	19.7
US	13.0	17.1
France	7.5	17.0
Italy	7.6	16.2
UK	6.3	13.6
Spain	4.7	11.5
Asian NIEs		5.8
Mexico		2.6

Source: US Department of Labor, World Competitiveness Report, May 1995.

Table 7.5b Wage costs per hour in European Union countries, 1995	
Country	**US$ per hour**
Germany	31
Belgium	26
Austria	25
Denmark	24
Netherlands	24
Sweden	21
France	20
Italy	16
Ireland	14
UK	14
Spain	13
Greece	8
Portugal	5

Source: Agarwal (1997, p. 103).

The key variable, of course, is the level of unit labor costs rather than wages *per se*, that is the cost of labor taking into account productivity. It is clear that differences in wage rates around the world are not due merely to differences in productivity. Erickson and Kuruvilla (1995) show that even in western Europe, there are considerable differences in unit labor costs that would provide an incentive for the movement of capital in search of lower costs. Differences between western and central/eastern Europe are even more marked: in 1993 the average cost of workers in the VW–Skoda factory in the Czech Republic was ten times lower than in plants in Germany, but productivity was 60 per cent of German levels and rising fast (Schwab and Smadja 1994, p. 42).

Labor market rigidity

The rigidity or flexibility of labor regulation is frequently seen as a crucial element in the "attractiveness" of locations to foreign capital (for example Schwab and Smadja 1994). Germany is characteristically presented as a country with a highly regulated labor market, and a World Economic Forum survey claimed that labor legislation was more rigid only in Italy (compare Agarwal 1997, p. 102). A statutory framework of employee involvement in Germany grants employees participation at supervisory board level, and provides for works councils whose rights range from information through consultation to co-determination. Legislation and sectoral collective agreements make for a high degree of regulation of recruitment and redundancy, and the works council has an important role in the implementation of redundancy plans. In Spain, likewise, the functioning of the labor market has long been presented by employers and the government as excessively rigid; the lengthy administrative processes and high costs involved in making workers redundant have been cited as a major deterrent to job creation and to foreign investment. At times during the 1990s, commentators have predicted the inevitable exodus of foreign investors from Spain (for example Allard 1994).

Conversely, the deregulation of labor markets in the UK – the cutting back of individual employees' rights with regard to unfair dismissal, for example, and the strict legislative regulation of union action (notably of strike action and picketing) – has been seen as one factor in making the UK attractive to foreign investment (compare Pain 1996, p. 7). The ability of this lopsided deregulation (freeing labor markets, shackling unions) to help reduce industrial conflict in Britain has also been seen as an incentive to foreign companies in contrast, say, to Spain, with its continuing relatively high level of strikes (p. 30).

The focus on the competitiveness of different national models of labor market regulation and industrial relations has been particularly controversial within the European Union, leading to academic analyses of "regime competition" (Streeck 1991). Streeck argued that European integration raised the spectre of "social dumping" within the EU – the flow of capital from countries with more regulated labor markets to those with lower labor standards (see *EIRR* 1993, pp. 17–20). British Conservative governments (up until the Conservatives' electoral defeat in May 1997) polarized debate by presenting a stark contrast between, on the one hand, a liberalized, deregulated, relatively low-wage model – epitomized by Britain's opt-out from the social chapter of the Maastricht Treaty – and, on the other hand, the more regulated social market model of much of continental Europe, notably of Germany. In a Europe of high unemployment, it was claimed that the "British model" was much more successful in creating employment by attracting FDI (particularly from Japanese and other east Asian MNCs). The polarization of positions has led to fears of a competitive devaluation of labor standards as countries strive to attract (or retain) capital and hence jobs.

7.4.   AN ASSESSMENT OF THE IMPACT OF RELOCATION

We have so far discussed the debate on relocation, and the analytical arguments underlying the phenomenon. But how significant is it in reality? On the face of it, there is considerable evidence for relocation. According to data cited by Woodall (1994), US MNCs cut their domestic manufacturing employment by 14 per cent in the period 1977–89, compared with a 1 per cent fall in the US economy as a whole, and the employment in their European subsidiaries fell even more sharply; by contrast, numbers in their subsidiaries in developing countries were up by 6 per cent. UNCTAD's data on MNC employment (1994, ch. IV) show a similar picture among MNCs more generally. While employment in home countries stagnated, that in foreign affiliates expanded rapidly, the great bulk of the increase in developing countries. In China alone, the number of employees involved in inward FDI rose from 4.8 million in 1991 to 16 million in 1995 (UNCTAD 1996, p. 56).

The concerns about relocation have been intensified by a number of "high-profile" cases, of which the ABB, Ford and Renault decisions are only the most recent, of MNCs moving production to other sites both within and outside Europe (see Box 7.1). The transfer of Hoover's production from Dijon in France to Cambuslang in Scotland (*EIRR* 1993) was commonly seen as a prime example of this process, motivated by an alleged 37 per cent difference in labor costs, and by the willingness of the Scottish workforce to make major concessions on working practices in order to win the investment: a pay freeze; the recruitment of new employees on fixed-term contracts at lower wages; and the introduction of work flexibility, including multiskilling, the ending of restrictions on the use of contractors, and changes to the organization of working time. The decision provoked outrage in France, and the Scottish unions were seen to be negotiating "with a gun to their heads" (p. 14).

	Box 7.1 Some recent examples of "relocation" of multinational operations		
Year	**Company**	**Relocation plan**	**MNC's rationale**
1993	Hoover	Relocation of production of vacuum cleaners from Dijon to Scotland with 600 job losses in France	Lower labor costs and willingness of Scottish unions to make concessions on pay and working practices
1995	Sabena	Proposal to relocate 450 Sabena pilots to Luxembourg through a cooperation agreement with Luxair	Employers' social security contributions were 12% of salary in Luxembourg compared with 34% in Belgium
1996	TNT	TNT moves its European distribution hub from Cologne to Liège, with 600 job losses in Germany	The campaign of the Social Democratic–Green coalition government of North Rhine-Westphalia for a night fly ban; and differences in wage costs and social security contributions
1996	Moulinex	Plan to relocate production from Normandy plants to Mexico, with the loss of several hundred jobs	Lower wage costs
1996	Semperit	Plan by the German-owned company, the biggest tyre manufacturer in Austria, to relocate half of car-tyre production to the Czech Republic, with the loss of "a considerable proportion of the 2,400 strong workforce"	Loss of export markets to Japan after Austria's accession to the EU, requiring major cost-cutting
1997	Renault	Decision to close Vilvoorde plant with the loss of 3,000 jobs and relocate work in France and Spain	Excessive levels of non-wage labor costs in Belgium
1997	ABB	Five-year plan to shed 20–30 thousand jobs in western Europe and to create a similar number of posts in India, China and eastern Europe	Drive to increase efficiency, reduce labor costs, and get closer to expanding new markets in emerging economies

7.4.1.   The Exaggerated Threat of Relocation?

Despite such prominent illustrations of *délocalisation*, reports of the death of Europe as an investment location appear to be grossly exaggerated.

The continuing dominance of FDI in the developed world

First, to put matters into perspective, some two-thirds of FDI inflows still go to developed countries (UNCTAD 1996, p. 4), and a high proportion of the investment in the developing countries of Asia is Japanese rather than European in origin. In terms of employment, the great bulk of the foreign workforce of European MNCs continues to be in developed countries – 72 per cent of foreign workers in French MNCs, 75 per cent in German, 86 per cent in Swedish, 80 per cent in Swiss (UNCTAD 1994, p. 183). Even in France, the home of the *délocalisation* debate, the evidence is thin. Critics of the Arthuis thesis suggest that only 5 per cent of French FDI represents strict *délocalisation*, that is, the shifting of production abroad coupled with closure of domestic capacity (and sometimes the import of products into France); French affiliates in South-East Asia – the alleged prime site for relocated activities – account for only 5 per cent of all employees in French MNCs abroad (UNCTAD 1994, p. 189).

The domestic employment-generating effects of international integration

Second, a major element in relocation concerns companies rationalizing and integrating productive activities transnationally. In search of "efficiency" savings, MNCs may move particular operations to where they may be performed most cheaply. This was an aspect of *délocalisation* highlighted by the Arthuis report. However, a number of analysts have argued that relocation abroad resulting from efficiency-seeking behaviour by internationally integrated MNCs does not necessarily lead to net losses of employment in the home country. This is because it stimulates exports, particularly within large diversified conglomerate MNCs in which the home country operation is likely to be a major supplier of inputs to production facilities abroad. For example, the decision by the French producer of household equipment, Moulinex, to relocate a part of production from Normandy to low-cost Mexico, and to import Mexican-made products back into the French market (*Le Monde*, 19 June 1996), may mean the loss of relatively low-skill French jobs, but it is also likely to generate demand for exports from France of capital equipment, knowledge-intensive components, management services, and know-how.

Data on Japanese and US MNCs support the supposition that compensating employment may be generated in the home country by outward FDI (Agarwal 1997, pp. 106–7; Dunning 1993, pp. 363–5). Dunning, in his synthesis of research on the issue, concludes that there was a "neutral" to "marginally favourable" home-country employment effect of FDI from the US and UK, and that US and UK companies surveyed increased home employment more (or decreased it less) than domestic "uninational" firms. In addition, outflows of FDI set up future flows of income in the form of repatriated earnings on foreign assets, providing funds for domestic capital formation (Agarwal 1997, p. 104–5): indeed, the surplus of repatriated earnings (particularly by US MNCs) over inward flows of FDI in underdeveloped areas was a major bone of political contention in Latin America and elsewhere in the 1960s and 1970s. Agarwal (1997, p. 109) argues that FDI outflows from Germany "do not appear to have impaired domestic fixed capital formation" and have generated demand for capital and intermediate goods.

One impact of FDI does seem, however, to be to change the composition of domestic employment, reducing production-related and less-skilled jobs as more labor-intensive operations are relocated abroad (Dunning 1993, p. 365), and replacing them with skilled, professional and managerial jobs. This has implications for government policy, which are dealt with in the final section.

The importance of market presence in explaining relocation

Third, it is questionable how far differences in labor costs and in industrial relations regimes drive the relocation of production. One of the key criticisms of the relocation thesis is that many investment decisions are not driven by locational cost advantages, but by the need to be in particular markets ("market-seeking"), for both political and economic reasons (for example, Edwards et al. 1996). The massive relocation of German companies to central and eastern Europe is thus seen to reflect the need to gain early access to large new markets with heightened growth prospects, and the opportunities represented by massive privatization programmes, rather than the desire to exploit labor cost advantages (Barrell and Pain 1997, p. 67; Agarwal 1997, p. 108; *Financial Times*, 13 February 1997). In defence and other sectors based on public procurement, a direct presence in the national market is often imperative if companies are to win orders. Moreover, according to Woodall (1994), about half of all FDI in developing countries is in mining (and thus motivated by the need to access immovable and often scarce raw materials) and in services such as hotels and bank branches, which could not be exported from home countries; it is thus not displacing home investment.

The declining significance of labor costs

Fourth, even where cost, rather than market presence, is the main consideration in location decisions, the impact of *labor* costs may well be limited. Labor costs, even taking into account productivity (that is, unit labor costs), are only one element in the equations facing corporate decision-makers. Such costs are a small and decreasing percentage of total production costs for most industries and many services (Oman 1994, pp. 89–91). In particular, the share of low-skilled labor has fallen to only 5–10 per cent of total production costs in developed economies, from 25 per cent in the 1970s; the share of capital, R&D and marketing costs has been increasing (Woodall 1994). In other words, the competitive advantage of low wages has been eroded. Although direct labor accounts for about a third of total production costs in clothing and footwear, it is only about 3 per cent of total costs in semiconductors, 8 per cent in chemicals, 5 per cent in the production of colour televisions, and 10–15 per cent in cars. The advantages proffered by lower wage costs may be swamped by the host country's cost disadvantages in infrastructure, proximity to markets, language, skills, and so on. Moreover, partly as a result of changes in the organization of production – particularly the rise of flexible manufacturing, "lean production", just-in-time organization, etc., the quality and reliability of labor (and indeed of physical infrastructure such as transport and communications systems and the electricity supply) have become increasingly paramount (Oman 1994, 86-91).

A further point is that labor-cost differentials are not static, but are dynamically affected by the process of development itself. Thus the advantages enjoyed by central European countries, for example, are likely to be eroded rather rapidly as their economies expand and the gap between their wage rates and those in the west consequently closes. Already, there are indications of rising wage rates: for example, between 1990 and 1995, hourly labor costs in the textile industry nearly doubled in Hungary and practically trebled in Poland (*Financial Times*, 21 September 1995).

The questionable impact of labor market rigidities on relocation

Fifth, the role of inflexible regimes of labor regulation in stimulating relocation is highly uncertain, and despite the scope for relocation within Europe, the fears of capital flight and social dumping need to be put into perspective. On the one hand, high levels of FDI (by British MNCs among others) into countries such as Belgium and France (Barrell and Pain 1997, pp. 65, 74) suggest that rigid labor regulation need not be a deterrent to investment. Indeed, France – despite its extensive labor market regulation, minimum wage, and statutory framework of company-level collective bargaining and worker representation – has now overtaken Britain as a favoured destination of foreign investment in Europe, while Belgium, the Netherlands, Sweden and Switzerland all have higher per capita FDI inflows than the UK (p. 64). Although a regulated labor market, together with strict environmental regulation and high corporate tax rates, may make Germany relatively less attractive to investors, their impact should not be exaggerated: Agarwal (1997, p. 109) suggests the key factor deterring foreign investment – at least in sectors such as engineering – is the technological superiority of German enterprises.

On the other hand, the attractions of deregulated systems are open to question. Barrell and Pain (1997, p. 70) puncture the claims of the deregulated British model: "in spite of the supposed advantages offered by the flexible labor market in the UK and the deregulated business environment", UK firms have more assets located overseas than foreign firms have in the UK and the drift to EU destinations is accelerating; British MNCs are in the front rank of foreign investors in more highly regulated countries such as Belgium. This does not suggest "that the Social Chapter and the myriad of different labor market regulations in many European countries are seen by large multinational firms as obstacles that cannot be overcome".

Moreover, Barrell and Pain raise doubts about the *quality* of the jobs created by inward FDI in deregulated economies such as Britain's. Important skills shortages exist in the UK, for example for intermediate craft skills, an area where the German engineering industry is particularly strong. As far as German investment in the UK is concerned, the UK "appears to have performed relatively poorly in attracting investments from those sectors in Germany where innovations have risen most rapidly" (p. 68). Factors other than labor markets account for more than 80 per cent of the growth in UK inward investment from Germany since the mid-1980s.

In general, although relatively successful in attracting labor-intensive projects, the UK has lost out on investment of a high capital and R&D intensity: R&D expenditure as a proportion of sales in foreign affiliates in Britain is lower than the European average (p. 69). Such factors may trigger the movement of direct investment out of Britain. An example of what might be called "reverse delocation" is Texas Instruments' closure of its London plant and the transfer of technological development teams to Germany and France from the UK in 1994 (*Financial Times*, 6 May 1994).

Indeed the impact of labor market regulation on location may be "perverse". The Ford Halewood case provides a striking example. In March 1997, Ford management announced that the Merseyside plant would not produce the new generation of Ford Escort, and that 1,300 jobs (later reduced to 1,000) would be lost. One factor in management's decision appears to have been the much greater ease and lower cost of making workers redundant in Britain compared with Spain and Germany. The decision was taken despite the fact that the workforce had done all that had been asked of it to change working practices and raise productivity, and despite labor costs in the British plant being much lower than in Saarlouis in Germany (and, according to union sources, lower even than in the Spanish plant in Valencia) (EIRO 1997b). The ironic outcome is that although liberalized labor regimes may attract foreign capital more easily, they are also more vulnerable to losing it: deregulation is a double-edged sword. Conversely, foreign investment may be "locked in" to regulated systems.

Although the Ford relocation is a small incident compared with the continuing massive inflow of foreign capital into the UK, the ease of exit may be a key factor should Britain's attractiveness diminish as an inward FDI destination. Given that one of the main motivations for investment by non-EU MNCs in Britain is access to EU markets, failure to remain at the "heart of Europe" could trigger a rapid process of disinvestment in the future. Already, industrialists from Japan and elsewhere have issued warnings about the future of their British investments if Britain fails to join monetary union (see, for example, the president of Toyota, reported in *Financial Times*, 31 January 1997; compare Barrell and Pain 1997, p. 68).

7.4.2. The Challenges Posed by Relocation

None the less, concerns about relocation cannot simply be dismissed. There are a number of key areas where movement of capital between countries has had an impact on employment in European countries, or where future developments are likely to be highly significant.

First, as we have already seen, in certain industries such as clothing and textiles, where capital and technology are easily transferable and where labor input is both high and relatively unskilled, relocation has meant a serious and sometimes extremely rapid decline in production and employment in European countries. Considerable relocation took place in such industries from the 1970s, as Fröbel et al. (1980) detailed in the case of Germany, and the expansion of possible locations such as eastern Europe and China has sustained the process more recently.

Second, as argued earlier, the possibilities of relocation rest on advances in the technology and coordination of production that allow labor-intensive, and low-skill, elements in the production process to be split off, and to be produced at locations remote from the point of consumption. Given the rise of attractive new FDI locations in developing countries, together with continuing advances in technology, these tendencies appear likely to intensify, exposing increasingly broad areas of employment to transfer abroad, and exacerbating the insecurity of important segments of the labor force in European countries. For example, activities as diverse as the provision of customer inquiry services by telephone, type-setting, aircraft maintenance and data entry are susceptible to relocation to countries remote from the point of delivery, often through subcontracting arrangements; thus Swissair has reportedly transferred all revenue accounting to Bombay (Woodall 1994), while the judgements of the French Court of Appeal are put on an electronic database by data entry workers in China (Arthuis 1993, p. 20). The relocation to developing countries in the far East and the Caribbean of other electronic data services such as the management of magazine subscriptions, tax returns, library catalogues and insurance claims has also been reported. Within Europe, countries such as Ireland – benefiting from the use of English and relatively cheap skilled labor – have set themselves up in recent years as advantageous sites for the location of such activities (several major computer and communications giants such as IBM, Digital, and Bertelsmann have or plan pan-European customer help centres in Dublin – see *Financial Times*, 8 October 1996).

Third, arguments about relocation have generally built on the supposition that primarily lower-skilled, lower-paid work would be relocated, and that higher-skilled jobs would not be threatened, given the enormous education and training gap between developed and developing countries. According to Woodall (1994), the average worker in the developed world has eleven years' schooling, compared with five in China and Mexico; and the developed countries produce 85 scientists and technicians, and 19 university graduates per 1,000, compared with respective figures of nine and one in developing countries. However, the skill gap is closing. The EU is faced with a large pool of low-wage, flexible and relatively highly skilled labor on its doorstep in central and eastern Europe. Within NAFTA, there is a low-cost workforce of rising quality easily accessible in Mexico (compare UNCTAD 1994, p. 209). In absolute terms, the larger developing countries, notably China, Brazil and India, produce very large numbers of trained workers; China ranks third and Brazil fifth in the world in terms of numbers of university graduates (p. 206). These trends, combined with the advances in telecommunications and information technology referred to above, underlie a relatively new and ominous trend for workforces in Europe (and other developed regions): the relocation of *high-skill* work to *low-wage* economies (see, especially, Arthuis 1993). Thus, in a study of the Mexican automobile industry, Shaiken (1994) attacks earlier assumptions that less-developed countries such as Mexico would be unable to cope with the challenges of more complex production operations: the car plant studied by Shaiken, by careful recruitment of high-quality local labor, was able to achieve levels of productivity and quality comparable with the best in North America.

A recent example of such developments is the incredibly rapid growth of the computer software industry in India. Most US computer firms are now said to subcontract labor-intensive computer programming to Bangalore (Woodall 1994). Indian firms also cater to the expanding market for "remote maintenance". According to a special review in the *Financial Times* (6 November 1996), "Today, Indian software companies sell their services to an expanding international customer list which now includes Japanese and South Korean clients as well as those from north America and Europe, on the basis of quality, speed, innovation and skills as well as price" (compare Arthuis 1993, p. 21). With high labor costs and shortages of skilled software engineers in the West, the Indian industry's massive and rapidly growing pool of some 100,000 skilled and highly qualified software developers – at about one-fifth of the salaries of equivalent workers in Europe (ibid.) – has provided the opportunity for international "outsourcing" by western companies.

7.5. MNCS AND EMPLOYMENT: SOME POLICY ASPECTS

The threat, real or potential, of *délocalisation* has provoked a number of responses from policy-makers. Here we consider three issues: the validity of government attempts to cut labor costs in order to make European countries more attractive as an investment location; the proposed introduction of international minimum labor standards; and the implications of the Ford and Renault relocation decisions for policy-making within Europe – for the European Union, national governments and the social partners themselves.

7.5.1. Relocation and Labor-cost Competition

One policy approach to the threat of *délocalisation* has been to try to ensure that labor costs remain low. Exemplified by the strategy of British Conservative governments in the 1980s and 1990s, this has entailed cost containment through deregulation; as the president of the World Economic Forum,[3] Klaus Schwab, argued, "there is no way that the Western European nations will be able to ease their enduring unemployment problems without dealing with the structural rigidities in their labor systems" (Schwab and Smadja 1994, p. 42). While few other European countries have followed the radical deregulatory path of the UK, there has been widespread concern to reduce the cost particularly of less-skilled labor – the category most at risk from relocations. Arthuis's recommendations, for example, emphasize the need to lower employers' social contributions.

The limitation of such policies is, of course, that European countries ultimately can never compete on labor-cost terms with low-cost developing economies in sectors and activities susceptible to relocation. Such measures can at best be short-term palliatives. In the longer run, competition for investment from the developing world is likely to reinforce the shift in the developed countries from labor-intensive to high-tech, capital-intensive industries, and the decline in demand for unskilled workers (UNCTAD 1994, ch. IV). Thus MNCs add to pressures in developed economies to move to higher value-added activities.

Given the logic of international capitalist competition, UNCTAD may well be right to argue (1994, p. 211) that restrictions on MNCs' pursuit of integrated international production would be counterproductive because it would engender a loss of competitiveness and lead to substantial long-term falls in employment. But such a stance has critical short- and long-term policy implications. In the short term, there is a need for effective palliative measures to mitigate the human costs of displacement which, as in the case of textiles, may affect whole sectors of production. In the longer term, the crucial policy implication of the relocation dynamic appears to be the need to raise the quality of the labor force, through the promotion of appropriate education and training by the state and by firms. However, as suggested above, rapidly advancing skills in developing countries are likely to make the upgrading of skills in developed European countries a constant battle.

7.5.2. Controlling   Relocation   through   International   Labor Standards

A second policy reaction to the employment consequences of relocation has focused on renewed attempts to develop minimum international labor standards and codes of practice, in areas such as union rights, child and prison labor, to be included, for example, in trade agreements (see *EIRR* 1996). This, too, is controversial. From a free trade perspective, Schwab and Smadja argue (1994, p. 43) that low-wage newly-industrializing countries see western concern with social dumping, labor rights and environmental standards as a manifestation of bad faith and hypocrisy (see also *EIRR* 1996, pp. 27–8). There is an element of uncomfortable truth is such assertions: the rather parochial relocation debate in Europe does induce a sense of unease that entrenched interests are being defended at the expense of vastly poorer workers in developing regions. And, even on grounds of self-interest, it is possible to argue that rising living standards in the world's less-developed countries would be of benefit to the developed world itself by providing profitable new market opportunities.

Despite such reservations, however, it does seem reasonable to raise questions about the nature of labor regimes in competitor countries in Asia or wherever. It is highly debatable whether the use of child labor, horrendous working conditions, misery wages, intimidation by employers and repression of organized labor by the state are particularly advantageous to workforces in developing countries, even if they may serve longer-term goals of achieving capitalist "take-off". There now appears to be a broad coalition of interests in favour of such standards, including "multinational employers who have developed ethical codes of conduct for their suppliers and subcontractors (such as the US clothing company Levi-Strauss and the German mail order company Otto Versand), trade unions at national and international level, the ILO, governments and politicians in industrialised countries, and a wide range of international human rights organizations and charities" (ibid, p. 27).

The proponents of codes of conduct argue that they are necessary to avoid a global deterioration of labor standards as competition becomes increasingly internationalized, and to encourage developing countries to promote social development. However, while discussions may continue, the prospects for international agreement on such standards appear slim, given the hostility to them of many governments in the developing world. Even if they prove practicable in the future, it is questionable how far they will be effective in protecting employees in developed countries from "social dumping" – or workers in developing countries from exploitation. A major issue will be the effectiveness of any monitoring system to ensure compliance.

7.5.3. Relocation within the EU: the Policy Ramifications of Halewood and Vilvoorde

As we have seen, somewhat analogous issues of relocation also arise within the boundaries of Europe. The Vilvoorde and Halewood cases pinpoint some serious policy issues concerning the employment implications of MNCs' operations.

Social dumping and wage costs

First, they add fuel to the debate on social dumping and labor standards *within* the EU. While the defeat of the British Conservatives may mark the end of the extreme deregulationist project in the UK, and the new Labor government has adopted a more positive engagement with Europe, the issue of "regime competition" remains important. Vilvoorde focused attention not only on labor costs, but on the proportion of *non-wage* labor costs, particularly the contributions of employers to social security and pensions, and other welfare charges, which are particularly high in Belgium. In 1995, such costs varied very widely between EU countries as a proportion of pure wage costs – from as low as 6 per cent in Denmark to 18 per cent in the UK, 32 per cent in Germany, 34 in Spain, 44 in France and over 50 per cent in Italy (*Financial Times*, 18 July 1996; 8 October 1996).

One policy impact of such disparities has been to encourage a number of European states to reduce employer contributions, and cut back the welfare system of pensions and social security provision – already under scrutiny as countries try to meet the Maastricht criteria for economic and monetary union. The Belgian prime minister, Jean-Luc Dehaene, in the wake of the Vilvoorde decision, expressed the view that only European monetary union, followed by the rapid harmonization of tax and social laws, would prevent the competitive forcing down of standards as countries bid for the favours of MNCs such as Renault.

Controlling investment competition between EU countries

The second policy issue exemplified by Vilvoorde and Halewood concerns the competition between countries for MNC investment: Renault asked for Ecu 11 million for investment in its Valladolid plant, and Ford engaged in complex moves to win UK government aid for future investment in Halewood. These and other cases have raised concerns about MNCs "subsidy-chasing" across Europe – moving, or threatening to move, production in order to take advantage of EU and national government grants.

Brussels' response to Vilvoorde was to block Renault's application for investment aid in Spain, and to look at ways of ensuring that European funds could not be used to relocate viable operations to locations eligible for funding. Clearly, such aid-chasing relocations would create considerable instability while doing little to increase the efficiency of production in Europe. The regional commissioner, Monika Wulf-Mathies, suggested that European funds should be tied to long-term investment by companies, and announced that reforms of structural funds would be undertaken before 1999 to discourage relocation: "We want to promote regional development... but pure profiting from aid needs to be ruled out" (EIRO 1997a).

Relocation and the rights of the workforce

The third issue, raised particularly by the Renault closure announcement, concerns the effectiveness of the European framework of employee rights to consultation in major corporate decisions affecting their livelihoods. Renault apparently failed to consult properly with the workforce – in breach of the European Works Council Directive (94/45/EC) and of the Collective Redundancies Directive (75/129/EEC, amended 92/56/EEC) (see EIRO 1997a; *EWCB* 1997). In April, a French court ruled that Renault's European works council (EWC) agreement establishing its "European Group Committee" implied an obligation to "inform and consult [the Committee] over a decision to be taken affecting its strategic orientations and the major development of a European subsidiary such as to have repercussions at European level", and that this obligation had not been respected (*EWCB* 1997, p. 11).

However, while Renault was ordered to cease implementing the closure until it had fulfilled its obligation to inform and consult (and was ordered to pay a nominal fine), the Vilvoorde affair has raised serious doubts about the adequacy of existing EU regulation, prompting a review of social policy within the European Commission. The social affairs commissioner, Padraig Flynn, told the European Parliament that "there has to be a serious question mark over whether the scale of sanctions envisaged under national law are sufficient to act as a real deterrent against non-compliance", and a number of voices have called for the strengthening of provisions on information and consultation (*EWCB* 1997 p. 12). The Commission has used the opportunity to push forward a proposed directive on national works councils and to revive the long-delayed European Company statute. The latter would allow MNCs to incorporate themselves as a single EU-wide entity, avoiding the complexities of national corporation law; in return, however, employees would be covered by strengthened provisions for worker consultation and information. Progress has been blocked by differences on the extent of such participation (*Financial Times*, 12 July 1996), although Britain's new more positive stance towards "Social Europe" may give impetus to the initiative.

The wider political ramifications of the whole episode for Europe are significant:

> The ability of a multinational company to overtly [flout] the spirit of EU legislation in such blatant disregard of the social implications of its actions, highlights the persistent gap between the reality of economic and social Europe. In the run up to economic and monetary union the Commission is aware that it can ill afford to ignore the impact of... the location decisions of multinational companies on employment opportunities and social inequality, if it is to engender further support for the European project.
>
> (EIRO 1997a)

In other words, if European social regulation proves ineffectual in controlling the social aspects of relocation, disaffection with regard to the European Union is likely to grow.

Relocation and employee commitment

Fourth, relocation – and in particular the Ford and Renault experiences – raises general questions for managers about their relationship with their workforces. Modern production increasingly depends on successful strategies for gaining the commitment and involvement of a skilled and flexible workforce. The rationale of relocation decisions threatens to undermine, in the longer term, the foundations of such commitment, and perhaps to weaken the social legitimacy of international business both among workforces and in wider public opinion.

One aspect of this is the way in which the Halewood and Vilvoorde decisions call into question the value of "best-practice comparisons" across countries (see above). Such comparisons ultimately function as a lever of labor flexibility and productivity increases because employees believe that compliance will be rewarded (that is through new or continued investment). But the Ford Halewood case shows that workforce responsiveness is not sufficient to secure jobs: since "virtue" is not necessarily rewarded, the motivation to be virtuous may be reduced.

Similarly, at Renault Vilvoorde, the plant had been held up as a model of good practice; earlier investment had been accompanied by a new flexible shiftworking system (*Financial Times*, 6 March 1997) – to no avail, despite the plant's profitability, when the company decided to cut costs in Europe.

The implications for unions

A final question concerns the lessons of the relocation debate for unions and workforces. Their ability to combat the power of MNCs to play one plant off against another and to move employment around Europe has been a longstanding subject of concern (for an overview, see Hills 1997). The Vilvoorde events once again raise the question of the effectiveness of transnational workforce action. Vilvoorde was notable for stimulating the (alleged) first "Euro-demonstrations" in Brussels and Paris, with the participation of workers from around Europe; workers in Renault factories in France and Spain staged one-hour token stoppages in support of their Belgian colleagues.

Given the overwhelmingly national basis to labor organization, the effectiveness of such action is more open to doubt. Ultimately, French unions are likely to be more concerned about jobs for French workers than for Belgians, and there have been few instances of successful concerted international union action against MNCs. None the less, Hills cautions against the myth of labor powerlessness in the face of MNC "blackmail", and it is possible to envisage unions playing a role in avoiding the "no-win" round of competitive devaluations of working conditions driven by MNC strategy.

In addition, union resources are in some respects increasing. Electronic communications provide unions as well as managers with a greater ability to process information internationally (compare Hills 1997). The introduction of European works councils may prove to be an important mechanism for unions to achieve the international coordination and networking necessary to respond adequately to relocation and rationalization initiatives. For example, employee representatives on the EWC of a large German MNC have recently attempted to use the council to obtain a comprehensive country-by-country analysis of terms and conditions of employment in the company's European subsidiaries. Although few analytical studies have yet appeared of the practical functioning of EWCs, doubts must remain, however, as to how far they will aid cross-national union action; indeed, they are just as likely to provide management with a tool for convincing workforces more easily of the irresistible logic of international corporate restructuring.

7.6.   CONCLUSIONS

This chapter has argued that the increasing international integration of corporate operations, coupled with advances in the technology of production and of management control, and the expansion of the world market to encompass huge new regions of population, has unleashed a new wave of anxiety about the consequences of MNCs' behaviour for employment. It has focused on the question of *délocalisation* – the search by MNCs for investment locations, within Europe and outside it, where labor costs and standards are lower.

Our analysis of the evidence leads to the conclusion that in some respects the scale of the problem has been exaggerated. Many activities are not susceptible to relocation, FDI to lower-cost countries is often driven by a "market-seeking" rather than "efficiency-seeking" rationale, and outward investment often appears to have a net employment-generating effect in home economies. None the less, there are worrying aspects: the rise of low-labor-cost areas on the EU's eastern borders; the expanding range of economic activities which may be "hived off" from other productive processes and moved to remote locations; the increasing competition in *high*-skill, even "leading-edge", sectors such as computer software. More generally, while economists may argue that in the long run "efficiency seeking" by MNCs helps raise efficiency and competitiveness, and hence employment, in home countries, relocation generates sometimes massive social consequences in the short run. Arguments of economic efficiency are likely to be of little consolation to communities and workforces devastated by the abrupt termination of productive activities.

Relocation is not just a threat between Europe and the developing world, but within Europe itself, where the single market has prompted concerns about "regime competition" and social dumping. The redistribution of employment between countries may not affect *aggregate* employment levels in Europe; but it certainly matters if it leads to a competitive bidding down in labor terms and conditions, so that the same number of people are employed on worse pay and lower security. Obviously, at the margins, judgements can be made about whether wage costs are too high, working hours too low, or labor protection too rigid. But the pursuit of the logic of cost-based competition implies a relentless and *continuous* cycle of forcing down standards. In the long run, this has to be unsustainable – certainly if a semblance of social order and cohesion is to be preserved in Europe.

Finally, it is perhaps worth making the point that MNCs are not desiccated economic calculating machines pursuing some abstract notion of efficiency, but complex structures of power and influence in constant interaction with the environment in which they are to a greater or lesser extent embedded (Ferner and Edwards 1995). As such, they are susceptible to the application of countervailing power at different "pressure points" in the organization. National subsidiaries and their managers are enmeshed in local networks of influence and exchange – with local and national political structures, customers, suppliers, employees and unions. In cases of relocation, the interests and loyalties of local MNC managers may lie with other local actors rather more than with corporate headquarters in the home country. Such "embeddedness" provides the conditions for the construction of interest coalitions to respond to the decisions of MNCs. But if such action is to go beyond the parochial perspective of the locality affected, those wishing to channel and regulate the actions of MNCs will require the ability to formulate a coordinated response at a supranational level. Such a degree of coherence is not easy to foresee. However, one of the factors in the Renault–Vilvoorde case was the genuine outrage provoked by the decision – in France and the European Commission as well as in Belgium, among politicians as well as unions and workers. While the immediate effect on Renault may be limited, the more diffuse political costs for the company arising out of the débâcle may cause it, and other multinationals, to think again in similar circumstances, particularly if outrage is translated into effective regulation and constraints.

NOTES

*   I would like to thank Paul Edwards and Paul Marginson for their helpful comments on an earlier draft of this paper.
1   "Billion" is used in the Anglo-American sense of a thousand million.
2   Data on employment in MNCs within Europe are at best partial. In the absence of more reliable figures, it is hard to make even very rough 'guesstimates' as to the total directly employed by MNCs in Europe, but if Europe's share of MNC employment were approximately in line with its share of FDI stock, the figure could amount to tens of millions. UNCTAD data (see Table 7.3) suggest that in France, Germany, Italy, the Netherlands, Sweden and the UK, aggregate employment by home-country MNCs amounted to possibly nine million people in the 1980s. In addition, foreign MNCs operating in these six countries employed at least four million. These figures are likely to be significant underestimates since in a number of cases the data are based on samples of larger firms, or only include manufacturing. Moreover, they exclude figures for employment by MNCs in important host countries such as Spain, Belgium or Ireland.
3   The World Economic Forum aims to bring together business, government and academia to serve "the global public interest". It publishes the annual "World Competitiveness Report" ranking countries on factors including wage costs, quality and flexibility.

REFERENCES

Agarwal, J.P. (1997), "European integration and German FDI: implications for domestic investment and central European economies", *National Institute Economic Review*, **2** (160) April, 100–110.

Allard, G. (1994), "Loss of jobs from multinationals is posing a challenge for Spain", *Journal of Commerce and Commercial*, **4**, April, 7.

Arthuis, J. (1993), "Les délocalisations des activités industrielles et de services hors de France" (extraits d'un rapport sur l'incidence économique et fiscale des délocalisations hors du territoire national des activités industrielles et de services), *Problèmes économiques*, **2** (338), 25 August, 18–25.

Barrell, R. and N. Pain (1997), "The growth of foreign direct investment in Europe", *National Institute Economic Review*, **160**, February, 63–75.

Coller, X. (1996), "Managing flexibility in the food industry: a cross-national comparative case study in European multinational companies", *European Journal of Industrial Relations*, **2** (2), July, 153–72.

Dunning, J. (1993), *Multinational Enterprises and the Global Economy*. Wokingham: Addison-Wesley.

Edwards, P., A. Ferner and K. Sisson (1996), "The conditions for international human resource management: two case studies", *International Journal of Human Resource Management*, **7** (1), February, 20–40.

Erickson, C. and S. Kuruvilla (1995), "Labor cost incentives for capital mobility in the European Community", in S. Jacoby (ed.), *The Workers of Nations. Industrial Relations in a Global Economy*, New York/Oxford: Oxford University Press, 35–53.

European Industrial Relations Observatory (EIRO) (1997a), "The Renault case and the future of Social Europe", Record EU9703108F, EIRO, February.

European Industrial Relations Observatory (EIRO) (1997b), 'Ford case highlights the costs of inward and outward investment", Record UK9702101F, EIRO, February.

European Industrial Relations Review (EIRR) (1993), "The Hoover affair and social dumping", *EIRR*, **230**, March, 14-20.

European Industrial Relations Review (EIRR) (1996), "Including labor standards in international trade agreements", *EIRR*, **275**, December, 26–30.

European Works Councils Bulletin (EWCB) (1997), "The Renault Vilvoorde affair", *EWCB*, **9**, May/June, 10–13.

Ferner, A. and P. Edwards (1995), "Power and the diffusion of organizational change within multinational enterprises", *European Journal of Industrial Relations*, **1** (2), July, 229–58.

Ferner, A. and J. Quintanilla (1997), "Multinationals, national business systems, and the management of HRM: the enduring influence of national identity or a process of Anglo-Saxonisation?" Paper for European Regional Conference of the International Industrial Relations Association, Dublin, 26–29 August.

Fröbel, F., Heinrich, J. and Kreye, O., 1980. "The New International Division of Labor", Cambridge: Cambridge University Press.

Hills, J. (1997), "Taking on the CosmoCorps? Experiments in trans-national labor

organisation" Mimeo, Department of Geography, University of Southampton.
Marginson, P. and K. Sisson (1994), "The structure of transnational capital in Europe: the emerging Euro-company and its implications for industrial relations", in R. Hyman and A. Ferner (eds), *New Frontiers in European Industrial Relations*. Oxford: Blackwell, 15–51.
Marginson, P., P. Armstrong, P. Edwards and J. Purcell with N. Hubbard, (1993), "The control of industrial relations in large companies: an initial analysis of the second Company Level Industrial Relations Survey". *Warwick Papers in Industrial Relations* No. 45. Coventry: Industrial Relations Research Unit.
Martínez Lucio, M. and S. Weston (1995), "New management practices in a multinational corporation: the restructuring of worker representation and rights?" *Industrial Relations Journal*, **24** (3), 182–90.
Mueller, F. (1996), "National stakeholders in the global contest for corporate investment", *European Journal of Industrial Relations*, **2** (3), 345–68.
Mueller, F. and J. Purcell (1992), "The Europeanisation of manufacturing and the decentralisation of bargaining: multinational management strategies in the European automobile industry", *International Journal of Human Resource Management*, **3** (1), 15–34.
Oman, C. (1994), *Globalization and Regionalization: The Challenge for Developing Countries*. Paris: OECD.
Pain, N. (1996), "Continental Drift: European integration and the location of UK foreign direct investment", NIESR Discussion Paper No. 107, London: National Institute of Economic and Social Research.
Ruane, F. and H. Görg (1997), "The impact of foreign direct investment on sectoral adjustment in the Irish economy", *National Institute Economic Review*, **160**, February, 76–84.
Schwab, K. and C. Smadja (1994), "Power and policy: the new economic world order", *Harvard Business Review*, **72** (6), November–December, 40–50.
Shaiken, H. (1994), "The new international division of labor and its impact on unions: a case study of high-tech Mexican export production", in J. Bélanger, P.K. Edwards and L. Haiven (eds), *Workplace Industrial Relations and the Global Challenge*, Cornell: ILR Press, 224–39.
Streeck, W. (1991), "More uncertainties: West German unions facing 1992", *Industrial Relations*, **30**, 317–49.
United Nations Conference on Trade and Development (UNCTAD) (1994), *World Investment Report (1994): Transnational Corporations, Employment and the Workplace*, New York/Geneva: United Nations.
United Nations Conference on Trade and Development (UNCTAD) (1996), *World Investment Report 1996. Investment, Trade and International Policy Arrangements*, New York/Geneva: United Nations.
Woodall, P. (1994), "You ain't seen nothing yet: the biggest threat to workers is not from imports, but from a mass migration of investment", *The Economist*, 1 October.

Index